C000234162

PIRATES
BUCCANEERS, THE REPUBLIC & THE
CARIBBEAN

sona
BOOKS

First published in the UK 2019 by Sona Books
an imprint of Danann Publishing Ltd.

Editor: Hannah Westlake, Designer: Alexander Phoenix

Copy editor for Danann Tom O'Neill

CAT NO: SON0441

ISBN: 978-1-912918-06-5

Made in EU.

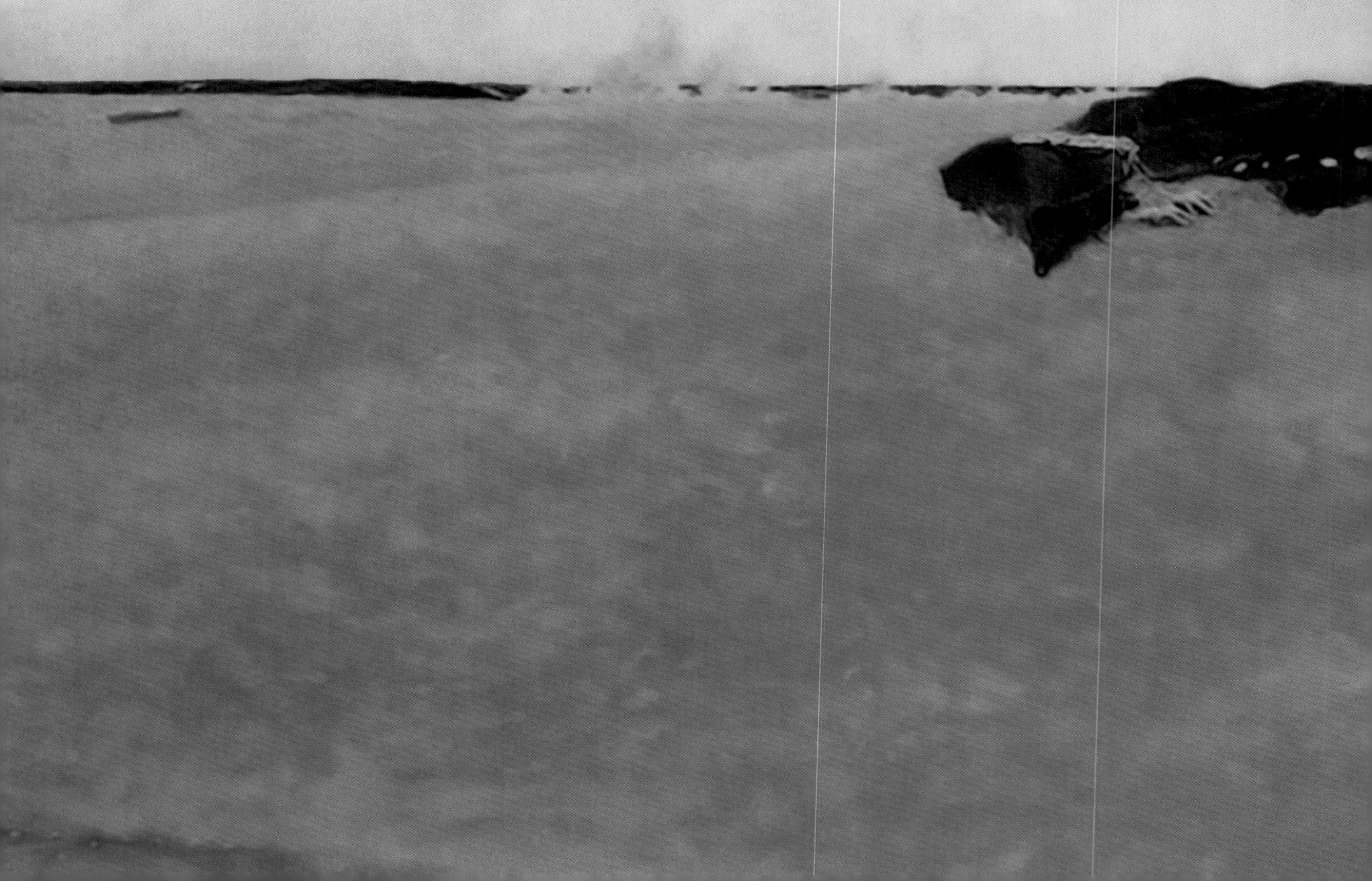

Welcome To

Pirates

Buccaneers, the Republic & the

Caribbean

In the 17th and 18th centuries, sailing from Europe or Africa to the Americas, or trading from India to Central America, was a risky undertaking. Ferocious storms and barely-understood diseases weren't the only threats; ruthless pirates lurked on the horizon, craving wealth and reputation.

In this book we cover everything you need to know about the legendary Golden Age of Piracy. Uncover the true stories of the bloodthirsty buccaneers who made their fortune plundering the high seas, from Captain Kidd and Edward 'Blackbeard' Teach to female pirates Anne Bonny and Mary Read. Find out what life was really like aboard a pirate ship, from the roles of the crew to divvying out the spoils. Investigate the founding and exploits of the notorious Flying Gang, a band of fierce pirate captains, and the piratical haven they founded on the island of New Providence in the Bahamas. Packed with incredible illustrations and insights into the period, this is the perfect guide for anyone who wants to learn about this famed Golden Age of Piracy.

Contents

The Golden Age of Piracy

Discover the true story behind history's bloodthirsty buccaneers

In the 1600s, the ghoulish sight of the Jolly Roger could strike fear into the hearts of even the bravest seamen. Pirates had existed for as long as man had sailed the seas, but it was at this time that they truly began to rule the waves.

The colonisation of the New World and the birth of the slave trade meant that the oceans were swarming with richly laden merchant ships, and many men and women turned to a life of crime on the high seas. And what a life it was! A bottle of rum at breakfast and a buxom wench at supper, and in between a day spent stalking ships and trading spoils in pirate havens.

These hives of villainy, hidden away on islands in the Caribbean and Indian Oceans, served as launch sites for raids on enemy outposts and merchant ships. Here, pirates could repair their vessels away from the watchful eye of the Navy, while taverns, gambling halls and brothels provided welcome respite for pirates who had spent months at sea.

Over the years, pirates' lives became easier and even more lucrative. Sailors knew these bandits were skilled, well-armed, and willing to risk it all – the chance of winning a battle with them was slim. Ships that did put up a fight were shown no mercy, so their best option was to raise the white flag and surrender.

However, as the problem of piracy grew, merchant communities began to take matters into their own hands, arming and equipping ships at their own expense to protect commerce. These ships, captained by 'privateers', were licensed by the crown and could attack any enemy vessel. Over time, the line between privateer and pirate became blurred.

In a world where native populations were being wiped out or bound in chains, pirate life represented freedom and democracy. It's easy to see why many found it hard to resist the spoils of the Golden Age of Piracy.

"Ships that did put up a fight were shown no mercy, so their best option was to surrender"

SPOILS OF THE NEW WORLD

The discovery of the Americas not only fuelled economies, but also a reign of terror

When Spanish explorer Christopher Columbus set sail on what he believed to be a westward route to Asia, no one could have predicted that instead he would stumble across one of the most resource-rich continents in the world.

He returned from the Americas laden with gold, pearls and a strange plant called 'tobacco', kick-starting an era of frantic colonisation by Spain and other European powers.. They quickly began stripping the new land and sending back ships laden with its bounties.

As wars between the colonisers waged, many settlers and sailors cottoned on to the riches that these galleons had to offer. By the 1630s, buccaneers were in operation in the Caribbean, mostly made up of Frenchmen who had been driven off the island of Hispaniola by the Spanish. They relocated to the island of Tortuga, which provided limited resources on which to live. It was partly in retaliation and partly out of necessity that these buccaneers began attacking Spanish ships, plundering them for every penny.

The English, French and Dutch embraced these newly established pirates as they dealt a much-needed blow to the strengthening Spanish. The English capture of Jamaica served to bolster piracy, as its governors semi-legitimised piracy and offered a safe haven in Port Royal – in return for a share of booty.

As Spain's power waned, the appeal of piracy faded with it, and letters stating legitimacy became harder to obtain. The buccaneers needed a new hunting ground. Rumours of ships laden with precious silks and spices sailing unprotected through Indian waters soon reached the rotten bunch, and in 1693, pirate captain Thomas Tew decided to seek one out. Setting sail from Bermuda, Tew cornered the Cape of Good Hope and cruised along the East African coast to the Red Sea, where he ran down a ship sailing from India to the Ottoman Empire. Despite its enormous crew, the ship surrendered and Tew's pirates helped themselves to £100,000 worth of gold and silver, as well as ivory, spices, gemstones and silk. The route, which was dubbed the Pirate Round, became one of the most profitable on the planet.

Pirate Henry Every captured a Mughal trading ship carrying £600,000 worth of goods

Manila galleons
These Spanish ships that sailed between Mexico and the Philippines provided a profitable link with Ming China and its spice trade.

North Atlantic
Piracy took place along the eastern coast of Canada and the US mainland. Newfoundland fisheries were notorious for pirate recruitment.

Tortuga
French and English buccaneers made this island the centre of Caribbean piracy, from which they launched countless attacks on Spanish colonies.

Sugar, Cotton

Tobacco, Sugar, Cotton

Slaves

Port Royal
This Jamaican town was crawling with criminals, with hundreds of brothels and taverns for pirates to spend their loot at.

PRECIOUS CARGO

Tobacco
Plunder like tobacco fetched a high price – if the pirate could bear to part with it.

Gold
Really lucky pirates might have stumbled across a vessel shipping Aztec treasures from Mexico to Spain.

Slaves
Not only could captured slaves be sold on, they could also be ransomed or made part of the crew.

Port Royal – a notorious pirate haven – before it was destroyed by an earthquake in 1692

TRADE ROUTES OF THE GOLDEN AGE

As shipping flourished between Europe and its colonies, so too did these pillaging pirates

Slave ships crossing the Middle Passage were often targeted by pirates

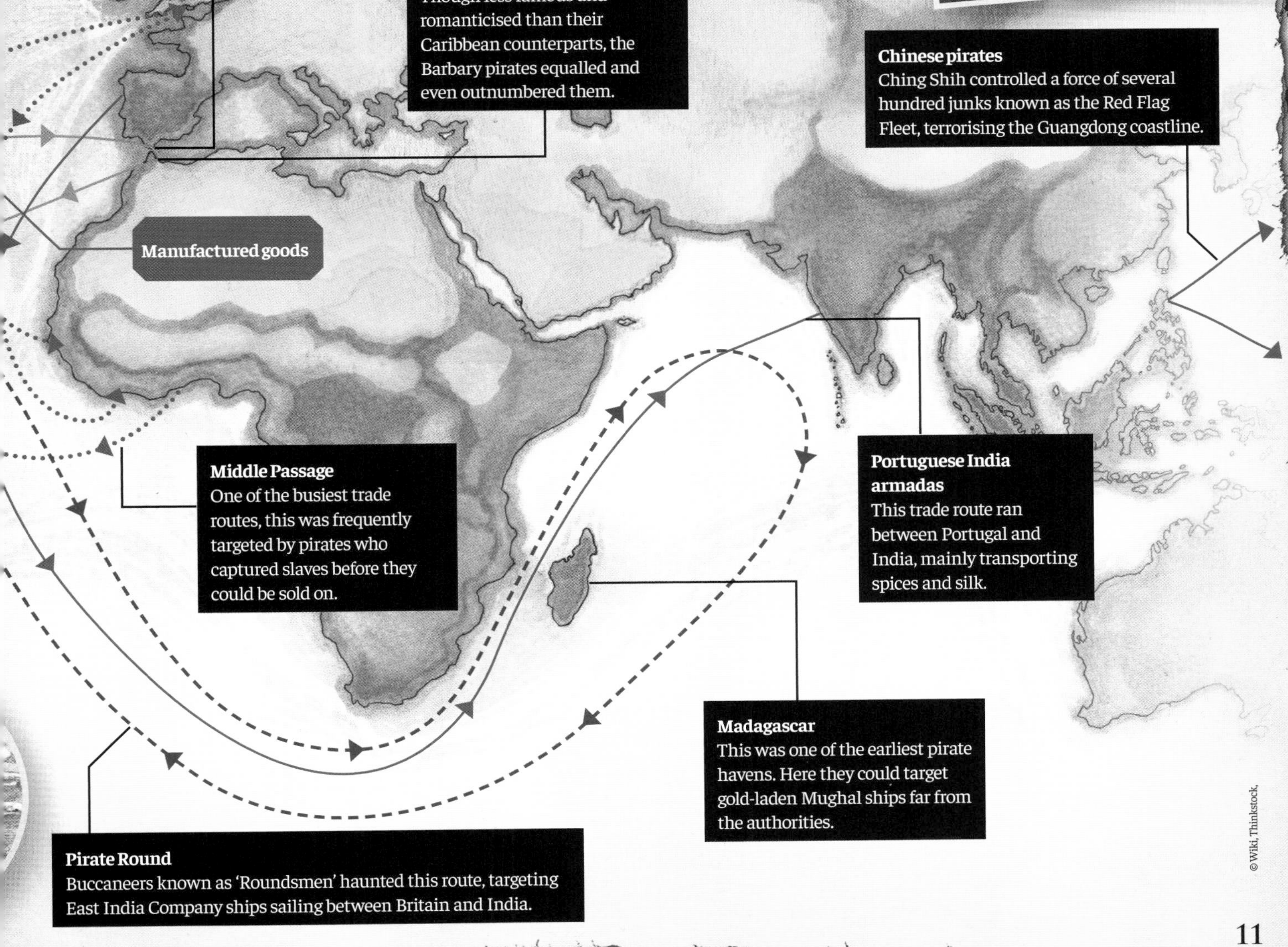

Spanish treasure fleets
Among the most sought-after ships were those that carried gold and silver from the New World to Seville.

Mediterranean corsairs
Though less famous and romanticised than their Caribbean counterparts, the Barbary pirates equalled and even outnumbered them.

Chinese pirates
Ching Shih controlled a force of several hundred junks known as the Red Flag Fleet, terrorising the Guangdong coastline.

Manufactured goods

Middle Passage
One of the busiest trade routes, this was frequently targeted by pirates who captured slaves before they could be sold on.

Portuguese India armadas
This trade route ran between Portugal and India, mainly transporting spices and silk.

Madagascar
This was one of the earliest pirate havens. Here they could target gold-laden Mughal ships far from the authorities.

Pirate Round
Buccaneers known as 'Roundsmen' haunted this route, targeting East India Company ships sailing between Britain and India.

THE ALLURE OF PIRACY

During the golden age of piracy, bandits and buccaneers reigned supreme across the seas

Across the late 17th and early 18th centuries, tremendous quantities of valuable cargo were being transported across the Atlantic Ocean, to and from the American colonies, which prompted experienced sailors and navigators to recklessly rebel and steal the goods for their own profit. The haul ranged widely in content and quantity, from treasure chests filled with gold, silver, and sparkling jewels, to tobacco, foods, ammunition, and barrels brimming with wine or brandy. Plenty of these imports, such as coffee, sugar, and fabrics, were in high demand and could be sold or traded for a substantial amount. Alongside precious gems, the plundered cargo was able to provide pirates with practical items, such as weaponry and ship equipment, and food and drink. For many, piracy was the only way in which they were able to earn money and survive, and it became as much of a livelihood as it did a chosen way of life.

For others, becoming a pirate wasn't a choice. Often, ships were seized during their crossings and its crews forced to serve under a new command, most especially those who were already experienced at sea or who could provide a particular skill, such as doctors, chefs, and carpenters. Mutiny, too, played a big part in piracy. There were many sailors who were unhappy with their living and working conditions, but who relied on their superiors and life on board the ship to survive. If the crew were able to group together and rebel, they could take over the ship, most often by overthrowing its officers and sailing it away from its routed course.

At the end of the War of the Spanish Succession at the beginning of the 18th century, thousands of men who had been recruited to serve in the navy were quickly dismissed and those who were able seamen became mutineers as a means of employment. Similarly, in 1856, most countries signed the Declaration of Paris, abolishing privateering. Prior to the

> "For many, piracy was the only way... to earn money and survive"

agreement, governments had supplied their navies with letters of marque, a licence which authorised the attack and capture of enemy vessels, allowing for legal plundering. When the treaty was signed and maritime warfare made illegal, the governments no longer had any need for the privateers and many of them turned to piracy as a means of avoiding further unemployment.

Amongst pirate crews, all men and women were treated as equal with no singular person outranking another. They elected their own captains, choosing whose leadership they wished to follow and everyone signed declarations of agreement to make sure that any bounty was divided equally. Piracy operated outside the governing law, under a different set of rules, and was a difficult activity for the authorities to control. For those who had no money, no prospects, and very little chance of climbing the class ladder, it presented an independent lifestyle of which individual wealth was a possibility. Being a pirate – or even just the thought of being a pirate – offered promise, opportunity, and adventure, away from a mundane existence on land. The sailing was a chance to travel and to explore, and pirates swarmed across the world, from the infamous Caribbean to the Ivory Coast.

With successful pillaging came riches – and with riches came pleasures. If it all went according to plan, a single voyage had the potential to earn a pirate more than they might have made across their entire lifetime, and there was no obligation for any of the profits to be handed over to government officials. Port Royal in Jamaica, was one of a handful of towns famed in the 17th century for its hedonism and debauchery; a pirate utopia where drinking, gambling, and prostitution could be freely indulged in, and for years it swarmed with buccaneers, although, more often than not, their wealth was lost as quickly as it had been found.

Above almost everything else, being a pirate meant a life of freedom; a chance for a person to live by their own rules and hand. An existence spent looting, exploring, and working outside of the law was one that appealed to many – and centuries after piracy's golden age, with its swashbuckling stories of treasure and adventure still being so prevalent in popular culture, it's safe to say that much of it still does today.

DRINK UP, ME HEARTIES

Hardtack

Also known as a sea biscuit, hardtack was part of the staple diet of any sailor. A plain and simple cracker made from wheat flour and water, it was cheap to produce, long-lasting, and ideal for lengthy voyages.

Salmagundi

Derived from the French word 'salmigondis', meaning a mixed concoction of things, this salad dish mostly comprised of meats, fish, and vegetables. Ship chefs would often use herbs and spices as a means of masking the rotten meat.

Salted beef

Salted beef was a principal ration aboard every ship and, like hardtack, it was easy to preserve for longer journeys. Where possible, all meats were either dried or salted and stored in a cask in order to extend their shelf life.

Rum

Rum, the drink probably most associated with pirates, was more accessible and affordable than other liquors, and it was more easily stored. In the mid-18th century, adding citrus to watered-down rum proved helpful in preventing outbreaks of scurvy.

ROGUES' GALLERY

These notorious buccaneers are representative of an era of defiance, independence, and adventure

Bartholomew Roberts

Nationality: Welsh **Born:** 1682 **Died:** 1722
Also known by his real name of John Roberts and his post-humous nickname of Black Bart, Roberts was one of the most successful buccaneers of his era. He was first conscripted under the leadership of captain Howell Davis, but his exceptional navigation skills allowed him to quickly climb the ranks and he soon came to thrive under the pirating lifestyle, plundering over 400 ships across his lifetime. Fearless and charismatic, he died in battle against privateer Chaloner Ogle and with his death came the grand culmination of piracy's golden age, as no other notorious figures followed him.

For a long time, Teach served as Hornigold's first mate, but it wasn't long before the skills and success of the student surpassed the teacher.

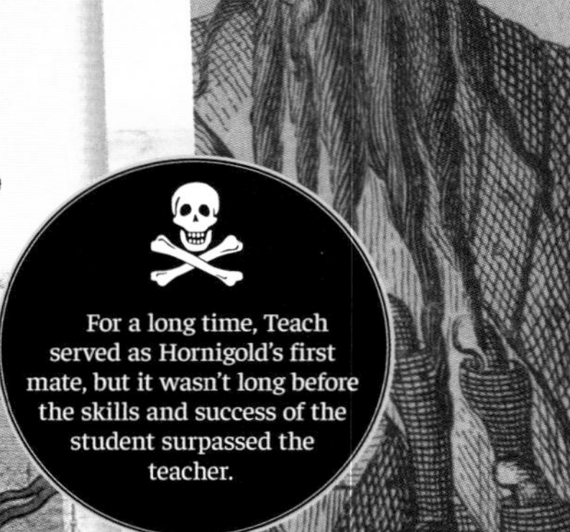

Edward Teach
Blackbeard

Nationality: English
Born: c.1680 **Died:** 1718
More commonly known by the name of Blackbeard, Teach is one of the most famous pirates in popular culture today, although he wasn't as successful as some of his other peers at the time. He first became a pirate under the command of Benjamin Hornigold and, at the peak of his career, he was in charge of four ships, commanded a pirate army of about 300, and had captured over 40 merchant ships across the Caribbean. He was eventually captured at his hideout on Ocracoke Island and killed by the Royal Navy, under the command of Robert Maynard.

Wynn began his pirating career during the Post Spanish Succession Period

Emanuel Wynn

Nationality: French **Born:** 1650 **Died:** Unknown
Very little is known about Wynn, but he is generally considered the first buccaneer to have sailed beneath the typical Jolly Roger pirate flag. His black-and-white design was a simple hourglass printed beneath a skull and crossbones, both of which became a common theme amongst pirates. His pirating career is believed to have commenced towards the end of the 17th century, when he began to raid merchant ships off the coast of America.

Soon after the death of Kidd, a sea shanty called *Captain Kidd's Farewell To The Seas* was written and printed, condemning his prosecution.

William Kidd

Nationality: Scottish **Born:** 1645 **Died:** 1701
Kidd began his sailing career as a privateer, engaged by the government to rid the seas of piracy, but he was forced into the trade after his crew elected him their pirate captain. When he captured Quedagh Merchant, an Armenian ship filled with reams of East Indies goods, he became a wanted man, and the Royal Navy set out to search for him. At the turn of the 17th century, he was captured in New York and sent to England for trial. He was found guilty, despite his reluctance as a pirate leader, and executed by hanging.

Mary Read

Nationality: English **Born:** c.1685 **Died:** 1721
Read was the daughter of a captain and first found employment aboard a ship disguised as a boy, before joining the Royal Navy and freely proving herself in battle, probably during the War of the Spanish Succession. Eventually, she joined forces with Rackham and Bonny, and the trio fought together until they were captured off the coast of West Indies. She died, pregnant, whilst in prison.

Black Caesar

Nationality: African
Born: Unknown **Died:** 1718
Black Caesar was one of the longest serving pirates of the golden age and his longevity is key in exploring social equality on the seas. Prior to sailing, he was a renowned war chieftain of a tribe and turned pirate captain only when a hurricane killed the crew who had enslaved him, and he mutinied. He ultimately joined Blackbeard's crew and, upon their eventual capture, was tried and hung alongside the others.

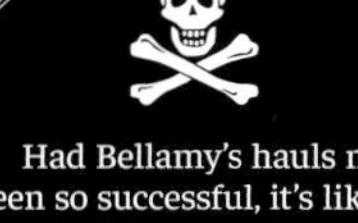

Had Bellamy's hauls not been so successful, it's likely that he'd have lived longer. The weight of the ship, laden with treasures, pulled it into high waves.

Samuel Bellamy

Nationality: English **Born:** 1689 **Died:** 1717
Bellamy, also known as Black Sam, sailed mostly in the West Indies for a little more than a year. He is widely regarded as the most successful pirate of the era, with a plundered estimate of over $130,000,000 and the capturing of over 50 ships. He was renowned for his skill in co-ordinating enemy attacks and minimising the loss of cargo. He was ultimately defeated by a storm, which sunk him and most of his crew.

Hornigold and his men once raided a ship to steal nothing but the crew's hats, after drinking too much the night before and throwing theirs overboard.

Benjamin Hornigold

Nationality: English **Born:** c.1680 **Died:** 1719
After pirating for three years, Hornigold accepted the 1718 Kings Pardon, offered to any man who wished to renounce, become an honest man, and assist in hunting down marauders. Prior to this reformation, he had founded the Republic of Pirates, a hideout haven in Nassau, but he soon became renowned for the betrayal of his former friends and his persecution of piracy. He died after his ship was destroyed in a hurricane.

Bonny was known to have blazing red hair and a matching temper

Anne Bonny

Nationality: Irish **Born:** c.1702 **Died:** c.1782
Although she never captained a ship of her own, Bonny is probably the most famous female pirate of her time. She was married to James Bonny, a poor sailor, but who craved adventure. Upon travelling to the Bahamas, she met Jack Packham, a pirate captain, and embarked upon an affair with him. She joined his crew, fighting alongside the men and fellow female buccaneer, Mary Read. Bonny was renowned for her skills in combat and was well-respected, regardless of her gender. When captured and sentenced, she claimed pregnancy, and was sent to prison instead. The timings and circumstances of her death are unknown.

As well as his enemies, Vane was infamously cruel to his own crew. He rarely followed the pirate code and often stole from his fellow sailors.

Vane was a savage pirate, known for his brutality towards captured crews

Charles Vane

Nationality: English
Born: c.1680 **Died:** 1721
Vane operated between 1717 and 1719, during the Post Spanish Succession Period, alongside other peers, such as Teach and Roberts. As with others, he was an able seaman and an ex-privateer, and was likely conscripted into piracy at the risk of unemployment after the War of the Spanish Succession. Although he was never particularly successful or wealthy, he was renowned for his bold nature and love of the pirate lifestyle. He was seized and tried after a shipwreck, and eventually executed over a year later. His body was hung on a gibbet at Port Royal as a warning to others.

ANATOMY OF A PIRATE SHIP

A ship was the most important thing a pirate could own, not only providing a means of transport, but also offering a life of freedom

As vital a practicality as a ship was to sail across the seas, to the crew, it meant much more; for many, it was their home. Pirates spent months, sometimes years, living and working aboard the vessel, and it was important that it was as well equipped as it could be, able to effectively carry all the required supplies, cargo, and equipment for a long voyage, and suitable to endure the harshest of weather conditions.

Each specific design of pirate ship possessed varying characteristics and was therefore useful in different scenarios. A brig, for example, was particularly favoured during piracy's golden age, more so than other ships, due to its speed and ease of navigation, although it wasn't so easy to manoeuvre in high winds. A frigate, too, was a popular type of warship, specifically built for combat. It came in a variety of sizes, but was typically larger than a brig and able to hold its cannons above its deck, which was ideal during an intense battle.

Generally speaking, ships became slower the bigger they were, and the more men and supplies which they carried onboard, especially if they were holding particularly heavy cargo. Pirate vessels, then, often travelled in fleets, with the tactic of a faster, and often smaller, ship sailing forwards to initially approach the enemy, while a bigger, heavier, and more well-armed ship could follow and attack. Although this was a clever strategic move, many merchant ships surrendered immediately at the mere sight of pirates, thereby managing to avoid naval warfare.

Adventure Galley was a particularly infamous ship, captained by William Kidd from the start of his privateering career at the end of the 17th century. The vessel itself was a hybrid of designs, combining square-rigged sails with oars, which was an unusual partnership in ships of the time. It was originally adapted from the frigate and built as such a warship in an effort to make it easily manoeuvrable in both blustery and calm conditions, as well as to generally increase its speed.

Over two years after its launch and as Kidd quickly succumbed to a life of piracy, the ship was finally successful in capturing two Indian vessels. Despite its innovative design, it began to deteriorate not long afterwards, however, with the hull gradually rotting and leaking. According to the accounts of Kidd and his crew, the ship was eventually sunk off the coast of Madagascar in 1698, three years after its launch, and the pirates quickly moved aboard one of their recent captures, Quedah Merchant. To this day, the final remains of Adventure Galley have never been located.

Quarterdeck
The quarterdeck was the uppermost part of a ship's deck, situated behind its main mast. It was where a captain would usually address his crew and where the vessel's flag was kept.

Captain's quarters
Situated at the ship's rear, the captain's cabin was the biggest room. As well as being used to dine and entertain, its large space was also useful in studying maps and charts.

Rudder
The rudder was a large wooden paddle located at the ship's stern. Used to steer the vessel, it was most often controlled by a wooden rod, known as a tiller.

SEVERNAJA
T I C O C E A N
Crow's nest
In piracy's early days, the crow's nest was simply a basket or barrel tied securely to the top of the ship's main mast. It was most often used as a lookout point.
Sails
Adventure Galley's unusual design, combining sails and oars, helped it to navigate against the wind and make progress in calmer weather. It could reach 14 knots under full sail and 3 knots under oar.
Bowsprit
The bowsprit was a slanted mast, which pointed forwards from the bow of the ship. Varying in size according to the vessel, it secured the rigging of the foremast.
Guns
Adventure Galley weighed over a staggering 284 tons in total, holding 34 cannons, 23 oars, and three masts. The huge warship needed over 100 crew members to properly sail it.
Anchor
Depending on the size of a ship, its anchor could often weigh over 1,000kg, meaning that even simply raising it took a lot of crewmen and a lot of time.
Hold
The ship's hold, also known as the cargo hold, was the space below deck, usually towards the hull, which was reserved for carrying the goods safely during a journey.

FIGHT LIKE A PIRATE

Across the centuries, pirates used a variety of weapons, each with a different purpose and level of usefulness

After boarding and attacking an enemy vessel, pirates would often find themselves engaging in a bout of hand-to-hand combat, fighting with many different smaller weapons, such as boarding axes, cutlasses, and daggers, in addition to often improvising on whatever was available at hand. These impromptu weapons were particularly useful after all the gunpowder and ammunition had run out, and the crew had to keep on fighting to either gain or keep control of the ship.

Hand weaponry was uninhibited by the weather conditions, with the rain often rendering all firearms useless, and they also allowed for a more controlled attack on enemies, because it was easier to manage their impact. This was especially important during boarding parties, in which pirates attempted to seize a ship and recruit its crew, without causing unnecessary injury or damage.

Light, short swords, such as the cutlass, were common weapons during piracy's golden age and were particularly popular with buccaneers. They were practical for close-combat fighting and simple to use, being easier to master than larger swords or rapiers. Warfare aside, they were also useful bits of equipment on deck, being sturdy enough to chop through rope, wood, and canvas.

There were other weapons which could be used as a form of defence, as well as a form of attack. Bucklers were shields used at the beginning of the 17th century. Although they were small and blunt, they were useful in deflecting blows, protecting the sword hand, and hindering the movements of the enemy.

Guns were often a pirate's first weapon of choice and their variety in size and range meant they were useful in many different situations and for different forms of attack. Prior to a boarding party, for example, pirates would often climb high up in the rigging and use a long-barrelled rifle, such as a musket, to target the enemy. This was usually done by sharpshooters; the name for those who were skilled in precision shooting from a long range and were less likely to waste bullets.

Smaller firearms, including handheld pistols, were most effective in close combat, such as when fighting aboard an enemy vessel, as they were easier to operate in cramped spaces, and they required less accuracy in their aim. They were also cheaper, as they held less ammunition than larger guns, but, as with all firearms, their efficiency depended on the weather, flints, and strength of gunpowder.

Developed in the early 17th century, the flintlock pistol was a revolutionary addition to naval warfare, becoming the dominant firing weapon for hundreds of years to follow. Before their arrival, pirates used a variety of matchlock, snaplock, and wheel lock mechanisms, all of which were reliant on gunpowder for their ignition. The variation in the production of calibre across nations, however, meant that captured bullets could not fit into the weaponry without being melted and recast. This was an incredibly laborious and time-consuming process, which didn't even always prove successful.

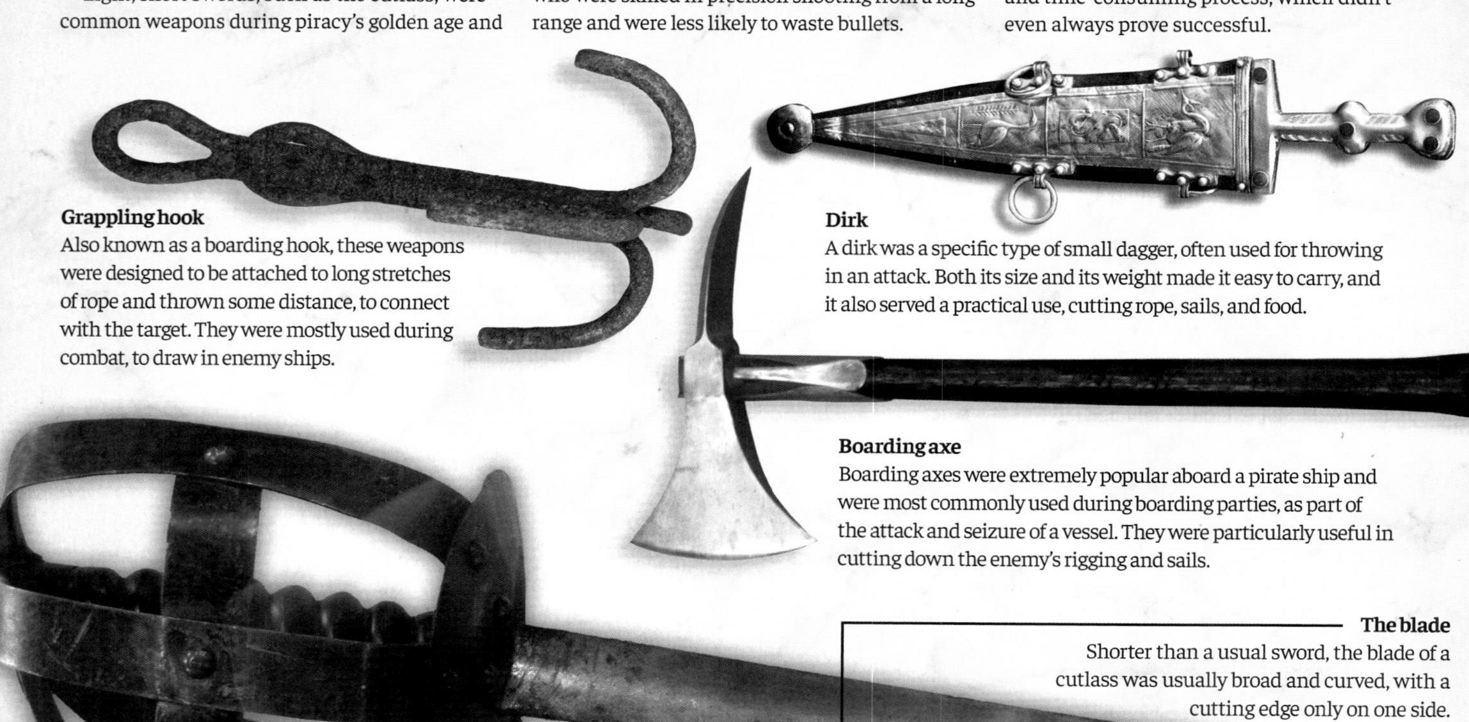

Grappling hook
Also known as a boarding hook, these weapons were designed to be attached to long stretches of rope and thrown some distance, to connect with the target. They were mostly used during combat, to draw in enemy ships.

Dirk
A dirk was a specific type of small dagger, often used for throwing in an attack. Both its size and its weight made it easy to carry, and it also served a practical use, cutting rope, sails, and food.

Boarding axe
Boarding axes were extremely popular aboard a pirate ship and were most commonly used during boarding parties, as part of the attack and seizure of a vessel. They were particularly useful in cutting down the enemy's rigging and sails.

The blade
Shorter than a usual sword, the blade of a cutlass was usually broad and curved, with a cutting edge only on one side.

Hilt
The handle of the cutlass, also known as the hilt, often had a cupped or basked-shaped guard, to protect the fighting hand.

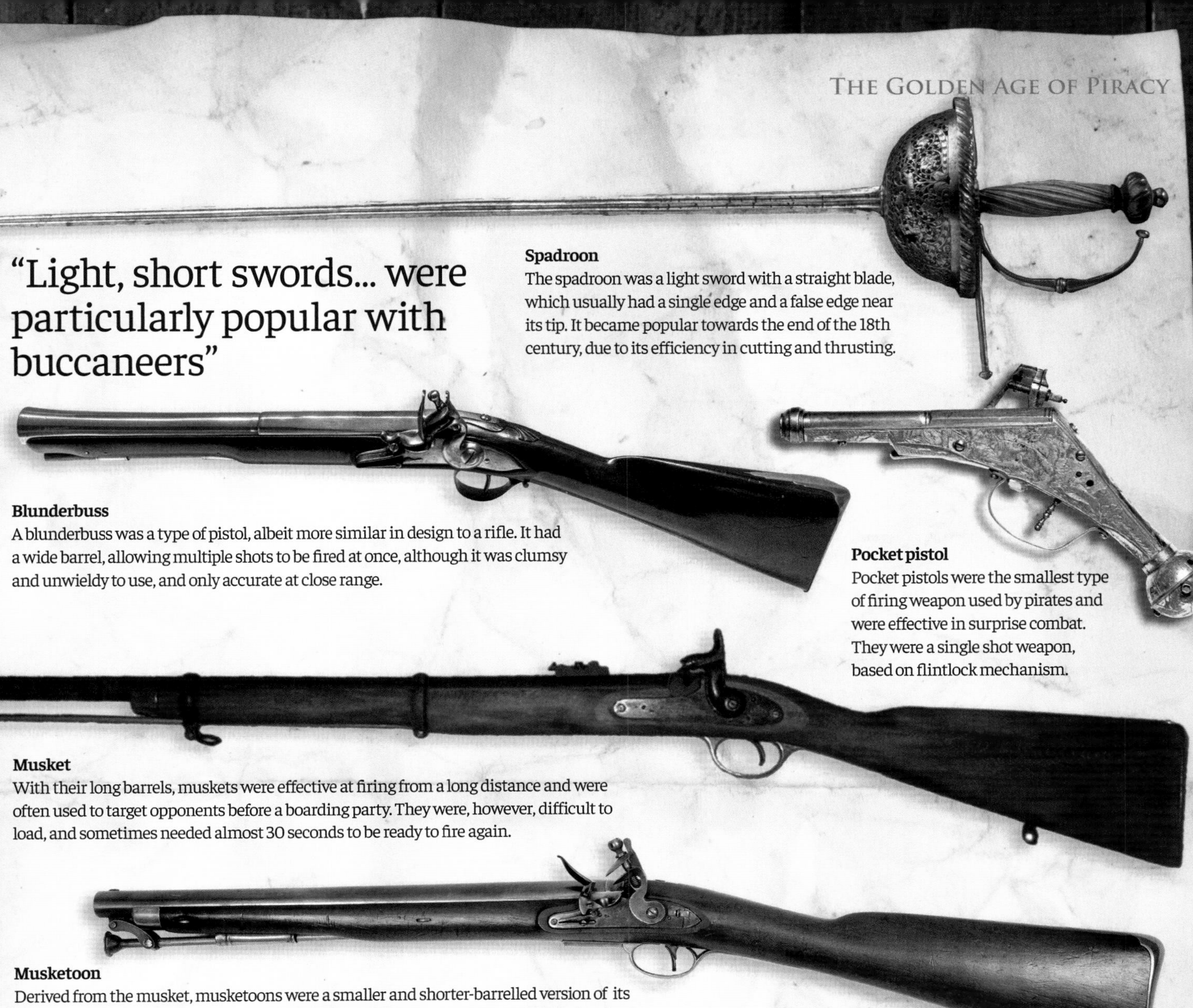

"Light, short swords... were particularly popular with buccaneers"

Spadroon
The spadroon was a light sword with a straight blade, which usually had a single edge and a false edge near its tip. It became popular towards the end of the 18th century, due to its efficiency in cutting and thrusting.

Blunderbuss
A blunderbuss was a type of pistol, albeit more similar in design to a rifle. It had a wide barrel, allowing multiple shots to be fired at once, although it was clumsy and unwieldy to use, and only accurate at close range.

Pocket pistol
Pocket pistols were the smallest type of firing weapon used by pirates and were effective in surprise combat. They were a single shot weapon, based on flintlock mechanism.

Musket
With their long barrels, muskets were effective at firing from a long distance and were often used to target opponents before a boarding party. They were, however, difficult to load, and sometimes needed almost 30 seconds to be ready to fire again.

Musketoon
Derived from the musket, musketoons were a smaller and shorter-barrelled version of its predecessor, and were popular in their size and practicality. Depending on their size, they could fire a singular or multiple musket balls.

Hammer
The hammer is the part of the pistol which holds and propels the flint forwards, to strike the frizzen.

Frizzen
The frizzen is the piece of steel which the flint strikes. The contact between the two produces a shower of sparks, which in turn ignites the gunpowder.

Jaws
The jaws clamp the piece of flint in place, ensuring it hits the frizzen hard enough for the metal to spark.

Frizzen spring
The frizzen spring holds down the cover of the pan containing the gunpowder, preventing it from becoming damp in bad weather.

Tip
The short, sharp sword was an effective weapon in battle, particularly useful in cutting and slashing at the enemy.

Pan
The pan is where the gunpowder sits. It is ignited when the flint strikes the frizzen, opening the pan and exposing sparks.

Trigger
When the trigger is pulled, the cock holding the piece of flint is released, throwing it forwards in order to hit the frizzen.

The Pirate Code

Being a pirate wasn't always carefree pillaging and plundering; some rules still had to be followed

The pirate code, generally speaking, was rules of conduct which were drawn up by a captain and their crew before a ship set sail. All pirates travelling aboard the vessel were to swear an oath of allegiance and sign the articles of agreement as a means of formal induction, which strictly documented what was to be done, what was not to be done, and the penalty or reimbursement as was appropriate. Usually, after a voyage, all evidence of the code was destroyed, so as not to be discovered and used during trial as proof of illegal collusion.

Serious misconduct such as theft, desertion or secrecy, was punishable by marooning or even death, but there were also less severe rules concerning curfews, drinking, and gambling aboard the ship. If someone was injured in combat, the code offered compensation, with the quantity of payment being dependent on the severity of the wound; the loss of a limb could fetch hundreds of pieces of silver.

> "Serious misconduct... was punishable by marooning or even death"

The listed articles also covered what share each pirate received of a successful raid, most often according to their rank aboard the ship. Usually, the captain received between five and six shares; senior individuals, such as the quartermaster, received two shares; crew members received one share, and junior individuals, such as the cabin boy, received half a share. Upon dispute or debate, the decision always remained with the captain, but just as with the rest of the crew, their position of authority could be lost (sometimes by mutiny) if it was abused or neglected.

Bartholomew Roberts, a notorious buccaneer of the early 18th century, often pushed captured crews into pirate conscription, forcing them to sign the code. To rebel against the written rules was, in a sense, to sign one's own death sentence, and the code was as much of a way to endure a life on the tough seas as it was a method of keeping rank order. Roberts' own pirate code survived, due to his untimely death in battle, and the documents were later used in court, as testimony against piracy.

Stolen goods were divided equally across the crew according to rank

Articles of Henry Morgan

The articles commonly attributed to Henry Morgan and his crew still exist today

I. The fund of all payments under the articles is the stock of what is gotten by the expedition, following the same law as other pirates, No prey, no pay.

II. Compensation is provided the Captain for the use of his ship, and the salary of the carpenter, or shipwright, who mended, careened, and rigged the vessel (usually about 150 pieces of eight). A sum for provisions and victuals is specified, usually 200 pieces of eight. A salary and compensation is specified for the surgeon and his medicine chest, usually 250 pieces of eight.

III. A standard compensation is provided for maimed and mutilated buccaneers. "Thus they order for the loss of a right arm 600 pieces of eight, or six slaves; for the loss of a left arm 500 pieces of eight, or five slaves; for a right leg 500 pieces of eight, or five slaves; for the left leg 400 pieces of eight, or four slaves; for an eye 100 pieces of eight, or one slave; for a finger of the hand the same reward as for the eye."

IV. Shares of booty are provided as follows: "the Captain, or chief Commander, is allotted five or six portions to what the ordinary seamen have; the Master's Mate only two; and Officers proportionate to their employment. After whom they draw equal parts from the highest even to the lowest mariner, the boys not being omitted. For even these draw half a share, by reason that, when they happen to take a better vessel than their own, it is the duty of the boys to set fire to the ship or boat wherein they are, and retire to the prize which they have taken."

V. In the prizes they take, it is severely prohibited to every one to usurp anything, in particular to themselves.... Yea, they make a solemn oath to each other not to abscond, or conceal the least thing they find amongst the prey. If afterwards any one is found unfaithful, who has contravened the oath, immediately he is separated and turned out.

All pirates signed a code of conduct before becoming part of a crew

SHIP-BOARD ROLES

A pirate's guide to the who's-who aboard a working ship

Captain

The pirate captain was elected by the crew and could be replaced at any time through a majority vote. They were expected to be bold, fearless, and skilled in battle.

Quartermaster

The quartermaster was second-in-command to the captain, with the authority to punish minor offences. They also managed the account books and kept general order.

Sailing master

The sailing master was in charge of sailing and navigating the ship across the oceans, adjusting its course as required, and taking care of all the necessary maps and charts.

Master gunner

The master gunner was in charge of the ship's weaponry and ammunition. Duties included keeping the powder dry and making sure all guns were in good repair.

Mate

There was often more than one mate aboard a large ship and they generally served as apprentices, raising the anchor and making sure the vessel had sufficient rigging.

Rigger

The rigger was specifically assigned to operate the rigging and to open and release the sails. This was one of the more dangerous roles to have, due to the risk of falling.

Carpenter

The carpenter took care of the ship's maintenance and repair, under the boatswain. They fixed the masts and yards, and checked the hull regularly to keep the vessel watertight.

Boatswain

The boatswain was responsible for supervising the ship's maintenance, checking its structure, sails, and rigging daily, as well as all activities on deck, including dropping the anchor.

Able-bodied sailor

The able-bodied sailor was a common and experienced seaman, familiar with reading the weather, steering and navigation, and handling the equipment of the ship.

Cabin boy

The cabin boy was usually a young child who worked aboard the ship as a servant. They were recruited either through kidnapping or from runaways who volunteered.

Pirates vs privateers

Tasked with keeping waters safe, privateers became as brutal as pirates themselves

Merchant vessels were a tempting target. It was the English who first commissioned privateers to protect their cargo while in transit, issuing them with licenses to attack any ship that posed a threat. Rather than a wage, privateers were paid with an agreed share of the takings, and the line between piracy and privateering became very blurred indeed.

On the face of it, the difference between these two vocations was simple. Pirates were criminals who acted alone, while privateers worked under the order of the crown. By allowing privateers to attack Spanish ships, Elizabeth I could deny any direct involvement, while still getting a share of the profits. Her 'sea dogs', as they became known, included Francis Drake and Walter Raleigh, but the Spanish saw them simply as state-sponsored pirates. Many captains and crews swung between privateer and pirate depending on the state of international affairs.

Many privateers were knighted, but others were not so lucky. In 1701, William Kidd was hanged for piracy. He had set sail years earlier with a government commission to suppress pirates in the Indian Ocean. Here, like many privateers of the time, he began to plunder foreign vessels indiscriminately, but conflict was growing among his crew. When they threatened mutiny, he struck the ship's gunner on the head, delivering him a slow and painful death. When Kidd returned to the West Indies, he had been declared a pirate, and was arrested and sent back to England. After his hanging, Kidd's body was gibbeted over the River Thames as a warning to any would-be pirates.

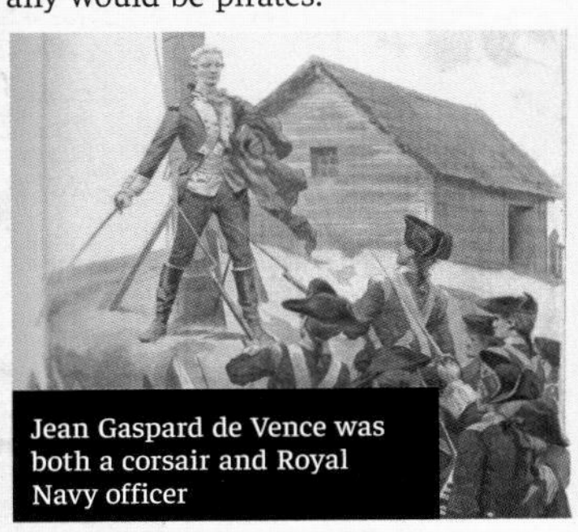

Jean Gaspard de Vence was both a corsair and Royal Navy officer

Day in the life

A PIRATE QUARTERMASTER

Keeping order in a lawless world, Caribbean, 18th century

Being a pirate in the 18th-century Golden Age of Piracy was not a glamorous job. Those who chose this perilous path (and those forced to against their will) risked life and limb. However, the rewards if successful were greater than any sailor in the Royal Navy could ever dream of. Although the ship's captain was in charge in battle, it was actually the quartermaster who held the real control. This figure, elected by the crew, even held command over the captain himself, and was responsible for the considerably hefty job of keeping the men and ship in order.

KEEP THE VESSEL SHIPSHAPE

Far from swashbuckling excitement, almost every day was filled with boring, monotonous tasks to maintain the ship. Pirates would fix the sails with pickers, seam rubbers and needles, work on repairing any holes in the ship by driving new oakum into the seams, and work the pump for hours. If the ship was in bad shape, they would find somewhere they could careen it to scrape off the barnacles and remove any worms in the hull.

FIND SOMETHING TO EAT

Food on board pirate ships was scarce, even for the authority figures. Because water in barrels would quickly go off, pirates would usually drink bumboo – a mixture of rum, water, sugar and nutmeg. The most common food was hardtack, which they ate in the dark to avoid seeing the weevils crawling over the biscuits, and some desperate crews even resorted to eating rats or their own leather satchels.

PUNISH LAWBREAKERS

Considering they were outlaws themselves, pirates had a surprisingly strict law code; the quartermaster was responsible for ensuring seamen stuck to it. It differed from ship to ship, but common laws included bans on gambling, rape and fighting. Punishments for rule breakers were harsh, from whippings to being sentenced to death. Walking the plank was actually very rare. One particularly grisly punishment was to be marooned with a gun loaded with a single shot.

It was more likely for lawbreakers to be simply thrown overboard than endure the psychological torture of walking the plank

The famous Jolly Roger flag was another form of intimidation

SETTLE A DISAGREEMENT

Quartermasters were keen to avoid any fighting on their ships, so any disagreements had to be settled on shore, and there was a set procedure for this. The quartermaster would accompany the men to land and turn them back to back. They would walk a set amount of paces, then, on his word, turn and fire. If both miss, they would draw their cutlasses. The intention wasn't to kill their opposition but to draw first blood.

CAPTURE A SHIP

Much of a crew's success depended on having a fierce reputation. Rather than slaughtering their way to victory, the aim was for the other ship to surrender peacefully, and terrifying reputations encouraged this. However, once surrendered, the enemy crew were usually spared. If it was known that pirates killed their prisoners, then crews would fight to the death, and this would make victory more costly in lives. Most were happy to surrender their booty peacefully.

SHARE OUT THE SPOILS

There was an agreed hierarchy on board pirate ships that determined how the captured riches were distributed. Pirates would even use early forms of modern-day checks and balances to keep everything fair. Ordinary seaman usually received a single share, while the captain, officers and quartermasters received larger amounts. Treasure was rarely, if ever, buried, and usually comprised food, weapons and clothing rather than chests of gold coins and jewels.

AVOID CAPTURE

Nearly all of the most famous pirates in history, such as Charles Vane and Blackbeard, only sailed for a few years before they were captured. Punishment for pirates was very harsh, and their executions served as a form of entertainment. Many would end up being hung or 'dancing the hempen jig', and some were placed in gibbets and starved to death. Their bodies would be left in the iron cages to swing and rot, serving as a gruesome deterrent for other would-be pirates.

OVERSEE MEDICAL CARE

Life at sea was not for the faint of heart – injuries and illness were just an accepted risk of the profession. The classic images of pirates with peg legs and hooks are not so farfetched – if untreatable, most injured limbs would be sawn off on board, with the patient being held down by his fellow pirates. If they could afford it, a lost leg would be replaced with a specially made peg leg to fit, but otherwise a stick was just tied to the stump. Hooks, meanwhile, were very expensive.

Despite their bloodthirsty reputation, pirate captains would usually be elected through a democratic vote

HOW TO CAPTURE A MERCHANT SHIP

A pirate's guide to plundering valuable cargo, Caribbean, Early 1700s

Everybody knows that pirates were only after one thing: treasure, right? In fact, during the Golden Age of Piracy, these bearded barnacles were looting all sorts of valuable cargo, from sugar and coffee to cocoa and silks. Pirates were a major problem for American colonists in the late 17th and early 18th centuries, strangling their essential trade routes between the New World, the Caribbean and Europe. Soon, however, the sea-bound scoundrels themselves were to become prizes worth hunting, with a rich reward given to any man who captured and killed them. With bounties on their heads, the pirates' reign of terror only lasted about 40 years.

What you'll need

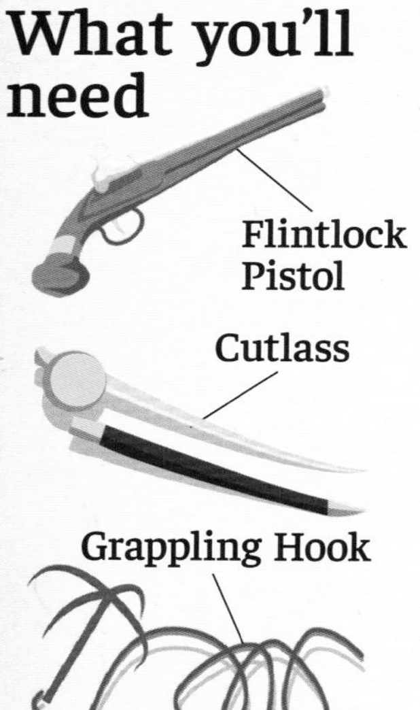

Ruling the waves

Speedy schooner

These ships were popular among pirates during the Golden Age because of their speed and ability to sail through shallow waters.

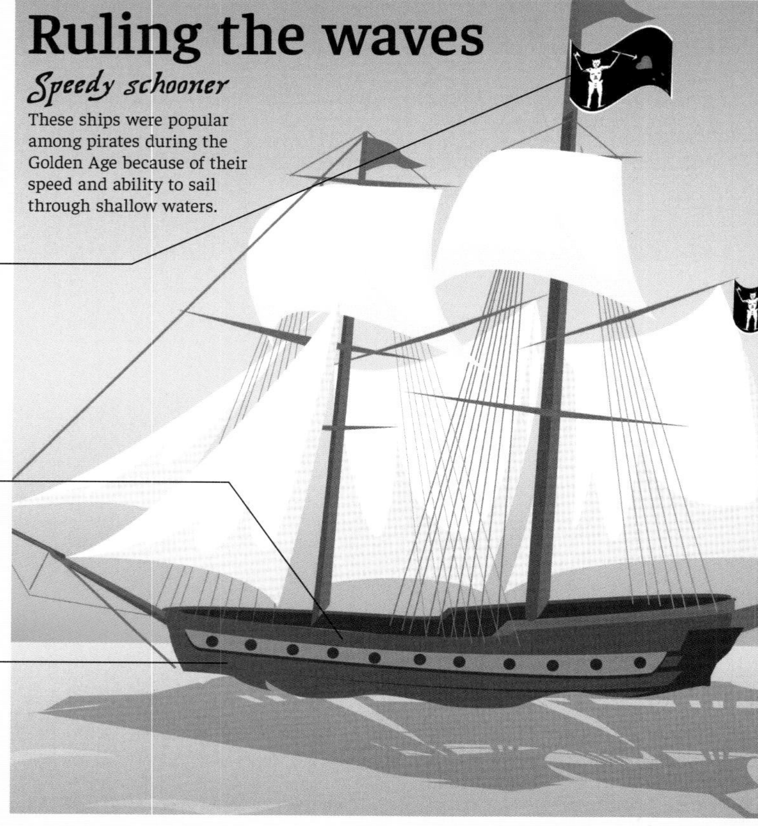

Fearsome flag

A pirate's flag was a symbol of death, sporting depictions of skeletons and devils. They hoped it would scare the enemy into surrendering.

Deadly weapons

It was not in the pirates' interest to waste expensive gunpowder, but cannons helped to intimidate the merchant ships.

Coveted cargo

Merchant ships carried anything from molasses to kegs of rum, but also plenty of useful supplies such as ammunition and food.

01 Get into position

Set sail in the Bahamas and keep a weather eye on the horizon for merchant ships. This is the perfect spot for unscrupulous operations since it's in line with trade routes and close to the cargo ports. There are also plenty of uninhabited islands and secluded coves in which to lie in wait for a passing cargo ship before ambushing them.

02 Follow your target

Shadow the merchant ship to see how many men are on board, what kind of cargo it carries and what armaments they could have. This could take several days, but a pirate must be patient; surprise is one of the greatest weapons on the open seas. Pirates were democratic, and would take a vote to make important decisions, like whether to attack.

How not to... loot if you want to live

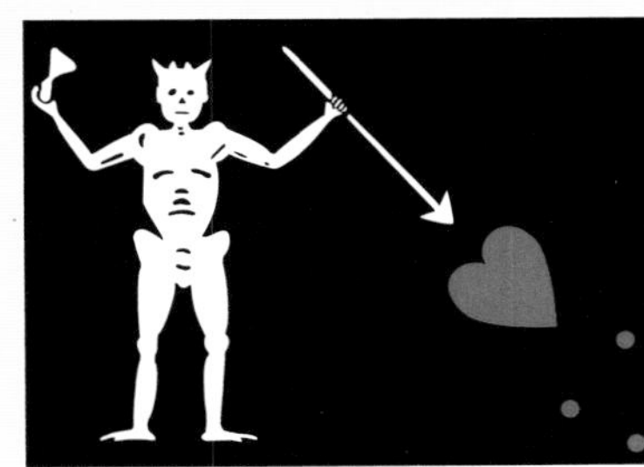

It was 1718 and of all the pirates in the Caribbean you were likely to meet, Edward Teach – better known as Blackbeard – was the most dreaded. As soon as sailors clocked the notorious flag – a skeleton stabbing a heart with a spear – they surrendered, trading their cargo for mercy.

Desperate, the locals went to the governor of Virginia, Alexander Spotswood, whose hatred of pirates sparked a manhunt. Once Blackbeard was within their sights, the sailors hid below deck, tricking the pirates into boarding their ship and using their own dirty tricks against them.

"Damnation seize my soul if I give you quarters, or take any from you," boomed Blackbeard, before bearing down on Royal Navy Officer Robert Maynard. But he didn't see the sailor that sprung from behind and hacked his head clean off. It was mounted on the bow of the ship that captured and killed the most infamous swashbuckler, but the legend of Blackbeard lived on.

03 Raise the flag

Wait until the dim light of dawn or dusk when the ship is difficult to see, and draw within firing range. Determine the ship's nationality and then raise that country's flag to lull them into a false sense of security. At the last moment, switch the flag for the pirate's true colours – usually black or blood red – and fire a warning shot.

04 Surrender or die

The flag is usually enough to frighten ships into surrendering without a fight. It's well known that a pirate flag usually means that no mercy will be shown once the ship has been boarded. Jam the rudder with wooden wedges so the ship can't be steered, and then use grappling hooks to pull the vessel close enough to climb aboard.

05 Take hostages

Ransack all the cargo, leaving no crate unturned, and offer the sailors a place on the pirate ship. They could have valuable skills or be used to press other crew members from merchant ships. If they refuse, toss them overboard, take them as slaves or hold them ransom. Always strip them of any jewels or money first, though.

06 Share the booty

Divide up the loot with your fellow crew, making sure that the captain receives a larger share of the stolen goods. Then either add the captured merchant ship to your fleet – making some adjustments to hide its identity, of course – or send it to the depths to destroy the evidence. There's a reward for captured pirates, so you can't be too careful.

4 Famous... Pirate ships

Adventure Galley

1695-98, WILLIAM KIDD

A hybrid ship combining sails and oars, Adventure Galley was poorly built, and was abandoned because of its rotting hull.

Fancy

1694-95, HENRY EVERY

After staging a mutiny and taking control of the ship, Every customised it to make it one of the fastest in the Indian Ocean.

Whydah

1716-17, SAMUEL BELLAMY

Originally a slave ship, the Whydah Gally was captured by Black Sam on the return leg of its maiden voyage. Its wreck is the only pirate ship authenticated beyond doubt.

Royal Fortune

1719-21, BLACK BART

This was just one of many ships acquired by notorious pirate Bartholomew Roberts to be renamed Royal Fortune.

THE SPOILS OF WAR

At the peak of the Golden Age, pirates were pillaging and plundering all over the world. Here are the biggest hauls of riches they picked up along the way

PRIZE 1

Year: **1695** **Location:** **Red Sea**
Victim: **Fateh Muhammed and Ganj-i-Sawai**
Pirate Captain: **Henry Every**
Spoils: **£500,000**

Every may not be as well remembered as some of his contemporaries, but over his lifetime, he earned more loot than most of them added together, and he is famous for what was quite possibly the richest singular haul in piracy's history. Towards the end of the 17th century, he headed north from the coast of Madagascar, in his ship Fancy, alongside other ships hoping to intercept a fleet of vessels owned by the Grand Mughal of India, which were returning from their annual pilgrimage to Mecca. The first one they attacked, Fateh Muhammed, was easily overrun, and the troop collected somewhere between £50,000 and £60,000. Greedy for more, Every quickly caught up with Ganj-i-Sawai, which carried the wealthiest of the treasures. After a bloody and lengthy battle, Every and his crew tricked the other ships and ran away with all the loot. A wanted man by the lawful and the lawless alike, Every disappeared from history shortly afterwards and the rest of his life remains a mystery. Sources of the time, however, suggest that he died penniless in London, having lost all of his riches.

PRIZE 2

Year: **1716** **Location:** **Florida coast**
Victim: **Sunken 1715 Spanish Treasure Fleet**
Pirate Captain: **Henry Jennings**
Spoils: **£87,000 (£600,000 in total, before division)**

In July 1715, a huge flotilla of Spanish galleons, loaded with mounds of treasure, was sunk by a hurricane off the Florida coast. Many of the sailors survived, were washed ashore, and hurried to collect as much of the riches as possible. News of the calamity spread and many ships sailed as fast as they were able towards the wreck. Amongst the pirates was Bersheba and its captain, Henry Jennings. Jennings was a privateer who had served during the War of Spanish Succession, and the looting of this Spanish shipwreck was his recorded foray into piracy. Bersheba and its crew arrived at the sunken vessels at the beginning of 1716, when most of the booty had already been salvaged. Jennings, however, found a big lump of it waiting to be shipped on a beach nearby, and he ambushed the camp, armed with three vessels and up to 300 men. Although he enjoyed the spoils of his raid, Jennings was one of the few pirates who accepted the 1718 King's Pardon, sailing to Bermuda and surrendering to the authorities himself. He retired from the sea and became a plantation owner, enjoying wealth and success on the land, although his ultimate fate is unknown.

PRIZE 3

Year: 1707 **Location:** Red Sea
Victim: British squadron of warships
Pirate Captain: John Halsey
Spoils: £50,000

John Halsey, like many, began his seafaring career as a privateer. As soon as the letter of marque was due to expire in 1704, Halsey and his crew set sail towards Madagascar in their ship, Charles, embracing the pirate lifestyle. During August 1707, as they travelled towards Mocha in the Red Sea, they encountered a fleet of heavily armed British warships. Despite having over 60 cannons aimed at them, Halsey decided to engage in battle. Surprisingly, the largest of the British vessels fled, breaking the formation, and allowing the pirates to overthrow the convoy. They managed to capture two of the ships, stealing an estimated £50,000 in loot. Charles was not Halsey's only vessel; he possessed a small flotilla, after capturing two merchant ships a year earlier. All of these sank soon after the victory in a hurricane and Halsey would die himself not long after, in 1708, of a fever. He was a well-respected man amongst his fellows and was buried with great ceremony.

PRIZE 4

Year: 1719 **Location:** Brazilian coast
Victim: Fleet of Portuguese warships
Pirate Captain: Bartholomew Roberts
Spoils: £40,000-£90,000

During the summer of 1719, Roberts and his crew spent over two months sailing the length of the Brazilian coast, but they failed to spot a single ship until they were just about to return to the Caribbean. In All Saints' Bay, there was a fleet of 42 Portuguese ships, loaded with treasure. Roberts, brazenly flying a Portuguese flag, sailed straight into the middle of the convoy, picked a ship at random, and took its officer hostage. He demanded to know the richest vessel and the prisoner pointed out Sagrada Familia, which carried 40 guns and almost 200 men. The treasure ship was boarded and captured by the pirates, and they sailed away with a plethora of riches, including tens of thousands of Portuguese coins and reams of jewellery.

Year: 1693 **Location:** Red Sea
Victim: Indian trading ship
Pirate Captain: Thomas Tew
Spoils: £100,000

Thomas Tew only ever set sail on two major piratical voyages during his lifetime, but they were both significant. Tew was one of the few to pioneer the route known as the Pirate Round, which led from the Atlantic, to Africa, then on to India. His first expedition went underway towards the end of 1693. As they sailed through the Red Sea in their ship Amity, Tew and his men came across a fleet of Indian ships, laden with treasure. Although the convoy carried as many as 300 soldiers, it surrendered without fight, and both parties escaped uninjured. Amity carried away £100,000 in goods. As per the pirate code, the loot was divided equally amongst the crew, with each member receiving between £1,200 and £3,000, according to their position, and Tew taking £8,000.

THE PIRATE HUNTERS

At the peak of piracy, vast quantities of goods were being looted and halting the progression of world trade. In response, the government employed anyone who wished to help

The 1718 Kings Pardon was first delivered by Woodes Rogers, the governor of the Bahamas territory. It was issued in retaliation to the growing activity of piracy across the regions and its introduction marked the beginning of the golden age's decline. The Kings Pardon was offered to anyone who wished to reject the buccaneering lifestyle and return to work in accordance with the law, in exchange for turning on their fellow pirates and helping authorities to hunt them down.

Although many pirates had served as privateers during the War of the Spanish Succession and had been considered useful by the government, in peacetime, they had become dangerous, volatile, and damaging to economic trade. The pardon worked particularly well with those who feared capture, but for others, pursuing was the only way to stop them – even then, it didn't always work.

Many renowned pirates, including Benjamin Hornigold, accepted the pardon, and took no issue with betraying his fellow men. Others, like Charles Vane, initially agreed to the offer, only to rebel almost immediately afterwards. In theory, the pardon was the perfect way to employ able seaman and cull levels of piracy; in practice, it incurred complications, not only in fighting some of the most notorious pirates alive, but also in terms of the rewards it could offer.

> "Not all hunters were pirates... many were government officials"

Without the democracy of the pirate code to guide them and the ability to swindle whatever loot they liked, there were many fights amongst the hunters as to how to divide the rewards and recognition of a successful chase. There was much less structural integrity to the way in which they operated, and the crew members regularly stole from and lied to one another.

Not all hunters were reformed pirates, however; many were governmental officials or naval captains, keen to curb the problem of piracy. Colonel William Rhett is one such figure, most famous for his capture of Stede Bonnet, who was also known as the Gentlemen Pirate and who often collaborated with Blackbeard on many successful voyages. Bonnet had a £700 bounty on his head when he surrendered to Rhett in 1718. He pleaded for clemency at his trial, vowing never to engage in acts of piracy again, but he was condemned to death and hanged alongside the rest of his crew in the Province of South Carolina.

Bonnet had somewhat of an easy death in comparison to his ally Blackbeard, who was also executed at the hand of a pirate hunter – the lieutenant Robert Maynard. The infamous

The Navy raids New Providence, a pirate sanctuary in the Bahamas

Hanged bodies wer often tied with chains t prolong public displa

Warfare on the open ocean was a deadly affair

Blackbeard's death was a major win for the pirate hunters

A French ship is sunk by the English Navy

seafarer was killed towards the end of 1718, at Ocracoke Island, after suffering five gunshot wounds and almost 20 slashes from a knife or cutlass. After Blackbeard's death, Maynard and his crew cut off his head, displayed it on the bow of the ship as a warning to other pirates, and then threw his corpse into the ocean.

Unless they were killed at sea, most captured pirates were sent to prison for a short time, then put on trial for their crimes, before almost certainly being found guilty of them. Crew members were often found to turn on one another and try to bargain their way out of the hangman's noose, whether it was with information or their share of loot, but the ploy rarely succeeded. The evidence against a captain and his men was usually overwhelming, and the majority of the crew was often hanged together.

William Kidd's arrest and death was one of the more unusual sentences of the piracy era, because he originated as a pirate hunter himself. His first voyages were sailed hesitantly as a privateer and he failed to capture any pirates for a long time, refusing to attack passing ships and losing many of his crew members to desertion along the way. On an occasion when Kidd did seize a ship, he discovered that its captain was an Englishman and he attempted to convince his crew to relinquish the vessel and its stolen valuables. They refused, he acquiesced, and he was immediately branded a pirate by the navy.

As soon as Kidd was arrested, his crew turned against him and he took the blame as their captain. He was imprisoned for a year in solitary confinement, before heading to trial, which had all the evidence to support him removed and two of his fellow soldiers testifying against him in exchange for pardons, helping to seal his fate. Kidd, the pirate hunter, was hanged as a pirate in 1701, after being betrayed by the government he'd helped to protect.

Punishment in the Golden Age

Marooning

This punishment was often reserved for those who deserted the post in battle. The culprit was abandoned on a desert island, with nothing but the clothes they had on, a small can of water, a pistol, powder, and shot.

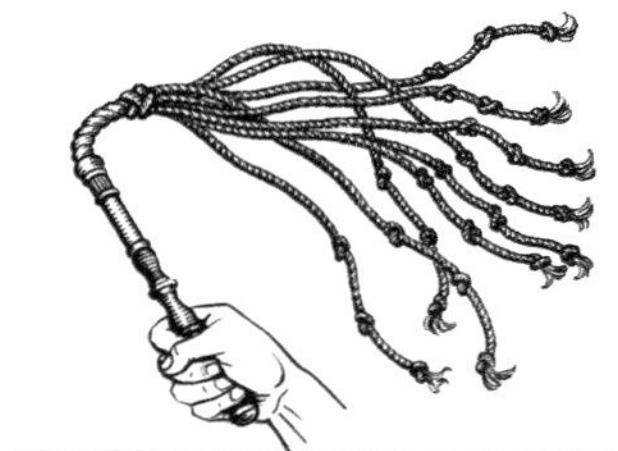

Cat o'nine tails

This was a particular method of whipping, which used an unwound rope of nine strands with a barbed end, usually either of fish hooks or musket balls. Afterwards, the raw skin was often doused in salt and vinegar to cause further pain.

Hanging

Hanging was the most common form of pirate execution and it often took place at gallows close to water, whether the sea or a river. To prolong public display, corpses were usually coated in tar or tied up in chains.

Clapping in irons

If a crew member misbehaved aboard the ship, they would often be clamped into wrist and leg irons, and either tossed into the ship's hold or tied to the ship's mast. The latter was especially popular if there were bad weather conditions.

LEGENDS OF THE SEAS

Pirates were a rather superstitious bunch, with a big list of dos and don'ts whilst at sea. Not all of their origins are known, but some prevail to this day

HAVING A CAT ABOARD A SHIP BROUGHT GOOD LUCK

Many pirates considered felines, particularly black ones, bringers of good fortune and would often take them aboard a vessel as a result. There were also particular superstitions regarding the behaviour of the cat whilst at sea, quite often in regards to the weather. If it walked towards a crew member, for example, this was an indication of good luck; if it turned away at the halfway point instead, they were convinced that bad luck was to follow. If it went overboard, whether through falling or being thrown, then a storm was sure to come; if the ship survived the tempest, then it would instead be cursed with nine years of misfortune. Polydactyl cats, which are cats with extra toes, were considered especially fortuitous, as well as being highly valued for their ability to climb and hunt, making them particularly useful in controlling the quantity of rodents aboard the ship.

DAVY JONES' LOCKER WAS A HELL WHICH RESTED AT THE BOTTOM OF THE SEA

The term 'Davy Jones' Locker' dates back to at least the mid-18th century, when it was first known to have been written down, although it is widely assumed to have circulated orally prior to this time. Succinctly speaking, Davy Jones is a synonym for the devil of the sea and his locker deep at the bottom of it. To be sent to Davy Jones' Locker was to be condemned to death; to perish, often drowned, in the ocean's depths, with no hope of return. The name of Davy Jones is first referenced in Tobias Smollett's *The Adventures Of Peregrine Pickle*, an adventure novel published in 1751, and it follows in much popular nautical literature of the time. Smollett describes the evil spirit by "his saucer eyes, his three rows of teeth, his horns and tail, and the blue smoke that came out of his nostrils."

THE FLYING DUTCHMAN WAS A GHOST SHIP, UNABLE TO EVER RETURN TO PORT

The origins of this particular superstition are unclear, although it makes up a huge section of maritime lore. It is said to be fleetingly spotted by sailors, often through the gloom at night, or swathed in fog, as a bearer of ill fate. The ship is often attributed to a 17th century Dutch captain called Bernard Fokke, who was a real sailor. Fokke worked for the Dutch East India Company and was famous for his incredibly fast voyages, making his trips in record time. Towards the end of the 1700s, he and his crew were sunk in a particularly bad storm, and his ship – or whatever remained of it – was never found. Although the beginnings of The Flying Dutchman aren't definitively known, the Fokke theory does make some sense, as the legendary ship is, as well as being cursed to forever sail the seas, renowned for its notable speed.

A SHIP'S FIGUREHEAD, ESPECIALLY IF IT WAS A WOMAN, HELPED TO KEEP IT AFLOAT

Seafarers have always regarded the naked body of a woman as a harbinger of good fortune and this often manifested itself onto the ship's figurehead, regarded as the spirit of the vessel. Folklore indicated that a woman had the ability to calm an angry ocean and, as so much of a sailing voyage was dependent on the weather conditions, the presence of the carving was intended to protect the ship and crew. However, this thinking wasn't extended to actual human women, as explained in the box at the bottom of this page.

It was widely believed that as long as the figurehead remained attached to the bow, then however strong a storm might be, the ship couldn't sink. The height of ornate figureheads is considered to be around 1700, near the beginning of piracy's golden age, but pirates themselves, of course, rarely got to choose their own – it really depended on the ship they stole.

THE KRAKEN WAS A FEARSOME SEA MONSTER, ABLE TO CAPSIZE SHIPS

The first mention of the kraken in print dates back to around the middle of the 18th century, but there are stories about such a monster dating back to 12th century Norway. Generally, the kraken is usually described as a giant octopus or squid, and it is believed to have the ability to sink a ship. It is likely that the basis for this particular myth is grounded in the giant squid or other large sea creatures. Although nowhere near as huge as the mythical kraken, giant squids can reach 12-15 metres in length – large enough to capsize a small boat – and it's not difficult to see how the sighting of one could aid a seaman in making a superstitious leap. The word 'kraken' is never explicitly used, but the beast is acknowledged in Jules Vernes' 20,000 Leagues Under The Sea, described as "a horrible monster worthy to figure in the legends of the marvellous."

WHISTLING ABOARD A SHIP BROUGHT MISFORTUNE AND BAD WEATHER

During sail, a lot of the ship's luck and safety was dependent on the weather, and it was a factoring basis for many of the superstitions. It was commonly regarded amongst pirates and other seafarers, for example, that to whistle aboard a ship would bring ill fortune to the vessel and its crew, especially in the form of bad weather, and it was therefore a forbidden activity. Furthermore, it was specifically believed that to whistle during calm weather would produce wind and that to whistle when it was already windy would generate even stronger gales, hence the popular phrase 'whistling up a storm'. Whistling wasn't the only prohibited activity aboard a sailing ship, however. There were many other superstitious acts including re-naming the ship, setting sail on a Friday, having a person die on-board, and the ringing of an untouched wine glass, all of which were believed to incur misfortune.

IT WAS BAD LUCK FOR A WOMAN TO BE ABOARD A VESSEL

Although the figurehead of a naked female was widely regarded to be the guiding spirit of a ship, women generally weren't welcomed as passengers, as they were ironically believed to be harbingers of misfortune. Across multiple myths, females have been depicted as cruel, dangerous, and threatening to sailors. Calypso, a Greek sea nymph, is described as having the ability to distract seaman with her beauty, leading them to ruin. Women, therefore, weren't always kindly acknowledged across the seas, although that doesn't mean they weren't always there. Superstitions aside, it was much more likely that their presence simply presented the men with too much distraction, as well as possibly provoking fights.

FACT AND FICTION

With years of pirate history, it seems only natural that with their legacies comes one or two legends. Some are true and some are complete myths...

CAPTIVES AND MUTINEERS WERE FORCED TO WALK THE PLANK

Despite the common belief that walking the plank was the preferred method of torture amongst pirates, there are actually no primary historical records of prisoners or dishonoured crew members walking the plank. More favoured means of punishment included marooning, simply tossing the victim overboard, or the much more gruesome method of keelhauling. This involved tying the person to a rope and dragging them behind the ship, resulting in death either by wounds from repeatedly hitting the hull or by slow drowning. Punishments were often threatened to those who could offer something, such as goods or valuable information, and pirates were tactical in their execution of penalties, according to how it could benefit them; walking the plank would have been far too easy and painless. Disagreements amongst the crew were mostly settled through discussion and a democratic vote, as the law of their pirate code prevailed.

> "Favoured means of punishment included marooning, simply tossing the victim overboard or the gruesome keelhauling"

PIRATES BURIED THEIR TREASURE SO THAT NO ONE COULD FIND IT

According to historical records, there are very few instances of pirates burying their valuables – and even fewer instances of these valuables being buried in an old wooden treasure on a faraway island. Towards the end of the 17th century, William Kidd discovered that he was a wanted man and that the Royal Navy was searching for him and his crew, so he hid some of his loot near New York, planning to later use it as leverage during his trial. It was discovered and dug up by the English before Kidd had the chance to, and it was instead used as condemning evidence against him. Rumours of reams of hidden treasure buried across the world naturally followed, but no proof, either physical or written, has ever been found. Generally speaking, pirates were more likely to enjoy, spend, and trade their riches, rather than to hoard it.

ALL PIRATES WOULD SAIL UNDER THE INFAMOUS SKULL AND CROSSBONES FLAG

Although it's one of the most recognised symbols of piracy in modern day, not every pirate ship hoisted the exact same flag. Crews sailed underneath flags in a variety of shapes, sizes and colours, with various elements representative of different things. A plain black flag, for example, was indicative of the death of a member of the crew. Vessels often had a multitude of flags, which they would use at different points during their route, according to country or region. A part of the flag's intent was to scare enemies, thereby minimising damages and allowing a ship to be plundered with limited loss of goods. It often worked; for some merchant ships, the sight of a pirate's flag alone was enough to instil fear. Emblems were also often raised in the midst of battle, as a means of encouraging morale within its crew, as well as inciting panic in the enemy.

PIRATES HAD PARROTS AS PETS ABOARD THEIR SHIPS

Although they are often depicted squawking upon a pirate's shoulder in popular fiction, parrots were not always a common choice of pet whilst sailing across the seas, although they would have made more of an appearance than might be expected. Across the 17th and 18th centuries, pirate crews were part of major economical and geographical movements, travelling far and wide and exploring new horizons. They tended to follow the popular trade routes, staying near to where the goods were – such as the Caribbean, Indian Ocean, and the coast of West Africa, and with these new and tropical places came new and tropical animals. The exotic pet trade meant that people back home would have paid a reasonable amount of money for parrots and other unusual animals, and pirates could easily purchase them in foreign ports. In most instances, they were less of a pet and more a means of gaining wealth.

PIRATES WERE BRUTAL AND BLOODTHIRSTY TYRANTS

For almost all pirates, their buccaneering lifestyle wasn't founded on a love of violence. They viewed themselves as businessmen, working for trade and profit, and battles were only participated in when they were either tactical or necessary to gaining wealth. Combat always carried the risk of injury or death, as well as damage to or loss of the vessel or the prospective prize, and pirates were keen to minimise as casualties as much as they could; if plunder could be taken without a fight, it would be. In many instances, merchant ships would surrender at the sight of a pirate flag and the sound of a firing shot, rendering warfare unnecessary and allowing the goods to be easily taken. If merchant crews were prepared to put up a fight, pirates would often threaten to slaughter anyone who resisted them and to accept those who obeyed them as prisoners.

BUSTED

PIRATES WOULD OFTEN HAVE A WOODEN LEG

This is another popular cliché for whom Robert Louis Stevenson's *Treasure Island* is to thank; his main antagonist, Long John Silver, is infamous for having only one leg. Historically speaking, however, there were few recorded instances of such injuries on whom Stevenson may have based his character. Francois Le Clerc, for example, was a 16th century French pirate who lost his leg fighting in Guernsey. As such, he was subsequently given the nickname of Pie de Palo by the Spaniards and Jambe de Bois by his fellow Frenchman, both phrases of which roughly translate as 'peg leg'. The myth, therefore, has some basis in fact, as such injuries could very easily occur when in battle, or during an accident while carrying out normal duties. In reality, though, pirates were no more prone to losing a limb than any other seafarer was; it was just as likely to happen to law-abiding sailors.

ALL PIRATES WERE RENOWNED FOR WEARING EYE PATCHES

This is, in fact, true for some pirates, but it wasn't necessarily always because they had been injured or lost an eye in battle. Although there are few first-hand accounts for the reasoning behind it, there is consensus among historians that it's plausible that eye patches would have more commonly been worn as a way of helping the crew to see better in the dark. This was especially important during a battle, when they were constantly moving above and below deck, as it can take eyes up to 25 minutes to completely adapt from bright light to darkness. If the eye beneath the patch had already been conditioned to the darkness, they would be able to quickly swap the eye patch to the 'outdoor' eye, exposing the one which had already adjusted to the low light and therefore helping to strengthen the pirate's attack.

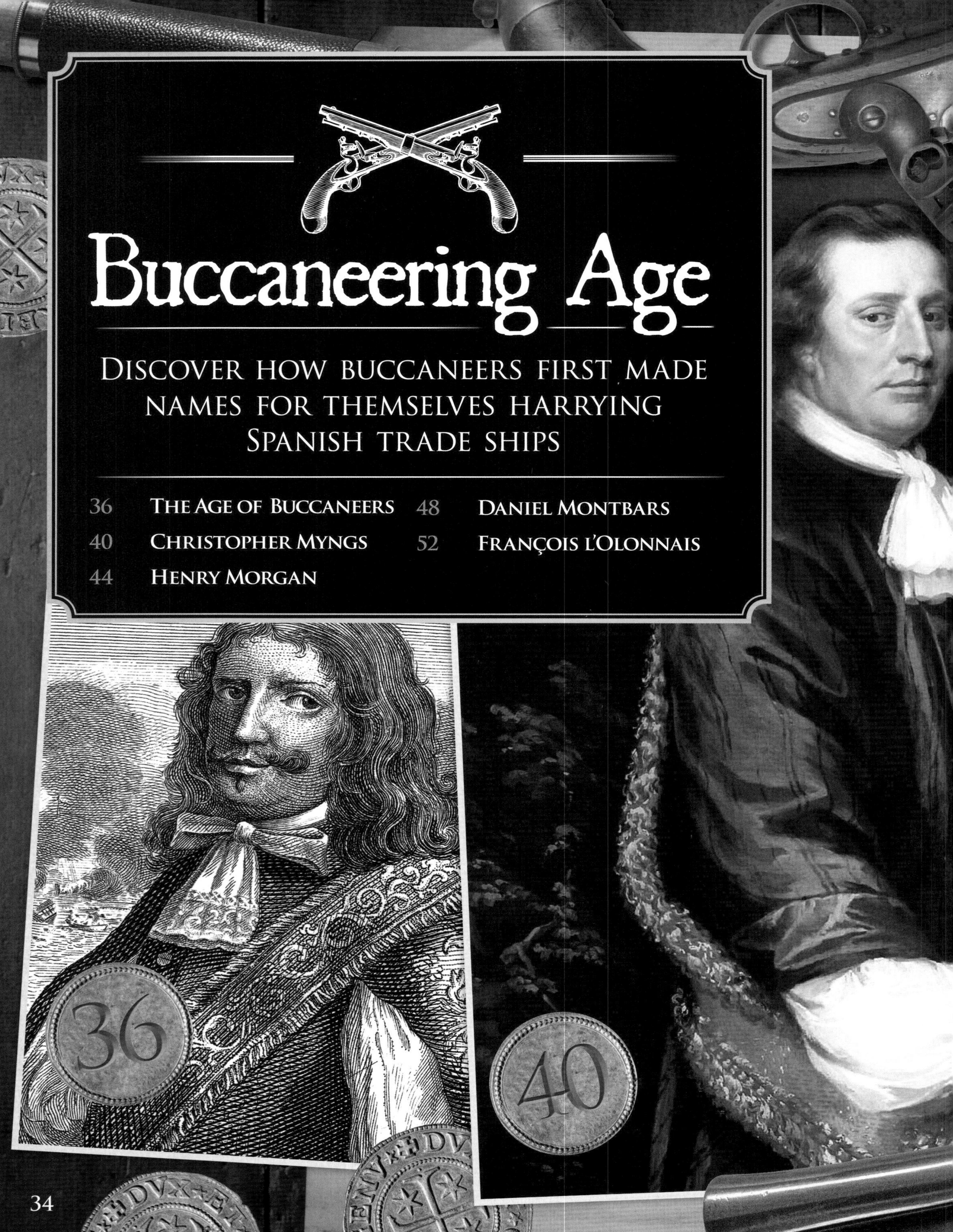

Buccaneering Age

Discover how buccaneers first made names for themselves harrying Spanish trade ships

44
48
52

THE AGE OF BUCCANEERS

With their attacks on French and Spanish possessions in the New World, the buccaneers were the real-life pirates of the Caribbean

Though the term has become something of a catch-all, a true buccaneer was a pirate that operated in the Caribbean and along the South American coast during the mid to late 1600s and early 1700s. The term has also come to include those who acted within the law and those who operated without.

Some prominent buccaneers like Henry Morgan were actually privateers, sailing ships that were licensed to seize the goods and chattels on board enemy vessels, in Morgan's case Spanish. Privateers carried a 'letter of marque and reprisal', an elaborate document that was studded with important-sounding legalese, and they were expected to maintain journals of their exploits and to turn over a healthy portion of their prizes to the crown.

The term buccaneer was originally applied to the lawless hunters and mountain men who worked and foraged inland, among the hills and valleys of Hispaniola (which today incorporates the Dominican Republic and Haiti). They are thought to have been men of French origin and took their name from the way they cooked in the style of the Caribbean Arawak natives, using a wooden frame called a buccan to cure and smoke their meat.

The Anglicised form, buccaneer, became more widely known with the 1684 publication in English of the book by Alexandre Exquemelin, *De Americaensche Zee-Roovers*, which was translated as *The Buccaneers Of America*. Many were fine marksmen, with their years as hunters honing their musket skills.

During the 1620s, these men, dressed in their leather hides and carrying their long hunters' knives, began migrating across the island, drifting towards the northern coast and circa 1630, many of them settled on the offshore island of Tortuga, named as such by Columbus who thought the land mass resembled the shape of a turtle's shell. The island had a good natural harbour and would prove an effective launch pad to raid the shipping lines that rode through the Windward Passage between Cuba and Hispaniola.

On Tortuga, the first leader of note was the Frenchman Jean le Vasseur, and it is he who is widely credited with turning the island into a base for more than half a century's worth of lawless piratical activity. A former military engineer, in 1642 he oversaw the construction of a fort on an outcrop above the harbour. With its own source of spring water, coupled with the protection provided by the fort, Tortuga had the potential to become a permanent base of operations. This powerful bastion Le Vasseur described as his 'dovecote'.

The Spanish were not impressed with his actions and in 1643 they sent six ships and 500 men to take the fort and put Le Vasseur and his fellows in their place. But so effective was the Frenchman's defensive system he sank one ship and scattered the rest. The Spaniards' amphibious landing was also a disaster and the invaders were ambushed, losing 200 men.

Le Vasseur's success saw his reputation spread and seamen, runaway slaves, escaped criminals and all kinds of desperate outlaws from other nations, particularly the English and the Dutch, soon swelled his numbers. From here they began to launch attacks on Spanish shipping, using small boats to target the great galleons laden with gold and valuables from the New World.

The Frenchman's autocratic rule soon angered the French authorities, however, as he refused to share his prizes, and eventually he fell foul of his own men. Still, he established Tortuga as a haven for buccaneering and this loose and ragtag group found some cohesion, on occasion referring to themselves as the Brethren of the Coast. Every once in a while they appointed an Admiral as they banded together to attack major targets, such as Panama, which was thoroughly sacked by Henry Morgan's men in 1671.

> "He established Tortuga as a haven for buccaneering"

The liveliest account of the buccaneers' antics are found in Exquemelin's *The Buccaneers Of America*, and though he often muddles dates and includes much hearsay, undoubtedly gathered among hard-drinking tavern-dwellers in the ports that he visited, much of his history is corroborated by bona fide Spanish sources.

Exquemelin travelled to Tortuga in 1666 as an indentured servant with the French West India Company and he joined the buccaneers three years later, working as a surgeon, a truly valuable commodity aboard ships at the time. He lived among the buccaneers for more than 12 years and at some point moved from Tortuga to Port Royal in Jamaica where he had a hand in the most noted adventures of Henry Morgan (whom he cast in a very unfavourable light in the pages of his book).

For all his inaccuracies and exaggerations, however, Exquemelin's account remains a valuable first-hand source and it is littered with tales of buccaneering bravado and bravery. He tells of Bartholomew the Portuguese, for example, whose myriad successes were invariably tempered by wretched ill fortune, one notable example being his capture of a Spanish ship off the coast of Cuba, which saw him grab 70,000 pieces of eight and 54,431 kilograms of cacao beans. As he sailed away with his prize, three Spaniards journeying to Havana subsequently set upon his ship and his plunder was in turn plundered.

When a severe storm forced him to find a harbour in Mexico, meanwhile, the townsfolk recognised him as the man who had been marauding their coast and he was held captive and set to be hanged. The night before his hanging, however, he escaped from the ship on which he was held and leaped overboard, using two earthenware wine jars as buoyancy aids. Though he got away, his bad luck continued to dog him and Exquemelin records that he made many violent attacks on the Spaniards without ever becoming rich, "for I saw him dying in the greatest wretchedness in the world."

Bartholomew the Portugese established a set of rules known as 'The Pirate's Code'

Buccaneers used small boats for speed in their attacks

The buccaneer Roche Brasiliano was a blight on the Spaniards with a terrifying reputation for torture

Pirates in the Caribbean

Island-hopping pirates spent much of their career in the Caribbean

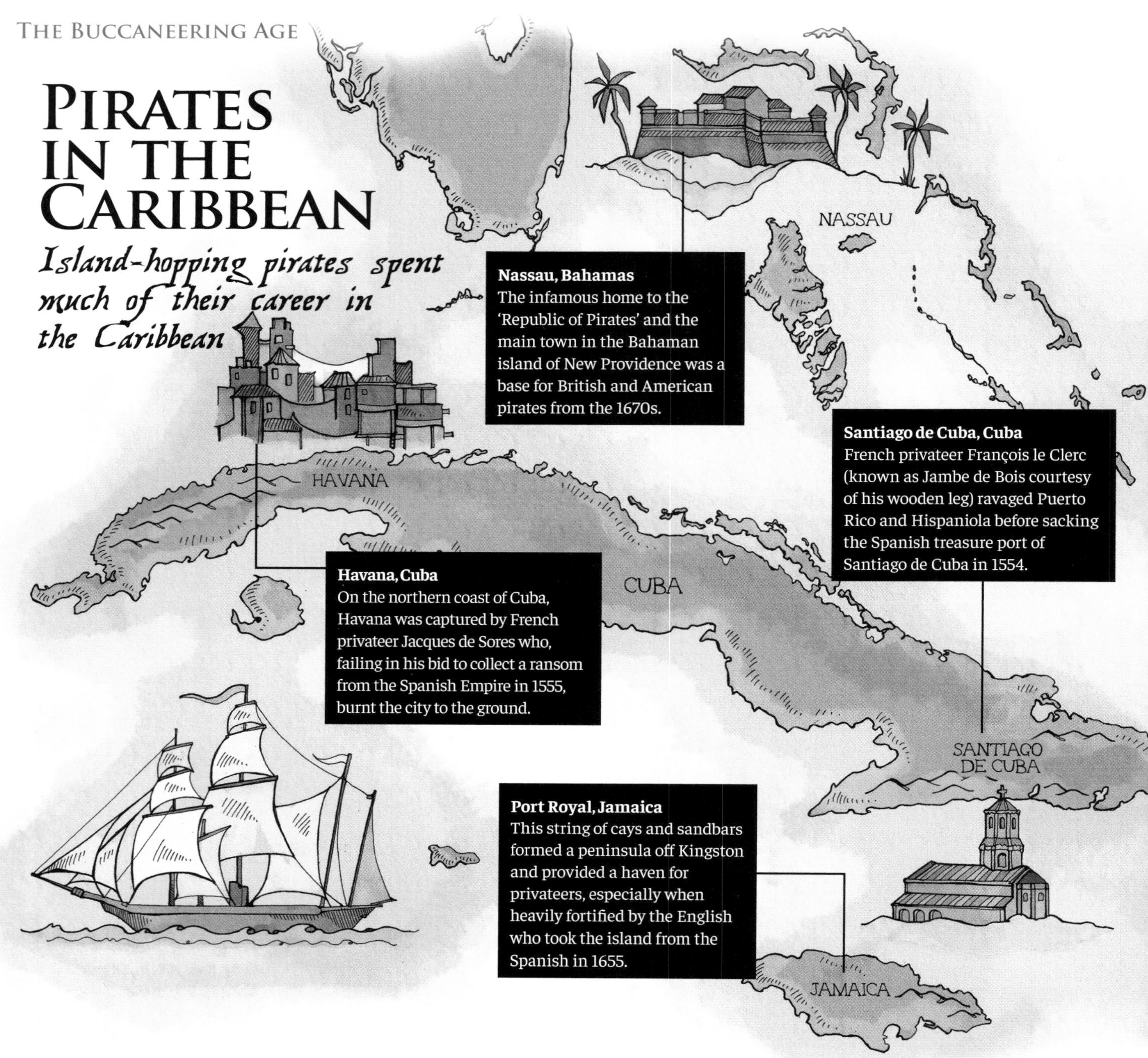

Nassau, Bahamas
The infamous home to the 'Republic of Pirates' and the main town in the Bahaman island of New Providence was a base for British and American pirates from the 1670s.

Santiago de Cuba, Cuba
French privateer François le Clerc (known as Jambe de Bois courtesy of his wooden leg) ravaged Puerto Rico and Hispaniola before sacking the Spanish treasure port of Santiago de Cuba in 1554.

Havana, Cuba
On the northern coast of Cuba, Havana was captured by French privateer Jacques de Sores who, failing in his bid to collect a ransom from the Spanish Empire in 1555, burnt the city to the ground.

Port Royal, Jamaica
This string of cays and sandbars formed a peninsula off Kingston and provided a haven for privateers, especially when heavily fortified by the English who took the island from the Spanish in 1655.

The surgeon-cum-writer also records the deeds of the Dutch buccaneer Roche (or Rock) Brasiliano, who turned to buccaneering when the Portuguese expelled the Dutch invaders from Brazil in 1654. One of his most famous feats came five years later when his ship ran aground following a raid on a Mexican port. As he and his 30-man crew travelled overland on their way to a pirate safe haven, they ran into a large contingent of Spanish cavalry and Exquemelin notes that their musketry tore the Spaniards to pieces. Spanish accounts, on the other hand, record how Brasiliano and his men fled the horsemen and escaped in canoes.

> "He would roam Caribbean towns: regularly lopping off an innocent person's arm or leg"

Brasiliano's dislike for Spaniards, says Exquemelin, was legendary and he would roam Caribbean towns attacking anyone he pleased, regularly lopping off an innocent person's arm or leg, "for he was like a maniac." He also took a grisly pleasure in torturing the Spanish and is said to have roasted his enemies alive on wooden spits, "like killing a pig."

Also included in Exquemelin's account is the French buccaneer François l'Olonnais (see profile on page 52) who counted the sack of Maracaibo in Venezuela among his many piratical exploits. This man boasted some of the most gruesome sensibilities amongst his brethren, on a par with Brasiliano, regularly torturing his captives in a bid to learn where they had stashed their most valuable treasures. If they refused to succumb to the rack he would hack them to bits with his

Sir Henry Morgan sacked the city of Panama in the 1670s – this image shows a capture Spaniard bowing before him

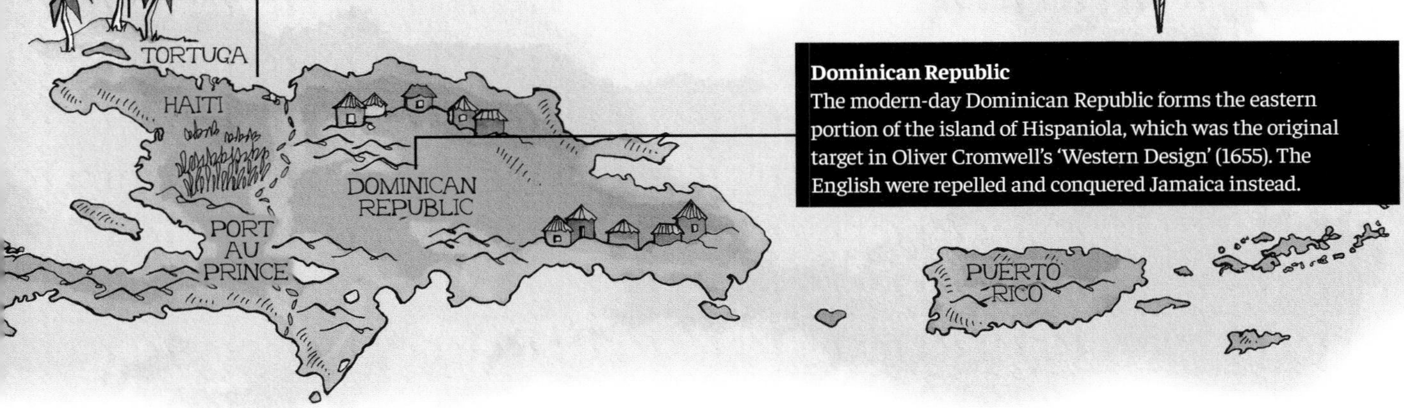

Tortuga
With mountains on the northern side of the island and only one harbour on the south, Tortuga offered safety to buccaneers who raided the shipping lines that rode through the Windward Passage between Cuba and Hispaniola.

Port au Prince, Haiti
The region that accommodates the modern-day city of Port au Prince was a pirate haven in the 17th century, with the Spanish seemingly surrendering the western part of the island of Hispaniola to the buccaneers.

Dominican Republic
The modern-day Dominican Republic forms the eastern portion of the island of Hispaniola, which was the original target in Oliver Cromwell's 'Western Design' (1655). The English were repelled and conquered Jamaica instead.

cutlass. Exquemelin devotes the largest amount of space to Henry Morgan (see profile on page 44) and his operations from Jamaica.

While Jamaica became a primary buccaneers' haven, Tortuga remained incredibly important to illegal operations, being l'Ollonais's base for his attack on Maracaibo. It continued to serve the buccaneers well for many years until the French authorities cracked down on piracy in 1713. That was an altogether different 'age' of piracy (what we commonly call 'the Golden Age'), a successor to the age of buccaneers which has its roots in the exploits of the mid to late 17th century. The English followed suit with the King's Pardon of 1717, which empowered the governor of the Bahamas to accept the surrender of, and to subsequently pardon, any known pirate.

The livelihoods of these men (and a few notable women), would not have existed without the pioneering of early buccaneers. They inherited the tactics, the sailing routes and the codes of honour left by their forebears. While many outlaws agreed to accept the King's Pardon, others either lied or just plain refused, and continued to terrorise the Caribbean throughout the early 18th century. Their days were numbered; the heirs to the original buccaneers were hunted men."

All pirates signed a code of conduct before becoming part of a ship's crew

CHRISTOPHER MYNGS

the mass murderer

How a respected naval officer and war hero became a feared killer and a buccaneer

Throughout the long and bloody history of buccaneering, very few buccaneers have been as feared and reviled as Sir Christopher Myngs. Having started his career completely legally as a British government-sanctioned naval officer, Myngs is a prime example of the effects of power and means going to one's head. During his lifetime, a 'kill or be killed' attitude and a series of extremely poor choices transformed Myngs from a respected, battle-worn vice admiral into a bloodthirsty mass murderer.

Born circa 1620-25 – the exact year of his birth remains unknown – in Norfolk, England, Myngs joined the Royal Navy as a cabin boy a couple of years before the start of the English Civil War (1642-51), and quickly worked his way up the ranks after siding with the Parliamentarians, who won. He was given a bit of a leg up by Oliver Cromwell, the then Lord Protector of England and Her Commonwealth, who wished to reward him for his loyalty to Parliament, and Myngs became the captain of his first ship, Elisabeth.

While Elisabeth was still under his command, he led a crew of soldiers into the first Anglo Dutch War (1652-54) and managed to capture a Dutch convoy, including two men-of-war. After the end of the war, Myngs's career continued to blossom further. Bestowed with a promotion to flag officer rank from Cromwell himself, Myngs was ordered to set sail to the Caribbean in 1655. His mission was to clean up the carnage left by noted angler and veteran of the Irish wars, Robert Venables, who had set off on an expedition to attack the Spanish in the West Indies during the war.

Seeking to use his puritan status to weaken Roman Catholic influence in the New World, Cromwell recruited Venables as the general commander of land forces and sent him on a special mission he called the Western Design. The aim was to secure a base of operations in the Caribbean, targeting Spanish colonies in the West Indies, to threaten trade and treasure routes in the Spanish Main. After some faulty advice from Thomas Gage, a renegade Dominican 'expert', Cromwell's hope was the Western Design would allow him and his men to attack the Spanish Empire in the Caribbean, thus avoiding a war in Europe.

Obviously, not everything went quite to plan. Venables was required to share his rule over the infantry – most of which were highly under qualified and incompetent – with General-at-Sea William Penn, and the pair often clashed. The hostile working environment made the mission almost impossible. The fact that Venables's overbearing wife joined them on the expedition, and was rumoured to have interfered with and criticised his plans, didn't help matters.

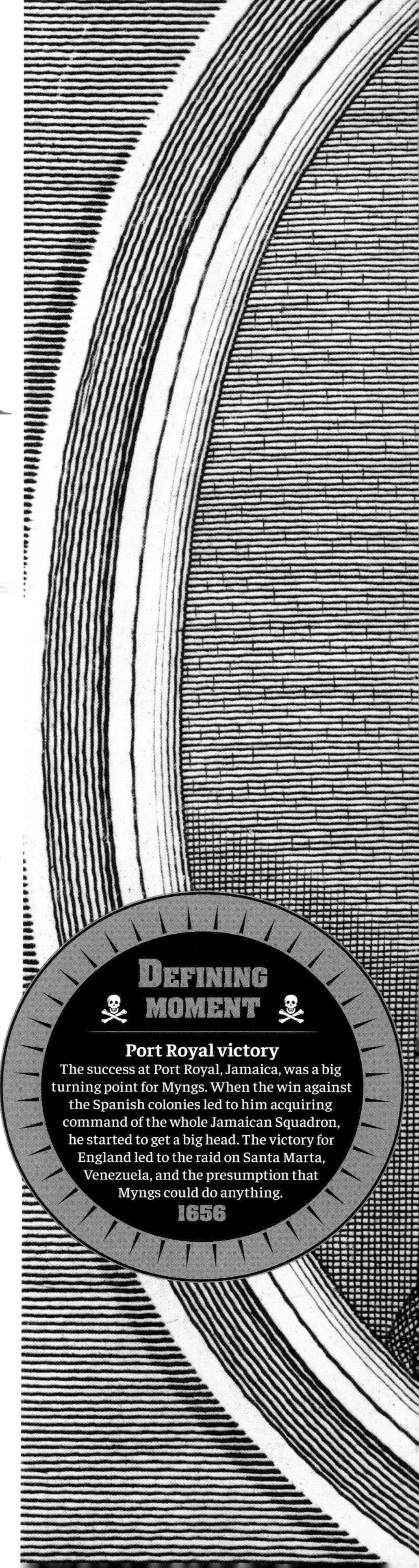

DEFINING MOMENT

Port Royal victory

The success at Port Royal, Jamaica, was a big turning point for Myngs. When the win against the Spanish colonies led to him acquiring command of the whole Jamaican Squadron, he started to get a big head. The victory for England led to the raid on Santa Marta, Venezuela, and the presumption that Myngs could do anything.

1656

"Even after all the trouble he caused for the English government, Myngs still received a knighthood"

Before he became a buccaneer, Sir Christopher Myngs was a respected war hero

The Anglo-Spanish War lasted from 1654-60

With supplies dangerously low, the soldiers suffering from thirst and heatstroke and Penn and Venables at the end of their tethers, the pair finally abandoned the mission after trying and failing to capture Hispaniola, the territory now know as Haiti and the Dominican Republic, which was ready and waiting for them. Giving up, they instead decided to capture the neighbouring island of Jamaica, which was being weakly defended by the Spanish. After their lacklustre and rather hollow victory, Venables and Penn departed the West Indies for England, and Cromwell sent Myngs in their place.

Myngs finally arrived in Port Royal, Jamaica, in 1656 as the captain of the 44-gun navy frigate, Marston Moor. His crew were on the verge of mutiny when he took them on, but he managed to subdue them with a firm hand. Whipped into shape, the reformed soldiers were ready for anything, which was great for them as the captain had quickly realised that the best defence for the powerful Spanish forces that now surrounded Jamaica was to take the offense. The crew were to attack before they could be attacked themselves.

> "His power kick reached a point where he would brutally massacre entire towns for no particular reason"

Some of the English forces from Venables's army remained around the island, but they would be of little help to Myngs's plan. Instead of recruiting them, Myngs turned to the local buccaneers of Port Royal and subsequently led a raid on Santa Marta in Venezuela. Everything went to plan and the crews were successful, with the Spanish experiencing a lot of bloody collateral damage.

After this win, Myngs was promoted and given command of the Jamaican Squadron of Commonwealth ships – the entire naval fleet of Port Royal – the following year, with Marston Moor becoming his flagship. He also kept the buccaneer vessels as auxiliaries, but it was not until October 1658 that Myngs could be considered a pirate.

With the new fleet at his fingertips, Myngs led several more attacks on the Spanish Empire throughout the Caribbean from late 1657 to early 1658, and invaded some of the bigger, richer towns of northern areas of South America. In February 1658, he returned to Jamaica as naval commander, and acting as a commerce raider during the remainder of the Anglo-Spanish War (1654-60).

During this time, Myngs began to get a bit of a reputation for often being crueller than necessary. His power kick reached a point where he would brutally massacre entire towns for no particular reason while in command of his fleets of buccaneers. Later in 1658, he readied his

Myngs and his buccaneering crew's plunder of South American towns caused chaos and destruction for the locals

DEFINING MOMENT

Myngs's legacy

Myngs successfully led the then-largest buccaneer fleet ever assembled, 14 ships and 1,400 pirates, to sack San Francisco de Campeche. After all the trouble Myngs had experienced with the law, this was a huge feat and demonstrates how much influence he had over the English government and the buccaneers of the Caribbean.

1663

squadron to attempt to scatter and capture a Spanish treasure fleet off the coast of Porto Bello. Failing to do either, Myngs destroyed the Columbian towns of Tolú and Santa Maria, more out of annoyance than anything else.

At some point during his time in the Caribbean, Myngs's havoc-wreaking command style underwent a significant change. Before he recruited his crew of buccaneers, all of his invasions had been with his naval fleet, and had therefore been completely legal under the government. With the assistance of the new crew, Myngs became naught but a criminal. Understandably, his actions more than miffed the Spanish government. They considered him a common pirate and mass murderer, and attempted to protest his conduct to the English government of Oliver Cromwell, but to no avail.

In 1659, Myngs successfully plundered and devastated Cumana, Puerto Caballos and Coro of Venezuela with his Port Royal buccaneers before returning to Jamaica, his temporary home, with about a quarter of a million English pounds' worth of silver and other valuable goods from Coro. The raid seemed like a success on the surface, but Myngs overlooked a rather large slip up: he had shared half the bounty, which was considered government property, with the buccaneers against the explicit orders of the English Commander of Jamaica, Edward D'Oyley, and so was subsequently arrested for embezzlement. Myngs was sent back to England in 1660 aboard Marston Moor, and ordered to stand trial as an ordinary pirate.

However, Myngs' luck changed again when the restoration of the monarchy brought political turmoil. His case was dropped in the confusion of it all and he became a free man. He was sent back to the Caribbean with a new fleet, this time on his flagship Centurion, and resumed his naval duties.

Myngs returned to Port Royal in 1662 and, despite the fact that the Anglo-Spanish War had ended with a new truce existing between England and Spain, he ordered his fleet to attack more Spanish colonies. His actions were believed to be part of a covert English policy with the aim to undermine the Spanish dominion of the area by destroying as much of the infrastructure as possible. Later that year, Myngs got his buccaneers back on board by promising them the opportunity to plunder some more. This time, however, Myngs had the support of the new governor, Lord Windsor.

An attack on Santiago de Cuba, Cuba's second largest city, ended in plunder and success despite its extremely strong defences, and attracted buccaneers from all over the Caribbean who wished to join Myngs on his 1663 mission to capture San Francisco de Campeche, which resulted in them acquiring a huge haul of booty. During the attack, Myngs was wounded and so returned to England to recover. He continued sailing for a few years more, serving as Vice Admiral of the White during the Second Anglo-Dutch War (1665-67), and even received a knighthood for his service.

The ex-buccaneer was finally defeated at what was known as the Four Days' Battle (11-14 June, 1666). During what became one of the longest naval engagements in history, Myngs was hit by two musket balls, one through his cheek and the other through his shoulder. He eventually succumbed to the wounds the following August.

Even after his knighthood and war hero status, Myngs's reputation as an unrelenting and formidable pirate is the one that has endured the most.

HENRY MORGAN

the best of the buccaneers

Whether hero or villain, loyal subject or bloodthirsty treasure-seeker, Henry Morgan lived a courageous and colourful life

When the English publisher of Alexandre Exquemelin's book The Buccaneers Of America printed its edition in 1686, Henry Morgan was outraged. He was described therein as a pirate, and he sued for libel. The case was settled out of court, the aggrieved party taking a handsome sum, for Morgan was a privateer, not a common pirate, and he made war on the Spanish Empire with a commission from the English governor of Jamaica. When the buccaneer died on his Jamaican estates in 1688, succumbing to ailments engendered by his heavy drinking and carousing, the governor ordered a state funeral. For Henry Morgan, in his eyes, was the very best of the buccaneers. History is inclined to agree.

The evidence is plentiful, and more than compelling. Morgan had sailed into Caribbean waters in 1654 with the troops committed to Oliver Cromwell's Western Design, and the successful invasion of Jamaica gave the English a newly acquired territory from which to terrorise Spanish shipping. During this period Morgan proved himself an able captain and war-leader, taking charge of several raids, including the 1663 sacking of Villahermosa and the looting of Gran Granada in Nicaragua. At the age of 32 he was named Admiral of the Brethren of the Coast.

His reputation was boosted further five years later, when in 1668 he led the famed attack on the Spanish treasure port of Portobello in Panama. The town was a staging post for Spain's Peruvian booty, launching the empire's treasure on the sea roads back to Spain. And the Portobello assault not only proved Morgan's tactical acuity, but also his audacity and his sheer ruthlessness.

The port was protected by two castles, one on either side of the bay. Unwilling to risk his ships, Morgan launched an amphibious assault, sailing his 12-ship fleet to the Bay of Boca del Toro before transferring his 500-man raiding party into canoes acquired in Cuba. Paddling through the night, they landed around 4.8 kilometres from their target and marched under the cover of darkness, arriving at Portobello just before dawn. A skirmish with a Spanish lookout post on the edge of town broke their cover, though they had managed to catch the garrison unawares.

Morgan's men split up, and one group took the town, rounding up the residents and locking them in one of the two churches. The others, meanwhile, turned their attention to the fortresses protecting the bay. The nearest was Santiago Castle with its garrison of 80 men. It looked a formidable obstacle, bristling with guns (that many did not work

DEFINING MOMENT

The Western Design

Oliver Cromwell's bid to capture a prominent Spanish territory in the West Indies stalled at first as the troops under General Venables and General-at-Sea Penn failed in their bid to take Hispaniola. However, a successful attack on Jamaica proved a strategic move, allowing privateers like Morgan to plunder millions from Spanish shipping.

1654

Morgan earned the title Admiral of the Brethren of the Coast

was unbeknownst to the assailants). Morgan, however, was concentrating on other things, for he had a cunning plan. It was also rather cruel.

Entering the church, he dragged out the mayor and several townsfolk, including some friars and nuns, and forced them to march towards the castle ahead of his buccaneers, acting as a human shield. The defenders fired cannon, killing one of Morgan's men and wounding civilians. The guns then fell silent and the attackers soon reached the castle walls. While the Spanish stared in horror at the motley gang of invaders stalking towards them, another group sneaked up on the seaward side and scaled the walls. The battle for the castle was on. The Spaniards fought gallantly and more than half their number died before they surrendered.

The following day, Morgan turned his attention to the bastion on the other side of the bay, the Castle of San Felipe, which soon fell into his hands. He then raised the English flag above the town and his fleet sailed in. Once in command of the town, Morgan and his men set about their looting and Exquemelin, the French surgeon and buccaneer who was ever-biased against his former leader, catalogued Morgan's crimes, claiming that he tortured women to find the whereabouts of their hidden cash. There is some corroborating evidence, though it is widely believed that Exquemelin exaggerated Morgan's brutality. Ironically, in so doing he actually boosted Morgan's standing.

Defining moment

The prisoner in London

Though arrested and returned to London in a bid to appease the Spanish after the sack of Panama, Morgan's standing in the eyes of English society became apparent. During his stay he was received in all the finest drawing rooms, and was never incarcerated. Indeed, he met King Charles II to receive his knighthood.

1672-1674

Whatever one makes of his morals, few could doubt Morgan's courage or his military acumen; the raid on Portobello is regarded as one of the most audacious amphibious operations of the 17th century. He sent a letter to the president of Panama demanding 350,000 pesos. Otherwise, he'd burn Portobello to the ground. After much wrangling he received around 100,000 pesos and with his booty from the sacking of the town, returned to Jamaica with somewhere in the region of 250,000. His critics claimed he had exceeded his remit, though the Admiralty, suitably impressed, declared that the Portobello haul was a legally accountable prize.

According to Exquemelin, when back in Jamaica Morgan and his men soon ran through their money with drunken orgies and it was not long before his men pressed him to launch another quest for loot. In October 1668, he set sail for a rendezvous off Hispaniola where he met up with some French buccaneers and the 34-gun frigate HMS Oxford, which had been donated by the governor of Jamaica.

Morgan's target was the wealthy Spanish treasure port of Cartagena and his squadron of ten ships and 800 men seemed more than

Morgan's attack on Maracaibo, Venezuela in March of 1669 was a sign of his growing audacity

Morgan's sack on Panama inspired the artist Allen True to paint this bloody picture

DEFINING MOMENT

Lieutenant Governor of Jamaica

Armed with his knighthood, he returned to Jamaica with the new governor, Lord Vaughan. However, the two did not get on with the latter complaining of the former's carousing lifestyle. That said, Morgan proved his worth with his military excellence coming to fore during a stint as acting governor when he boosted the island's defences.

1674-1682

Morgan's notoriety has seen several statues built in his honour

enough to ensure a positive outcome. However, things went awry after Morgan had transferred his base to Oxford. A rowdy party ensued ahead of the raid and someone set the magazine alight. The frigate was blown to smithereens. Only ten of the 200-strong crew survived the blast. One of them was Morgan.

The destruction of Oxford forced a change of plan and Morgan switched targets, sailing instead to Maracaibo on the Venezuelan coast, which proved easy prey. Exquemelin again reports hideous torture conducted for pleasure and for gain. News of Morgan's exploits reached the admiral of Spain's West Indian fleet who sent three warships to intercept the marauding buccaneer. Ever the cunning fox, however, Morgan won the day. He sailed a captured ship into the Spanish flagship and blew up both vessels.

His reputation was now soaring at dizzying heights, though Morgan was not yet done. In December 1670 the largest-ever buccaneer fleet – totalling almost 30 ships and 1,200 men – was bearing down on Panama, the primary Spanish treasure port on the Pacific coast. After a fierce battle to knock out the castle at the entrance to the River Chagres, Morgan sailed upstream before transferring his troops first to canoes and then onto foot.

On January 28, 1671, Morgan and his troops advanced across the plain outside Panama, which the Spaniards had defended with 1,200 infantry and 400 cavalry. These men were relatively inexperienced, however, and were no match for Morgan's war-hungry troops. The Spaniards launched a raggedy charge and were shot down by the dozen courtesy of Morgan's sharpshooters, French musketeers stationed in his vanguard, and the cavalry soon broke ranks and fled, leaving the infantry at the buccaneers' mercy. More than 400 fell as the invaders charged into the city. The buccaneers lost just 15 men.

> "The Spaniards launched a raggedy charge and were shot down by the dozen"

Aware that defeat was a distinct possibility, the Spanish had made contingency plans, moving out the vast majority of the treasure onto ships ahead of the battle. The fleeing militia, meanwhile, were ordered to set fire to the city should their defence fail. Again, the inhabitants were tortured to reveal the whereabouts of hidden treasure. According to Morgan, only £30,000 was taken in plunder, amounting to £15 per man. His buccaneers were by all accounts furious and many blamed Morgan for their paltry remuneration. Concerned about his safety, Morgan scampered back to Jamaica.

News of Panama's destruction was well received in Jamaica, though it soon became apparent that it had contravened the Treaty of Madrid, signed in July 1670. The Jamaican governor and Morgan had not received news of the treaty until after the fact, but still both men were to be punished by way of appeasing the Spanish. Morgan was arrested and sent home to England, though he never saw the inside of the Tower and was instead allowed to live freely in London.

In fact, in 1674 Morgan was actually knighted by Charles II for his services to the crown and returned to Jamaica as the Lieutenant Governor. There he lived well as an exceedingly wealthy man, owning plantations totalling over 6,000 acres. He was eventually removed from office in 1682 and died six years later, succumbing to the diseases caused as a result of his bawdy lifestyle. By the time of his death, though, his brave deeds, in addition to the horrors outlined in Exquemelin's book, ensured that he would forever leave an indelible imprint on the history of buccaneering.

DANIEL MONTBARS

the exterminator

His seething hatred for the Spanish made Daniel Montbars of Languedoc one of history's most vicious and bloodthirsty pirates

Some pirate legends are exactly that. The mists of time and centuries passing blur historical fact into tall tales. Rumours and whispers attain the veracity of facts. Reputations are forged, spurred on, accounts are written down and passed from generation to generation. Upon closer inspection, stories of mighty deeds ripple away into nothingness, like a reflection in a pond. Myths offer the illusion of greatness and the illusion can last a long time when left unquestioned. Some pirates, for sure, deserve their fearsome reputations. Some really did accrue huge amounts of treasure and would have spent it rather than buried it. Yet many were subject to aggrandisement in the eyes of writers and historians.

Daniel Montbars (1645 – c.1707), a French buccaneer who sailed around the West Indies on a personal bid to destroy everything and anything Spanish, was the real deal and acquired a legend in his own lifetime. A bloodthirsty buccaneer, his preferred method of torture and killing was gruesomely inventive. Now, movies and books have romanticised much of the life at sea, but make no mistake, pirates were tough brutes and could partake in sickening acts of barbarity when needs must. Their life was not an Errol Flynn movie.

Spanish sailors and garrison soldiers who were left over from battle – at sea and on land – were sure to fear the name 'Montbars'. A thorn in the side of the Spanish fleet, the pesky bee in their bonnet, the wasp around their sugary beverage, Captain Daniel Montbars terrorised Spanish settlements and townships for several decades, in a mad lust to exact revenge and mayhem against his sworn enemy.

Montbars's preferred method of killing was slow and very painful for the victim. It was also a gory spectacle for anybody forced to watch. This was precisely the point and effect Montbars wished. The punishment was a way of humiliating the person forced to endure it. Montbars would order a man to have his stomach sliced open, take out part of the guts and attach it to a wooden post. The indignity and horror didn't end there. With viscera extracted and nailed down, the cruel captain would then have the person dance around doing a jig, while smacking a burning log against said person's backside. As the man cried out in abject agony, his innards would spill out on the floor until the poor victim snuffed it. There's crazy and deranged, and then there's Daniel Montbars of Languedoc, scourge of the Spanish Main and whose violent manner earned him the name – in his own lifetime – 'Montbars the Exterminator.' Chances are, if you were unfortunate enough to come across

DEFINING MOMENT

Fighting the Spanish

Montbars sails from Le Havre, having signed up to the French Royal Navy. Serving with his uncle, they head to Santo Domingo in the Dominican Republic and fight a sea battle with two Spanish ships. It is here that the uncle is killed and Montbars's hatred of the Spanish increases even further to set him on his subsequent path.

1667

Legend has it, Montbars's hatred of the Spanish came from tales of Conquistador cruelties toward the natives of Central and South America

It is said Montbars buried treasure at Anse du Gouverneur beach, St Bart's island

Montbars and you were batting for the Spanish, things really wouldn't end well.

Montbars hailed from the southern French region of Languedoc, a place with its own blood-soaked history, as it was seat of the medieval Cathar heretics, for a short time deemed a major threat to Catholicism and the authority of the church. The Cathar religion was prominent in the area until massacre after massacre – known as the Albigensian Crusade – virtually erased their presence and their branch of worship. Raised in a wealthy family and receiving a gentleman's education, the story goes that Montbars developed a specific loathing for the Spanish after reading accounts of Conquistadors in the New World. How true this all is remains unprovable, but Montbars actions against the Spanish attest to a virulent hatred toward his Iberian neighbours and he plagued them incessantly, using British-run ports – because they would support attacks against the Spanish at given times.

Bidding adieu to France in 1667, Montbars joined the Royal French Navy as a midshipman and set off from the northern port of Le Havre with the intention of taking the fight to the Spanish overseas, in the pirate-infested waters of the Caribbean and Americas. On the other side of the world, which must have looked like heaven on earth to so many Europeans, Montbars distinguished himself in skirmishes and battles against the Spanish navy. One account described how the Frenchman fearlessly charged ahead but relished in the defeat of his enemy: "Montbars led the way to the decks of the enemy, where he carried injury and death; and when submission terminated the contest, his only pleasure seemed to be to contemplate, not the treasures of the vessel, but the number of dead and dying Spaniards, against whom he had vowed a deep and eternal hatred, which he maintained the whole of his life."

> **DEFINING MOMENT**
>
> **Terrorising the Spanish Main**
>
> **Montbars travels the Caribbean and Gulf of Mexico terrorising the Spanish Main. During this time, he sacks and plunders coastal towns in Colombia, Honduras, Mexico and Venezuela. He develops a reputation, not just as a fierce buccaneer, but as a torturer with a fine line in sadistic inventiveness.**
>
> **1670s-1707**

So how did Montbars operate and get away with his countless assaults against the Spanish? The region's unique geography and turbulent politics – empires at each other's throats – played a huge part. Exquemelin, the Dutch author, who wrote The Buccaneers Of America (1678), a pioneering work written by a pirate, one of Captain Henry Morgan's associates, dissected the allure of Caribbean waters, with their hidden coves, readily available food and water sources, and potential riches. It didn't take much for a pirate ship to disappear. 'There are so many uninhabited little islands and keys, with harbours convenient and secure for cleaning their vessels, and abounding with what they often want, provision: I mean water, sea-fowl, turtle, shell and other fish." He goes on to write about bigger catches: "Another reason these seas are chose by pirates is in the great commerce thither by French, Spaniards, Dutch

DEFINING MOMENT

Lost at sea?

Around 1707, Montbars disappears from history. It is said he drowned at sea, when his boat was caught in a storm. But in the years since, like many pirate tales, stories of buried treasure circulated. The island of Tortuga has been a focal point. Did Montbars bury his plunder on the beaches at Grand Saline or Anse du Gouverneur?

c. 1707

Montbars wearing the skull and crossbones, a 19th century engraving illustration by 19th century craftsman, René Rescalon

and especially English ships. They are sure, in the latitude of these trading islands, to meet with prizes, booties of provision, clothing, naval stores, and sometimes money."

Montbars turned to the pirate life after an uncle, who had accompanied him to the Caribbean, died at the hands of the Spanish one day. The narrative puts it that Daniel was ashore on Hispaniola at the time of his beloved uncle's untimely death, helping French buccaneers ambush Spanish horsemen. In the wake of grief, Montbars settled on becoming a full-time buccaneer and to exact retribution against all Spaniards in the colonies. Is this simply another apocryphal part of the ferocious Montbars biography? Perhaps, but Montbars did sign up to the Brethren of the Coast, a pirate collective, mustered nearly 1,000 men and set off in 15 ships to take the Spanish-held port of Maracaibo.

Montbars also left his mark on Colombia, Mexico, Honduras and Venezuela. The Spanish Main cowered in fear. It hadn't been too long since they'd rid themselves of another French menace, either. It was as if the Spanish administration were cursed by insanely violent Frenchmen. Before Montbars commenced his

> "Montbars settled on becoming a... buccaneer and to exact retribution against all Spaniards"

lucrative endeavours, they'd put up with the 'Bane of Spain' aka François l'Olonnais, another buccaneer known for his cruel methods and righteous slaughter. (He died in 1668 and was eaten by cannibals.)

Throughout his pirating career, Montbars only had eyes for the Spanish. He was, in effect, 'Bane of Spain: the sequel'. The siege of Maracaibo is among his most audacious and infamous episodes. The actual fighting lasted barely a couple of hours, with the townsfolk and garrison initially putting up a defence before fleeing into the hills to avoid capture. They'd also absconded with all their gold and silver. Montbars wasn't best pleased, so ordered his men into the foothills. He'd torture them into giving up the treasure.

When a Spanish fleet rocked up and blocked the exit route, Montbars decided upon two things. Firstly, he would ransom the town and, in exchange for 2,000 crowns, he promised not to burn the place to cinders. Secondly, Montbars knew he and his men could be taken down in a fight and, if they survived, sent to the gallows. As part of a diversion tactic, Montbars sent out a fire ship – literally a ship loaded with combustibles and set on fire – to cause mayhem and send the Spanish into a panic. It worked and Montbars sailed away in the ensuing chaos. Stories like this attract legend. Here was a man with his back against the wall, but who refused to give in and dug himself out of a tight spot to have the last laugh.

Montbars disappeared from history, as if he'd been a phantom of the imagination all along. Some say he died at sea during a violent storm, going down with the ship for an eternity resting in Davey Jones's locker, leaving behind all that buried treasure and a name – 'Montbars the Exterminator' – for the history books to remember. The year of his disappearance is usually given as 1707.

FRANÇOIS L'OLONNAIS

the most sadistic pirate

Rivals would rather die than put themselves in the hands of one of the most fearsome pirates to ever sail under the black flag

During his life, François l'Olonnais appeared to have two loves. One was a fondness for gathering large quantities of treasure and the other was a penchant for inflicting the worst kind of pain on those who stood in his way. As one of history's most notorious pirates, torture was merely part of his job and something he found to thoroughly enjoy. That he was rather good at it made it all the worse for his victims but it did, at the very least, earn him a great, if not fearful, respect from his fellow pirates.

Born Jean David Nau in the French seaside territory of Les Sables-d'Olonne circa 1635, l'Olonnais grew to show every sign of ruthless ambition and greed. He'd been sent to the Caribbean island of Martinique as an indentured servant in the 1650s, but after his time in servitude he became a free man and moved to the island of Hispaniola. There he joined the buccaneers in attacking wave upon wave of Spanish ships and sacking coastal settlements. He gained a reputation, not so much as an accomplished pirate, but as a cruel and heartless adversary.

Indeed, in his first few voyages, l'Olonnais showed little mercy. He and his fellow pirates were able to intercept many ships laden with goodies from the Spanish West Indies and Spanish Main, which earned him great riches and booty and turned him into a well-known figure in a good portion of the North Atlantic Ocean. Spaniards were said to prefer death to any thought of surrendering to him and it earned him the admiration of the Governor of Tortuga, a Caribbean island off the north-west coast of Haiti which was a known pirate refuge.

The governor, Monsieur de la Place, granted l'Olonnais the command of a small ship and allowed him to go forth and seek his fortune. He and his assembled crew ended up targeting a small Cuban village called De los Cayos. But even though they were spotted by fishermen who raised the alarm, prompting the inhabitants to ask Havana's Governor for assistance, the pirates overcame a well-armed vessel sent to deal with the situation, forcing the Spaniards to surrender.

L'Olonnais then showed them how ruthless he could be. He had his foes hanged one by one. He also turned his attention to a hangman who had travelled with the Spaniards and who was under orders to execute every pirate. L'Olonnais was to be the exception and taken to Havana alive, only the circumstances had changed somewhat. Shaking with fear, the hangman struck a deal, offering the pirates information in the hope of being spared. But after l'Olonnais listened and took note, the confessor was

DEFINING MOMENT

The day l'Olonnais played dead

Early in his pirating career, l'Olonnais's ship was battered in a storm and his fleeing crew was slaughtered by the Spaniards. He had to resort to smearing blood from his wounds across his face and body so he could hide among the dead. He escaped and found himself in the pirate refuge of Tortuga thanks to the assistance of French slaves.

c.1661

beheaded too. Just one man was kept alive, and sent back to the governor with a chilling note. It read: "I shall never henceforward give quarter to any Spaniard whatsoever; and I have great hopes I shall execute on your own person the very same punishment I have done upon those you sent against me. Thus I have retaliated the kindness you designed unto me and my companions." The governor was understandably rattled.

Yet that wasn't enough for l'Olonnais. Buoyed by his success and having embarked on a series of fruitful expeditions, l'Olonnais placed his eye on some bigger prizes. He decided he wanted to sack the city of Maracaibo, where he had already successfully ambushed a bounty-laden ship and so he found himself standing on board one of eight ships that were bobbing in the sea under the glaring heat of the sun, along with over 400 resolute men.

The Frenchman expected to pick up vast riches and untold resources and he was bolstered by the support of Michel de Basco, a successful pirate who had come to live a very comfortable life. Even though de Basco had no pressing need to go out to sea once more, he had been impressed by l'Olonnais's preparation, offering up men and his expertise for what was certain to be a bumper haul. It meant the fleet was eventually packed with some 600 pirates. It didn't take very long for their first success.

A couple of months into their voyage, l'Olonnais was alerted to a ship sailing from Puerto Rico to the colonial territory of New Spain, which had been established in 1521 following the conquest of the Aztec Empire. He ordered all but his own ship to hang back as he went to meet it alone, sparking a fierce battle against the Spaniards that lasted three hours. Once l'Olonnais emerged victorious, with his foes surrendering, the pirates bagged themselves a huge quantity of cacao, 40,000 pieces of eight and an extremely lucrative amount of jewels.

For this reason, the inhabitants of Maracaibo had every right to be fearful. First of all, the pirates targeted the supposedly impregnable fort of San Carlos de la Barra, which was defended by 16 large guns. Carrying pistols and swords, they slaughtered a group of men trying to stop them and then, with the fort destroyed and fires burning, they continued to the city. Heading towards land in canoes, dodging fire from a ship sent to protect against invasion, l'Olonnais's men went ashore and marched towards the town. By this time, most of the inhabitants had fled with their goods and money but they left behind more than enough food for a hearty feast and the pirates were able to seize their houses.

Showing the kind of leadership which would define him and solidify his reputation,

DEFINING MOMENT

The eating of a heart

If there was any doubt about his brutality, l'Olonnais's encounter with a group of Spaniards on the way to San Pedro would fix that. When they would not tell him of a safe route, he slashed the chest of a Spaniard, pulled out his heart and began to chew on it. "I will serve you all alike if you show me not another way," he told the others.

c.1666

"As one of history's most notorious pirates, torture was merely part of his job and something he found to thoroughly enjoy"

When l'Ollonais sacked cities. he also tortured citizens for information regarding their wealth and goods

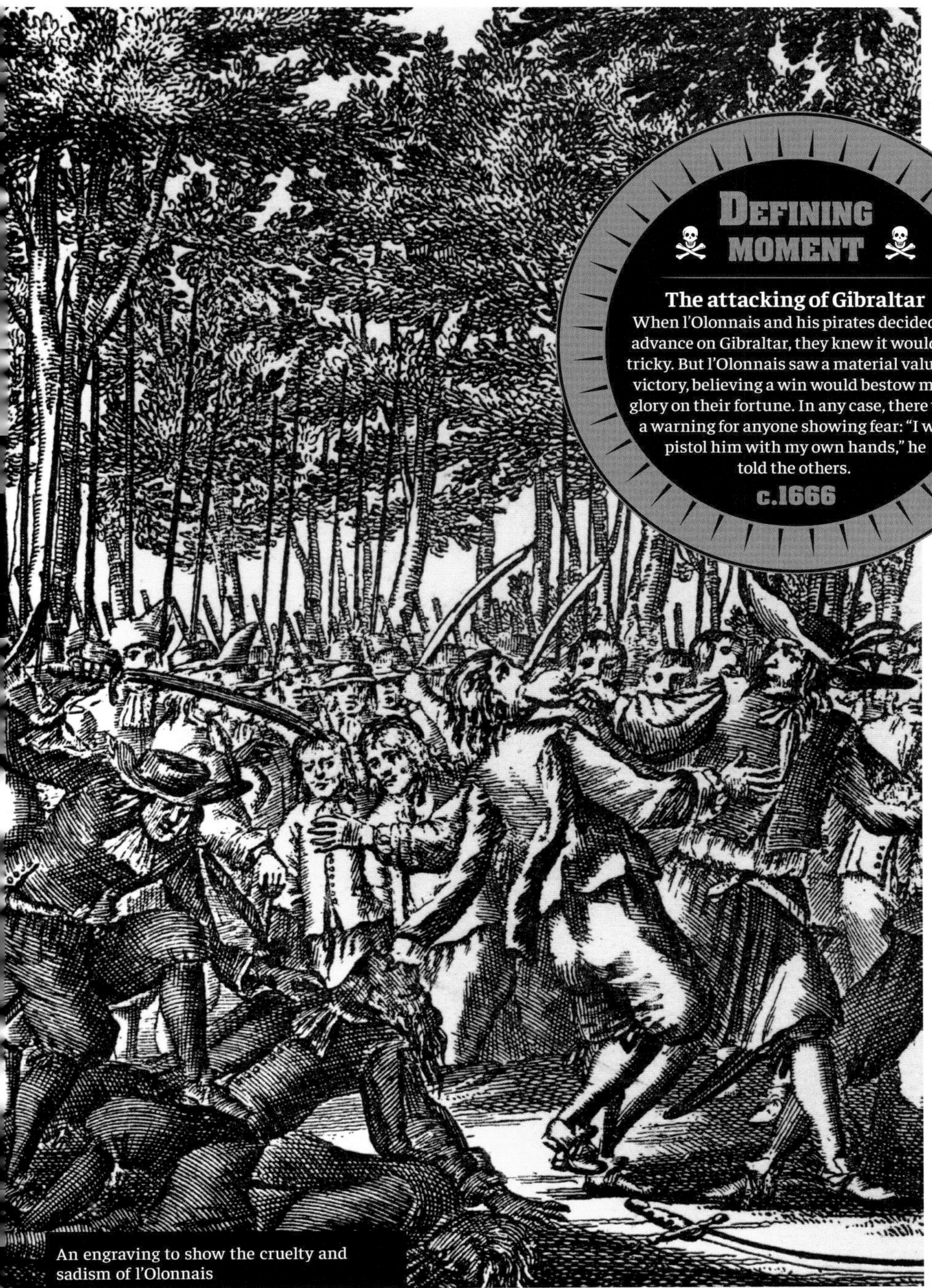
An engraving to show the cruelty and sadism of l'Olonnais

DEFINING MOMENT

The attacking of Gibraltar
When l'Olonnais and his pirates decided to advance on Gibraltar, they knew it would be tricky. But l'Olonnais saw a material value in victory, believing a win would bestow more glory on their fortune. In any case, there was a warning for anyone showing fear: "I will pistol him with my own hands," he told the others.
c.1666

l'Olonnais had 160 pirates go into the woods in search for the fleeing inhabitants. According to Alexandre Olivier Exquemelin's 1678 account of l'Olonnais and the sacking of Maracaibo, The History Of The Buccaneers Of America, they returned with "20,000 pieces of eight, several mules laden with household goods and merchandise, and 20 prisoners." Some of the prisoners were tortured using the dreaded rack in the hope of getting them to pinpoint where many of their goods had been hidden. When they gave little information away, l'Olonnais used his cutlass to slash a hapless prisoner into bits in front of the others as a warning.

It seemed to do the trick. One of the prisoners said he would show the pirates the hiding place. Yet the fleeing inhabitants had moved the items for fear of them being found. So after two weeks and with rape, pillaging and wholesale destruction underway, the pirates decided to head for the town of Gibraltar where they believed Maracaibo's residents were hiding. Getting wind of this, the governor seized his chance and sent 400 men to meet them there. He also ordered the residents of this town to take up arms and join the fight.

L'Olonnais took stock of the situation. He and the pirates decided the potential riches in Gibraltar were too great to give up without a fight and so they headed to the town with their cutlasses and pistols. At one stage, l'Olonnais ordered the pirates to flee and the Spaniards began to follow. The pirates turned and slaughtered their pursuers. Gibraltar was theirs and they took prisoners and grabbed as much booty as they could.

Some of the female prisoners were abused by their captors and other prisoners were tortured. L'Olonnais did not care that many captives were dying of disease and hunger – money and treasure was more important. After a month, he sent four of his prisoners to demand a ransom on behalf of the pirates. If the governor did not pay a significant ransom, they said, the town would be burned to the ground. Fires raged after a couple of days and eventually the pirates left with their treasures and slaves, stopping off at Maracaibo on the way for further plundering.

On their return to Tortuga, l'Olonnais and his men were given a hero's welcome but the spoils were soon spent, so embarked on another expedition. As before, the pirate showed his inhuman nature, allowing prisoners to be severely tortured. L'Olonnais would cut the tongues of prisoners failing to divulge information; he would wrap knotted rope around men's heads so tight that their eyes would pop; and he would peel flesh from victims and chop away their arms and legs. Once Spaniards answered his questions, he would simply kill them.

Yet he wouldn't entirely get away with his crimes. When l'Olonnais's ship ran aground close to the islands of De Las Pertas in the Gulf of Honduras, he and his crew were forced to break up the vessel and build a boat big enough to allow half of them to leave the shore. Unfortunately this took time and they ran into the Kuna tribe in Darien, a province of Panama. After being captured, l'Olonnais was ripped to pieces by the natives, his limbs torn away and burned and his ashes thrown to the air. As Exquemelin notes, it was done, "to the intent no trace nor memory might remain of such an infamous, inhuman creature." There was no question, l'Olonnais's pirating days were well and truly over.

The Pirate Round

Pirates hunted ships on the richest trade route, the passage from India to the Caribbean known as the Round

74
66
70
76

SAILING ON A ROUTE TO RICHES

The Pirate Round existed only for a brief period of time but it allowed for some of the richest pickings the world has ever known

The day Thomas Tew asked his men to steer a fresh course for the Cape of Good Hope in January 1693, he became more than a privateer; he became one of history's most innovative pirates. Tew may not have liked his association with piracy but when his crew shouted their approval and allowed him to forget about attacking French holdings in West Africa in favour of pursuing riches in the Indian Ocean and the Arabian Sea, his stock not only grew, he inspired a whole new wave of piracy.

Prior to Tew's decision to head for fresh waters, piracy had mainly flourished in the Caribbean. The pirates generally had the blessing of the European powers who handed them letters of legitimacy and they tended to target Spanish ships, intercepting them as they made their way across the sea so that they could relieve them of their plentiful booty. For the rival colonial powers, it was a way of engaging Spain in a proxy war of sorts but it wasn't to last.

Spanish power began to wane and peace started to take hold at a governmental level. Opportunities for pirates in the Caribbean were therefore getting ever more scarce. Faced with a particularly dangerous mission to Africa, Tew felt there were better, easier pickings elsewhere. He'd heard that ships packed with silks and spices were sailing through Indian waters and he believed the time was right to target one. Even better, he had got wind that the ships were unprotected and it made the new mission all the more enticing.

Starting from Bermuda, Tew and his crew sailed around the Cape of Good Hope, along the East African coast, en route to the Red Sea. They ran down the flagship of the Mughal Empire that had been sailing from India and found it to be the most easy of pickings. Rather than defend the huge quantities of gold, spices, ivory, silk and jewellery on board, the ship's 300-strong

The Navy pursues pirates to their island hideout

crew decided not to put up a fight. In doing so, Tew and his men collected booty valued at some £100,000.

It hadn't taken long for word to get around that Tew's men had divided up their spoils once they arrived at Île Sainte-Marie, off the coast of Madagascar. They each had taken goods worth at least £1,200 – a life-changing amount – and it only served to encourage other pirates to follow the same route. Tew's chosen path became known as the Pirate Round and the buccaneers who followed it were referred to as 'Roundsmen'. Scores of East India Company ships sailing between Britain and India became prime prey as a result.

The potential of the Pirate Round was stark but it was another pirate, Henry Every, who turned it into something of a holy grail. It was 1695 and Tew had ventured out once more to raid a Muslim ship, this time facing fierce resistance, which ended with him being killed. Every was in the same waters, commanding the warship, Fancy, backed by his 150-strong crew and 46 guns. With these, he took possession of Fateh Muhammad, bagging gold and silver worth £40,000. But it was the follow-up that reaped the rewards. Battling hard against the Ganj-i-Sawai ship, he seized an incredible haul worth as much as £525,000 – arguably the largest booty ever taken by a pirate crew.

That was it. Captains everywhere sensed a jackpot and a chance to bag some serious treasure of their own and so they set off in their droves. The pirates would leave from one of a number of colonial America's Atlantic ports, depending on where they were usually based, be it New York, Boston, Philadelphia, Rhode Island or Bermuda. They would then head south-east down the west coast of Africa via Madeira, round the Cape of Good Hope, northwards up the African coast and on to Madagascar, Mauritius or Réunion. As they did so, they had the full support of those back home.

> "Captains everywhere sensed a jackpot"

Indeed, people living in the American ports were very amenable to the pirates. In many cases, that was because they were far from being a respectable bunch themselves – New York was certainly a smaller, rougher and a very different place to the city we know today. As such, the pirates were seen as essential for day-to-day life since they brought wealth, cut-priced goods and trade. They were more than welcome to maintain and repair their ships in the ports and stock up on vital items for their arduous journeys.

The pirates were certainly glad of this assistance, because the Pirate Round entailed a far longer journey for the sailors than the forays in the Caribbean. They needed all the provisions, assistance and time for careening as they could muster to lessen the dangers they would face, since being at sea for months at a time was dull, the food was usually terrible and there was also the chance of developing scurvy through a lack of vitamin C. There was also a danger of high fever, gangrene and being caught, so support and supplies was vital.

The stop-off points on the Pirate Round were great trading posts, too. A rocky island base was claimed and established by buccaneer Adam Baldridge at Île Sainte-Marie. It was perfectly located since it was close to the route of the maritime ships as they returned from the East Indies laden with goods. Baldridge would offer supplies and trade their plunder for cattle and food, with the pirates loving the secluded, safe bays. Hundreds of their fellow men made it home and they were able to get along without hassle. Many of them raised families there, burying their dead in the infamous pirate graveyard.

The waters around Mecca in the Mughal Empire were busy with people making the Hajj pilgrimage

Around 30 headstones remain at the pirate cemetery on the island of Île Sainte-Marie, otherwise known as the island of pirates

The grave of a pirate called Joseph Pierre Lechartier in the pirate cemetery at Île Sainte-Marie; note the skull and crossbones

THE PIRATE ROUND

Trace the route that Thomas Tew and his associates made famous

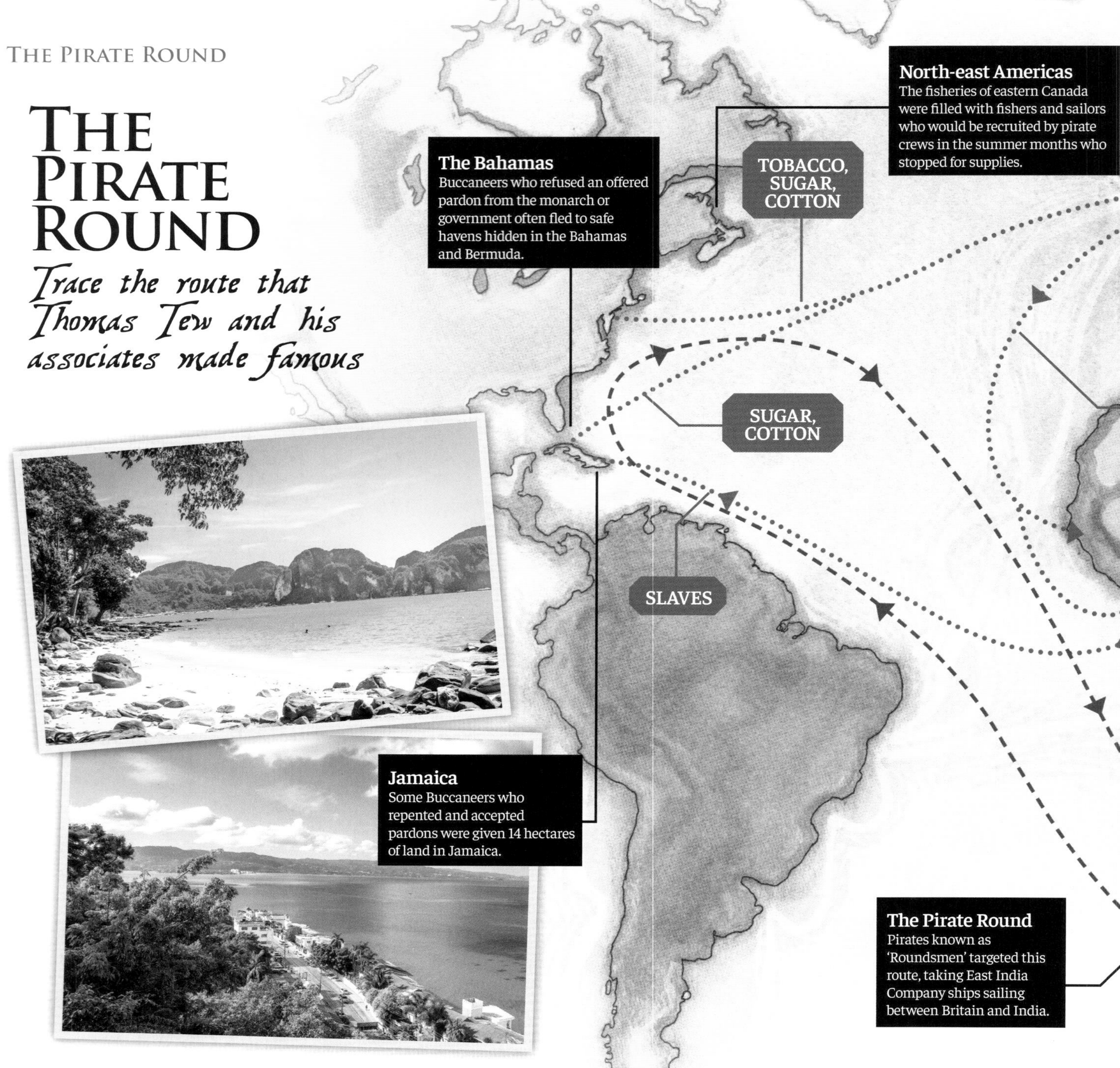

> "William Kidd, who was sent to capture Every, ended up becoming a pirate"

Another base was created by James Plantain at Ranter Bay in the north of Madagascar. The island became a key pirate haunt, providing the breathing space needed ahead of the targeting of ships from the rich Mughal Empire. The pirates would head for the Red Sea to attack vessels which set sail from Surat, north of Mumbai in India, to Mecca on the west coast of Saudi Arabia. As they made their way back with their spoils, they often sailed east of Madagascar where they could find other ships to plunder, maximising the amount of booty.

It was all straightforward and led to years of success. The pirates knew when Muslims would be on their way to Mecca for the annual pilgrimage, taking advantage of a stretch of sea just 30.5 kilometres across. Understandably, the Mughal Empire was incensed at what was going on and it pressured the British government to take action, having initially blamed the British East India Company for the attack. The Privy Council and East India Company offered a bounty of £1,000 for the capture of Henry Every. But the Pirate Round continued. Indeed, even the notorious Scottish privateer, William Kidd, who was sent to capture Every, ended up becoming a pirate. His downfall came when he looted Quedagh Merchant, captained by an Englishman which, in circumstances you'll read elsewhere in this book, eventually led to him being executed.

For all that, though, the Pirate Round was brief. Baldbridge lost his base on Madagascar in

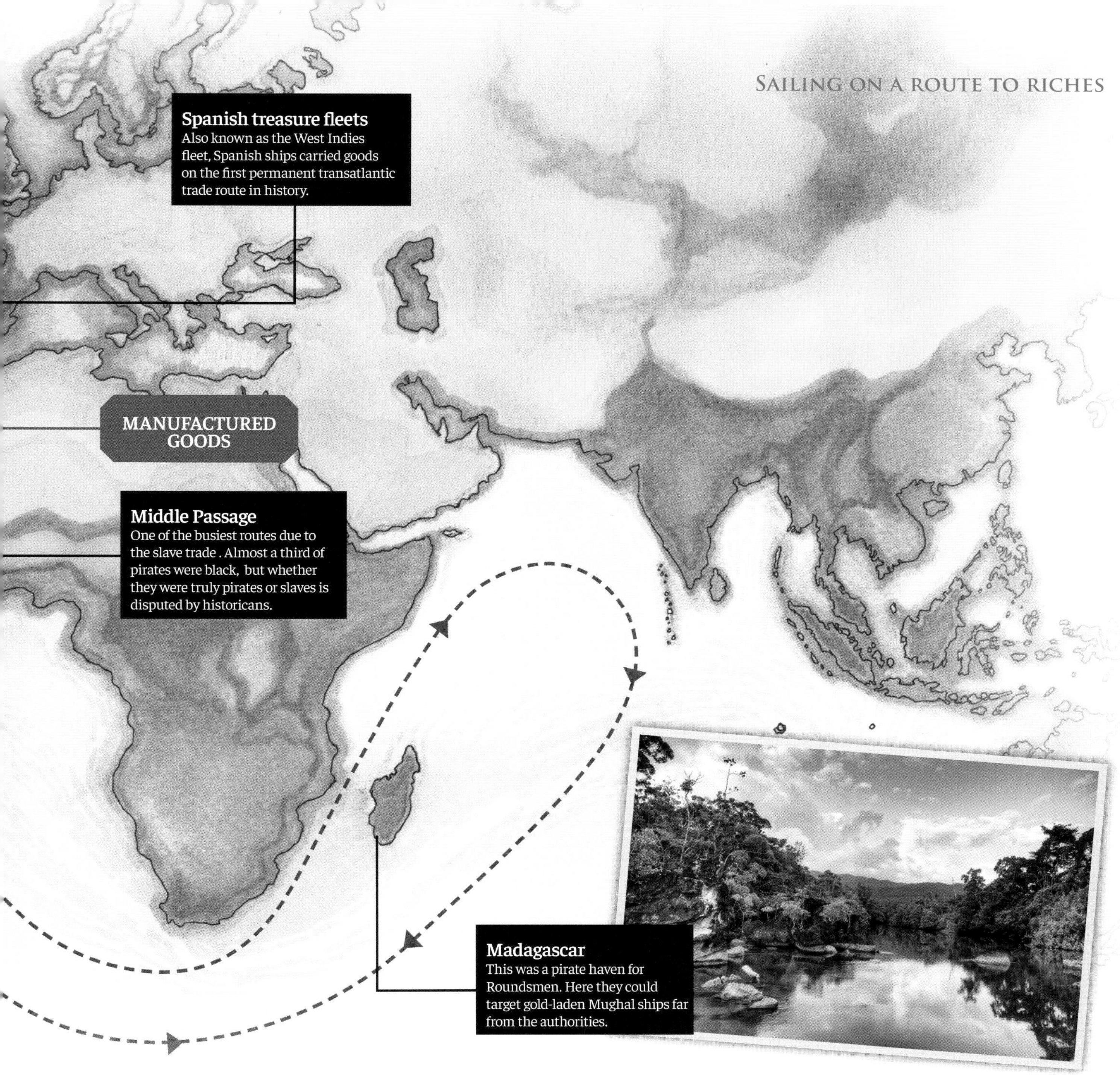

Spanish treasure fleets
Also known as the West Indies fleet, Spanish ships carried goods on the first permanent transatlantic trade route in history.

MANUFACTURED GOODS

Middle Passage
One of the busiest routes due to the slave trade . Almost a third of pirates were black, but whether they were truly pirates or slaves is disputed by historicans.

Madagascar
This was a pirate haven for Roundsmen. Here they could target gold-laden Mughal ships far from the authorities.

1697 when local tribes discovered he had sold a group of natives into slavery, and the ships became more guarded, which meant expeditions were more dangerous. Thomas Howard seized upon a ship which had run aground on a reef off Madagascar in 1699, while Abraham Samuel led a kingdom of pirates and Antanosy people in southeastern Madagascar from 1697. But the War of Spanish Succession put the Pirate Round to bed. Waged between 1701 and 1714, triggered by the death of the last Habsburg King of Spain in 1700, it opened opportunities for pirates in the Bahamas and made it easier to plunder as a member of the naval services. Legal backing meant not being caught.

It wasn't until 1719 that the Pirate Round became popular once more, even if only for a couple of years. Pirates such as Edward England, Olivier La Buse, Christopher Condent and John Taylor were active during this period. Indeed, La Buse and Taylor captured Nossa Senhora Do Cabo at Réunion in 1721 and took away £800,000 worth of treasures from Portuguese East Indiaman. But it simply proved too arduous a route and it didn't help that native Indian pirates were looking for their own share of the spoils in the area. There's no doubt it was good while it lasted, though.

Henry Every receives treasure during a successful expedition in the Indian Ocean

DEFINING MOMENT

Tew lands in Bermuda

Little is known of Tew's early life, not even where and when he was born. He is said to have had family in Rhode Island. Traveller John Groves wrote to the Council for Trade and Plantations in 1697, and said he had seen Tew in Jamaica in 1682, but it was his landing in Bermuda in 1691 that proved so pivotal: he built a reputation as a privateer.

1691

THOMAS TEW

the seafaring Robin Hood

He went after the richest ships in previously uncharted waters, and distributed the wealth among the people

It was 1692 and Captain Thomas Tew was standing on the deck of a 70-tonne, eight-gun sloop, facing his 46 strong crew as the hot sun burned their skin. He regaled them of the purpose of their expedition: to make their way to the River Gambia where they were to take a French factory at Goorie, yet he had, in his mind, plans for something else entirely. Although Isaac Richier, the Governor of Bermuda, had sent both Tew and Captain George Dew on separate ships to carry out the mission, Dew's topmast was destroyed in a violent storm. It meant that Dew had to travel back for repairs, and that had left Tew and his crew to voyage alone. This, he surmised, paved the way for a golden opportunity.

Getting ready for the expedition had been no easy task, even for such an experienced voyager as Tew. His raid had been commissioned and funded by a private group of individuals eager to boost their own wealth and, while he was confident that his years as a privateer would enable him to pull it off, Tew had spent many months preparing for it. With an official granting a 'letter of marque', he and Dew had set off from Bermuda, but Dew's premature departure caused a rethink. Sensing the benefits to himself to be outweighed by the danger, he made a decision to change course. In doing so, he not only altered the destination but the entire course of his career.

Up until that point, Tew had taken pride in being a privateer – that is, someone engaged in maritime warfare under a commission of law. He liked the air of respectability this gave him, and hated being labelled a pirate. Piracy was not, he would argue, why he had left his wife and two daughters behind in Newport, Rhode Island, to set up in Bermuda. Pirates were merely lawless in his eyes, even though they were, in actuality, often born as much out of necessity as greed. The Navigation Act of 1651, for instance, had banned the colonies of the British Empire from trading with the Netherlands, Spain, France and their colonies. This had strangled trade to the point that sailors were sitting around twiddling their thumbs for long periods of time.

With Dew out of the way, though, Tew was able to firmly stand on his own two feet. According to an account of Tew by Captain Charles Johnson in *A General History of the Pyrates* from 1724, he felt that targeting French holdings would have no benefit to the public, and only be of use to those funding it. He felt his and the crew's bravery would not be justly rewarded, so he asked a crucial question.

Rather than sail to The Gambia and carry out the mission under protection, he wanted to know if his crew would pursue a less dangerous

This image shows Thomas Tew (left) talking all about his exploits to the New York governor, Ben Fletcher

An illustration showing Thomas Tew successfully attacking a ship from India

expedition, one that would perhaps enhance their reputation and deliver riches that they would directly benefit from. He wanted them to forget the commission, effectively turning pirate. To his great pleasure, the crew is said to have shouted: "A gold chain or a wooden leg, we'll stand with you!" Whether they did actually say those words could never be truly verified, but it certainly adds to the drama surrounding such pirate endeavours.

With the crew having selected a quartermaster – someone who would give approval to the captain's decisions and look after their interests – the new band of pirates prepared themselves. They ventured to the Cape of Good Hope in the South Atlantic Ocean, and steered to the Mandeb Strait, which connects the Red Sea to the Gulf of Aden. The crew came across a richly laden ship travelling from the Indies to the Arabian Peninsula, and Tew convinced them that the 300 or so on board would not put up a fight. He was right. The enemy surrendered, and the pirates took away gold, silver, ivory, spices, gemstones and silk, sharing the lucrative spoils between them. The quarter master did not approve of taking the other five ships in the area, so they steered to Madagascar instead.

DEFINING MOMENT

The destruction of Dew's ship

Tew was commissioned to destroy a French factory near the River Gambia with Dew. They departed, sailing close together, but a storm damaged Dew's ship, forcing him to head back for repairs. This made it easier for Tew to propose to his men that they become pirates.

1692

But Tew's decision to take his crew into uncharted waters had paid off, with the value estimated to be worth more than £100,000, of which £8,000 was retained by Tew. Ever the gentleman, the captain eventually ensured the group of men who had financed the original expedition were also handed £5,000, which was 14 times the vessel's value. There were differences of opinion at Madagascar, though. The quarter master wanted to settle there, finding St Mary's Island perfect with an abundance of food and resources. Tew gave those who wanted to stay their share of the booty while the rest looked to return to Rhode Island. On their way back, they captured an Indian ship and increased their wealth. Their reputation grew and they arrived back in April 1694.

Tew was treated like a high-end celebrity, fawned over by those in power and applauded by all who met him. He'd opened people's eyes to the opportunities offered by the Arab ships, and he became solid friends with Benjamin Fletcher, the royal governor of the Province of New York. But while he now wanted a quiet, non-seafaring life, his crew – and others who dearly wanted to embark on an expedition with him – pestered for another trip. Their motivation was clear: unlike Tew, many

> "The crew was thirsty for treasure and absolutely hellbent on taking a ship"

DEFINING MOMENT

Tew relents and sails on a second pirate cruise

Tew didn't want to be seen as a pirate so he visited New York governor Ben Fletcher and persuaded him to grant a privateer commission. He set sail in 1695 and joined the fleet commanded by Henry Every. For Tew, however, the expedition came to a very bloody final end.

1695

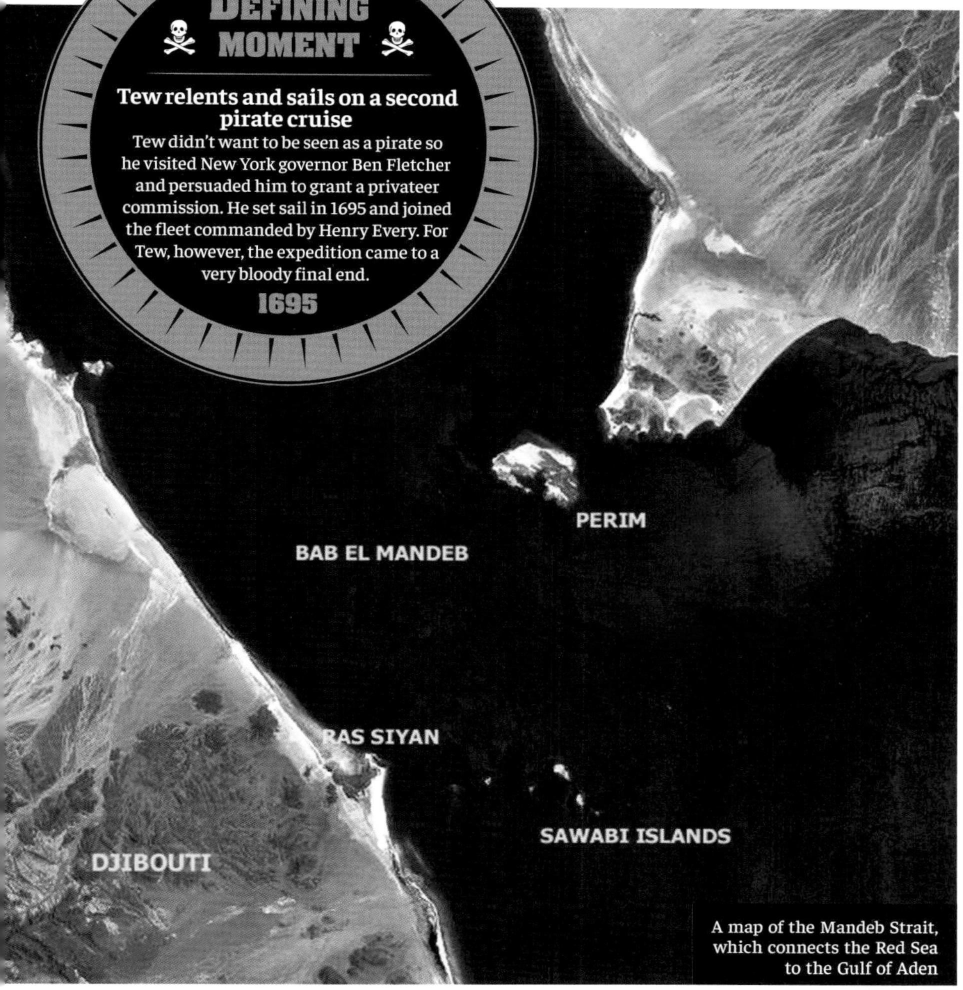

PERIM
BAB EL MANDEB
RAS SIYAN
SAWABI ISLANDS
DJIBOUTI

A map of the Mandeb Strait, which connects the Red Sea to the Gulf of Aden

Although Tew didn't like being referred to as a pirate, he still had a flag in-keeping with his piratical pursuits

crew members had squandered their shares. Eventually, Tew relented, and a second pirate cruise on board the Amity was planned. More than 40 men accompanied him initially, and a further 20 or so crew members had joined them by the time they reached Madagascar. With six new guns, they felt ready for anything.

Even now, though, Tew hated being labelled a pirate. Before he set off on this second expedition, he had ensured that he had the right paperwork – a new letter of marque from Fletcher, which he'd obtained following a bribe that nonetheless granted a level of legitimacy. They found they were not alone as they approached the Mandeb Strait, and aimed to enter the Red Sea. Other pirates had decided the Arab ships would be easy pickings too, having heard of Tew's tales, so they all went ahead together attacking a 25-ship Mogul convoy in September 1695, which was en route to Mecca. Among those joining Tew was the infamous pirate Henry Every. A chase between the pirates and the convoy ensued.

The crew was thirsty for treasure and absolutely hellbent on taking a ship. An attempt was made to overtake one of them – the Fateh Muhammad – and, as the captain's black flag fluttered in the breeze, there was great confidence, albeit mixed with a little fear, among his men that they would be able to seize it. All around them other pirates were jostling for position, hoping to capture ships as well. It was a major battle on the waves, and Tew – who intended this to be his last voyage – was on the cusp of another success.

Their ship got closer and Tew instructed the crew to fire. Another order to fire was heard, but it was in a foreign tongue. This enemy ship was fighting back. As Tew's crew scrambled for a fight, the Arab ship continued to fire. A cannonball travelled at high speed towards the Amity and struck a glancing blow across Tew's abdomen as he stood on the quarterdeck of his sloop. His stomach was ripped apart, and blood poured from the horrendous wound. Tew "held his bowels with his hands," according to *A General History of the Pyrates*, and within minutes he was dead. Panicking, his crew surrendered and were captured, although they were freed after Every seized the Fateh Muhammed. They then buried their captain at sea, mourning his loss and direction.

Yet Tew's legacy continued. The route he had selected for his expeditions became established as the Pirate Round, and he was hailed as a good man whose work – while displayed ruthlessness – had greatly benefited the poor. As Fletcher would write on 24 December 1698, three years after Tew's death: "This Tew appeared to me not only a man of courage and activity, but of the greatest sense and remembrance of what he had seen of any seaman that I ever met with." Indeed, his successes were so inspirational, they boosted the number of people becoming pirates. A golden age had begun.

HENRY EVERY
the pirate king

From seaman to notorious plunderer, how did 'The Arch Pirate' become one of the most renowned in the world?

One of the most notorious pirates of his era, Henry Every was a force to be reckoned with during his brief yet sensational career. Famed for achieving what most pirates could only dream of, Every survived the usual pitfalls of pirate life – namely capture and death – and was able to retire, it was said, with one of the largest fortunes known in pirating history.

Like many of his pirate brethren, Every fell into the way of life by chance. Devon born, it was perhaps natural that he would find life on the seas, and Every initially joined the Royal Navy, serving for only a short time between 1689 and 1690. During this period, however, he is said to have taken part in several of the main battles of the Nine Years' War, and did well enough for himself that he was chosen to serve on the HMS Albemarle – a 90-gun frigate – by the captain himself in June 1690.

A mere two months later, Every was discharged from the Navy. He remained at sea, switching his attentions to the morally dubious, albeit lucrative, slave trade. The slave coast of Africa provided a ready source of slaves, and Every found employment as first mate on board the Spanish warship Charles II in 1693, attacking French slave ships. Again, this was a short-lived post, as the crew mutinied in early May the following year over lack of pay and other grievances. Every is generally credited with having been instrumental in the mutiny and consequent removal of the captain, and – in a stroke of fate – Every himself was elected the captain of the newly named Fancy.

His career as a pirate was just as brief as his career in the Navy, lasting for just two years in total. However, it was this period of his life that made Every's name. Under his command, the Fancy quickly gained a reputation for being quick and unstoppable, early successes helping to swiftly build a reputation for luck and cunning that would turn out to be the foundation of his legend. Early on it was rather clear that he was going to be a thorn in the side of Anglo-Indian relations, as Every stated that he would only attack non-British ships, a pronouncement that was perceived as a threat despite English reassurances.

The most daring and notorious of Every's exploits, however, came six months after he became captain when he led the single most audacious and lucrative pirate attack recorded in history. Every and the Fancy, along with several other vessels, took on the 25-ship strong convoy of ships belonging to the Grand Mughal as it crossed the Red Sea in August 1695, heading for Mecca on pilgrimage. Escort ship the Fateh Muhammed was taken out with

DEFINING MOMENT

Every joins the Navy

It could be argued that without this early career choice, Every might never have found his way to a life of piracy. Clearly able and quickly earning himself a good reputation, this initial start on the seas was to point Every in the direction of his future, more-famed exploits. He enjoyed several posts, before being discharged the following year.

1689

It was his time as captain of the Fancy that earned Every his later title of The Pirate King

Said to have been the pirate flag of Henry Every during his brief but lucrative career

Every's exploits captured the popular imagination, inspiring a number of literary works

The daring capture of the Ganj-i-Sawai made Every's career, and left him the richest pirate known to history

ease, but ambitious Every had his sights set on the grand prize: the treasure-laden 1,600-tonne Ganj-i-Sawai.

A daunting prospect to a less bold man, the odds were not in Every's favour, with the Ganj-i-Sawai boasting 62 guns to the Fancy's 46. Luck was on Every's side, however, and an early and crippling blow to the enemy's mainmast quickly determined which way the wind blew. There was more good fortune to follow, when an exploding cannon killed many Ganj-i-Sawai's men, further reducing her chances and greatly increasing the odds in Every's favour. With his quarry unable or unwilling to put up much of a fight now, Every triumphed, having just achieved the seemingly impossible.

With this victory, Every became the wealthiest known pirate across the globe, with the booty from the capture of the Ganj-i-Sawai clocking in at an estimated value of £600,000, a staggering sum the equivalent of over 50 million pounds in modern currency. Those who also took part in the capture received around £1,000, untold wealth for your average seaman.

DEFINING MOMENT

Mutiny on Charles II

At the forefront of this bold move by disaffected and unpaid crew members, Every was quick to assert his position as a leader. When the either drunk or sick captain and his loyal followers chose to leave the ship rather than serve under the mutineers, Every was appointed captain in his place of the newly renamed Fancy.

1694

The myth of Every took off immediately, and there was no limit to the fabled daring of this famed pirate. He had, it was said, married the Great Mughal's daughter who had happened to be on board that day, duly fathering on her a number of children. (This is pure fabrication, as although it was reported there were women of high birth on board the Ganj-i-Sawai, there is nothing to support this extreme claim.) Every was also rumoured to have become royalty in his own right, and it was said he was treated as such by those who followed him. Despite the lack of evidence for any such claims, one thing was certain: Every's name was one of the most famed in the pirating world, and word of his exploits inspired many others to turn to the same way of life.

Despite the glamour and fame attached to Every's exploits, there is – as always – a darker side to the tale. It was said that when the Ganj-i-Sawai was captured, Every and his crew showed no mercy, murdering those who stood in their way and raping women who took their fancy, many of whom threw themselves overboard in desperation rather than face what the men had in store for them. Such reports could be dismissed as part of the legend that has surrounded Every, but – unlike other rumours – the violence that took place after the capture is supported by official records given by eyewitnesses, including members of Every's crew, not long after events took place. Every, on the other hand, is said to have said no harm came to the women.

Furthermore, there were fatal consequences to Every's bold move. Ever delicate at the best of times, the capture of the Ganj-i-Sawai proved

W R

PROCLAMATION

For Apprehending Henry Every, alias Bridgeman, and ſundry other Pirates.

WILLIAM By the Grace of GOD, King of Great-Britain, France and Ireland, Defender of the Faith, To Macers of Our Privy Council, Meſſengers at Arms, Our Sheriffs in that part Conjunctly and ſeverally, ſpecially Conſtitute Greeting. For as much as, We are Informed that Henry Every, alias Bridgeman, together with ſeveral other Perſons, Engliſh Men, Scots Men, and Foraigners, to the Number of about One Hundred and Thirty, did Steal, and Run away with the Ship called the Phanſie, alias Charles, of Fourty ſix Guns from the Port of Corunna in Spain, and Commit ſeveral Acts of Pyrracy under Engliſh Colours upon the Seas of India or Perſia Contrary to the Law of Nations, and of this Kingdom in particular; And that the ſaid Henry Every, and ſeverals of his Accomplices, ſince Committing of Pyrracy, having left the ſaid Ship in the Iſland of Providence, are Returned to, and have Diſperſed themſelves within this ...,thinking,and intending thereby to Save & Shelter themſelves from the Puniſhment & Execution of Law Due to ſuch Offenders: And We being Reſolved, that outmoſt Diligence ſhall be Uſed for Seizing, and Apprehending the Villanous Tranſgreſſors; Do therefore, with Advice of the Lords of Our Privy Council, Require, ... the ſeveral Shires, Stewarts of Stewartries, Baillies of Regalities, and their Reſpective Deputs, Magiſtrats of ... Commanders of Our Forces and Gariſons, and all others Imployed, or Truſted by Us in any Station what- ... this Kingdom, and Our Good Subjects whatſoever within the ſame, to do their outmoſt Indeavour and Dili- ... end the Perſons of the ſaid Henry Every, alias Bridgeman, together with James Cray, Thomas ... Down, John Reddy, John Stroger, Nathaniel Pike, Peter Soans, Henry Adams, Francis Frennier, Tho- ... Dauſon, James Lewis, John Sparks, Joseph Goſs, Charles Falconer, James Murray, Robert Rich, John Mi- ... Philips, Thomas Jope, and Thomas Beliſha his Accomplices, or any of them, and ſuch others as were ... be Probably known and Diſcovered by the Great Quantities of Perſian and Indian Gold and Silver ... ver him or them Priſoners to the next Magiſtrat of any of Our Burghs, to be by them keeped in ſafe ... bringing him or them to ſuch Condign Puniſhment as their Crime does Deſerve, and out of De- ... the Effect the ſame may not go Un-puniſhed; and for Incouraging the Magiſtrats above-named, and ... for, and Apprehend ſuch Nottorious Rogues: We with Advice foreſaid do make Offer, and ... undred Pounds Sterling for the ſaid Henry Every, alias Bridgman, and Fiftieth Pounds Sterling ... Perſons above-named to any Perſon or Perſons who ſhall Seize and Apprehend them or any of them, ... the Magiſtrats of Our Burghs, which ſhall be Truely and Faithfully payed, as a Reward to the ... d and Deliver Priſoner to any of Our Magiſtrats the ſaids Henry Every, or any other of his Acc ... eby all and every one of Our Subjects from any Hazard of Slaughter, Mutilation,or other Acts of ... the ſaid Henry Every, or any of his Accomplices, or any Perſons that ſhall Aſſiſt them, to Hinder ... And We with Advice foreſaid Peremptorly Inhibit and Diſcharge all, and every one of Our ... r, Conceal, or any ways Aſſiſt, or Supply the ſaid Henry Every, or any of his Accomplices above- ... WILL IS HEREFORE, and We Charge you Strictly, and Command, that Incontinent theſe Our ... of Edinburgh, and Remanent Mercat Croſſes of the Head-Burghs of the ſeveral Shires and Stewartries ... Name and Authority make Intimation hereof that none may pretend Ignorance. And Ordains theſe Pre- ...

... at Edinburgh the Eighteenth Day of Auguſt, and of Our Reign the Eighth Year. 1696.

Per Actum Dominorum Secreti Concilii:
DA. MONCRIEFF. Cls. Sti. Concilii.

GOD Save the King.

Edinburgh, Printed by the Heirs and Succeſſors of Andrew Anderſon, Printer to His moſt Excellent Majeſty, Anno DOM. 1696

The Privy Council offered £500 reward for the apprehension of Every, an amount that was met by the East India Company.

DEFINING MOMENT

Capture of the Ganj-i-Sawai

This most daring of escapades made Every's brief career as a pirate and earned him lasting renown as one of the richest and most successful marauders in history. The Mughal vessel was carrying jewels and other treasures to the worth of several hundred thousand pounds, and it is for this exploit that Every is best remembered.

1695

"One thing was certain: Every's name was one of the most famed in the pirating world"

a harsh blow to the shaky diplomatic relations between England and the Mughal powers, placing English authorities in a tricky position to say the least. Understandably greatly angered by what had transpired, the Mughal threatened retribution. If Every expected to be supported by his home country then he was to be mistaken, as a combined reward of £1,000 was offered to anyone who could capture the biggest threat to the safety of the seas. Every and his crew took moves to flee but, despite buying time by sailing to the Bahamas and bribing its governor, they could not escape the combined might of the Privy Council and The East India Company. After an attempt to obtain a pardon from the royally appointed Governor in Jamaica failed, he abandoned the attempt, returning to England. He also left another legacy: due to Every and his bold attack and capture of the Ganj-i-Sawai, the authorities for the first time decided to crack down on the increasingly frequent crime of piracy and all that it stood for. Every and his men were declared 'enemies of the human race' by parliament.

Retribution was brutal, as 24 of the pirates involved in the attack were arrested, and six found themselves before the courts. Tried and found guilty after an initial acquittal was overturned through bribery of the jury, the unfortunate men were eventually hanged in London in 1696.

Every himself, as fate would have it, managed to avoid sharing their sorry end, though many would no doubt say he deserved to meet a similar death for the trouble he had caused. Despite no firm evidence of what happened next, many supposed sightings were made of the infamous pirate over the months and years that followed.

The stories continued, fact weaving with fiction to create a legend that was further perpetuated by Daniel Defoe's 1719 *The King of Pirates* and other accounts that purported to tell the real story of this intriguing and terrifying individual. Over the years Every has been known by various names and aliases, some from during his lifetime and others that have been attributed to him posthumously, such as Benjamin Bridgeman, and the subsequent shortening of Long Ben, which can be linked to the real man. Others, such as John Avery, which cannot. Every himself signed his name as Henry Every.

There are conflicting stories about the eventual end of this bane of the establishment. Some say he escaped to the tropics where he lived out his days with the riches he had plundered, enjoying them well into his old age. Other versions of the tale have him getting at least some of what he deserved, being in turn conned out of his ill-gotten gains and retreating, penniless and alone, to die in poverty and squalor. If that were the case, what became of Every's famed treasure? Perhaps, as some believe, it is still out there somewhere, just waiting to be discovered by an intrepid treasure hunter, along with the remains of Every himself.

CAPTAIN WILLIAM KIDD

from privateer to pirate

Captain Kidd is undoubtedly among the most famous pirates of all time, but was it politics that ultimately brought him down?

Things were not going well for Captain William Kidd, a privateer about to upgrade to pirate. With the backing of rich lords in England, including King William III (in on the deal with a 10 per cent share), Kidd had set out on the open waves in Adventure Galley, with the remit to take down pirates, freebooters and sea rovers. Four notorious names mentioned in the king's commission, drawn up on 11 December 1695, included: Thomas Tew, Thomas Wake, William Maze and John Ireland. These pirates plagued shipping routes in the Indian Ocean. Kidd was, thanks to a letter of marque, also able to plunder any French merchant ships that crossed his path, under the 'commission of reprisals'.

Yet months and months had passed, fraught with disappointment after disappointment. Adventure Galley, a 34-gun ship, was in need of much repair, and the crew was increasingly in mutinous mood. Personal character defects in Kidd didn't help matters, either. He was deemed an arrogant man, a fine seaman but a tyrant on deck, whose obnoxious self-importance and airs annoyed just about everybody he met who was beneath him in social status. A shipping agent in the Indian port of Karwar attested to Kidd's argumentative nature and dealings with the crew. He described the captain as "a very lusty man, fighting with his men on any occasion, often calling for his pistols and threatening anyone that durst speak anything contrary to his mind to knock out their brains, causing them to dread him."

A series of miscalculations (in decision-making and course of action) sealed his fate and infamy as one of the most famous pirates of all time. Due to his connection to wealthy backers in New York and England, Kidd believed he had a level of protection. But moving forward into piracy was strange behaviour – even today the reasoning is unknown, and may be attributed to numerous factors, rather than a singular cause. Spurred on by a crew who may have cut their captain's throat if things didn't improve soon, Kidd failed to realise that once news of his piratical ways reached the ports around the Indian Ocean and back to the king's court, the privateering syndicate whose ship he commanded and who sent him out to capture pirates, would wash their hands of him and close ranks.

The myth of Captain Kidd as the greatest pirate of them all has endured. But the truth of the matter is different. Compared to others of his kind, he wasn't successful in endeavour or fortune, certainly not enough to justify his status in popular culture. What partly sealed

DEFINING MOMENT

The king's commission

The governor of New York, Massachusetts and New Hampshire, Governor Richard Coote, Earl of Bellomont, approached Captain Kidd to undertake a privateering mission with the backing of King William III. Given the letter of marque personally signed by the king, Kidd set off to take down pirates and enemy French ships he came across.

December 1695

"Kidd's obnoxious self-importance and airs annoyed just about everybody he met who was beneath him in social status"

Born in Scotland in 1645, William Kidd came from a sailing background, and his father was said to be lost at sea

the deal was the rumour in the years after his meeting with the hangman's noose, that he'd left behind buried treasure. A possible location for this bounty of silver and gold is Gardiners Island, off East Hampton, Long Island. A chest of treasure is a vital element in pirate mythology, hugely popularised by Robert Louis Stevenson's children's classic *Treasure Island* (1882). Much like Kidd's reputation down the years (somewhat overblown), actual historical accounts of sea dogs burying their ill-gotten pieces of eight and gold are a rarity. Feverish media attention during his capture and trial back in London ensured Kidd became something of a poster boy for this period of maritime history.

William Kidd was born in Greenock, Scotland, circa 1645. His father was a minister in the Presbyterian church, and by 1689 was at sea working as a privateer already straddling the line between hero and villain. Although he earned a name as a brave individual who went fearlessly into battle against the French, these early forays into plundering and rucking with the enemy indicate that his personality didn't endear him to folk. In command of Blessed William, the buccaneers mutinied and ditched their captain, sailing off without him after they docked at the isle of Saint Nevis.

Defining Moment

The killing of William Moore

With Kidd's men in a mutinous mood and their captain in a foul one, gunner William Moore told Kidd that they should capture a Dutch ship that had come into their midst. They quarrelled when Kidd threw an iron-hooped bucket at Moore, which struck him on the head. Moore died the following day.

October 1697

A romanticised portrait of a scene at New York Harbour aboard Captain Kidd's ship. Painted by Jean Leon Gerome Ferris (1863-1930)

Kidd wrote several letters to King William from his prison cell, requesting clemency

Setting off from Plymouth in May 1696, Kidd and his crew of 80 must have been in high hopes. Once in the Indian Ocean, deadly tropical diseases took hold. Illness and inaction (where were the pirates?) slowly began to gnaw at their collective spirit. Replacing the dead with new crew, many of them pirates, they set off for the Red Sea and Kidd's volte-face was near complete. First, venturing to the Red Sea was not in his mission statement. Second, he was now openly talking about making money from seizing any ships in the region.

On 14 August 1697, the 36-gun ship Spectre, captained by Edward Barlow, saw Adventure Galley and noted that it had a red flag raised (the pirate's flag). Attacking a fleet headed by the East India Company was an attack of lunacy as much as piracy, and Spectre, under Captain Barlow, won this skirmish. Kidd ordered his boat to get out of range and skulked off. For weeks, Adventure Galley went marauding, and tales of brutality regarding Adventure's crew were circulated.

Two weeks after the run-in with Spectre, Kidd landed the Big One. The 400-ton Quedagh Merchant was spied not far from the port of Cochin. Under the command of an Englishman, John Wright, Quedagh Merchant was carrying what to Captain Kidd must have been up to that point something of a motherlode: silk, opium, sugar, iron and calico. Adventure Galley was flying French flags this time, a routine deception as the idea behind it was a ship might not be seized by privateers. Using his letter of marque, he announced Quedagh Merchant was being taken as a prize for King William. It is estimated that Kidd earned £7,000 from this capture. He flogged its contents at Caliquilon and went on his merry way, the crew sated for now.

Soon after that, Kidd decided to ditch Adventure Galley, which was very much on

A 17th-century depiction of Captain Kidd burying his treasure at Gardiners Island, off Long Island

> "Captain Kidd turning pirate is among the stranger stories of the era. He had risen in the world from humble beginnings"

its last legs, and the newly acquired Quedagh Merchant became his man-of-war vessel. It was also around this time that he learned that his piratical adventuring had become common knowledge, not only in the region, but back in Europe. Kidd had frankly become a great source of embarrassment for the syndicate, if the stories were true.

Intending to flee the area and make for the West Indies, Captain Kidd made port at Sainte-Marie, Madagascar, and ran into Captain Robert Culliford of Resolution. This known pirate should have been detained, placed in irons, and his ship seized by Kidd. It was, after all, what he'd planned to do. Instead, they became pally, and Kidd assured Culliford he wasn't out to get him.

Captain Kidd turning pirate is among the stranger stories of the era. He had risen in the world from humble beginnings, had earned a reputation as a trustworthy man, was commended for acts of bravery in his dealings with the enemy France, had married a wealthy Manhattanite (Sarah Oort), and could call governors and lords friends and acquaintances. But the offer from the syndicate was a bind. He dared not refuse it, as to turn down such an opportunity would have attached a social stigma and dishonour. Conversely, it served to increase his standing in the world, if a success, and could make him a rich man who could afford to live a life of leisure or pursue some other land-based business.

Kidd didn't go quietly when arrested; he raged. Having taken stock of the captain's plunder – which was listed by the captured pirate during an interview before the eventual arrest – everybody from Bellomont to the East India Company was gripped by treasure fever, all wanting a slice. The total prize was estimated at a gargantuan sum: £400,000. As much as £14,000 was recovered in gold, silver and jewels. But was the estimate correct? And was there gold buried on Gardiners Island, where Kidd had set ashore twice in the weeks before his arrest?

On 14 April 1700, Kidd was back in London, holed up in Newgate Prison. There he stayed for 11 months, growing suicidal and knowing none of his former friends and allies wanted anything to do with him. In court, he faced charges of piracy and murder. Upon being found guilty and sentenced to be hanged, a stunned Kidd said: "My lord, it is a very hard sentence. For my part, I am the innocentest person of them all, only I have been sworn against perjured persons."

Kidd's death on 23 May 1701 at Execution Dock, Wapping, was gruesome and undignified. The first attempt to pass the sentence ended with the rope breaking. Strangled and delirious, the convict was strung from a ladder and hung a second time. His corpse was placed in a gibbet at Tilbury, where it rotted for years.

A galleon comes under attack by pirates; could it contain a fortune like that of the Great Mohamed?

ROBERT CULLIFORD

scourge of William Kidd

When Robert Culliford snatched Kidd's ship, the famed captain would stop at nothing to get him back

The mysterious Robert Culliford's life was one that was marked by some startling reversals of fortune, with mutiny, marooning and Marshalsea all playing their part. Culliford came from coastal Cornwall and, although his early years are lost to history, he soon left obscurity far behind. Culliford first came to notice in 1689 when he was serving as part of an Anglo-French crew, the Sainte Rose, a French privateer ship sailing the Caribbean seas. It was while on this crew that he met a fellow crewman named William Kidd, later to become famous in his own right, entering pirate legend as Captain Kidd.

When France and England declared war on one another, the crew of Sainte Rose mutinied and seized control of the vessel. Appointing William Kidd as captain, they renamed the ship Blessed William, yet things weren't rosy on deck for these English privateers. The sailors soon grew dissatisfied with Kidd's captaincy, and Culliford was at the head of a second mutiny against his former crew mate that took place in 1690. Waiting for Kidd to go ashore, Culliford's mutineers stole away in Blessed William and elected William Mason their captain. This proved a decisive moment in Culliford's career and, though he wasn't captain, he exercised enormous influence over Mason. Under Culliford's direction, the crew were granted a sought-after letter of marque, granting their privateering endeavours an official approval.

Culliford became a captain in his own right when the privateers captured a French frigate, L'Espérance, which Mason gave to his loyal crew mate. Blighted with bad luck that saw them lose much of their hard-won booty to French privateers, Culliford sailed for India, determined to refill their cargo hold with plenty of plunder. Instead, Culliford and his crew were soon captured by the Mughals and thrown in prison. Here they languished for nearly four years before they were released, and Culliford led his men out to sea, once more aboard a ship stolen from the mighty East India Company.

No doubt believing that his bad luck was behind him, Culliford must have been surprised to find himself on land all over again, when the crew of the stolen vessel took back their ship and marooned him. Luckily for Culliford, he was rescued by Mocha, a ship whose captaincy he inherited in 1697. With his ill fortune finally a thing of the past, Robert Culliford's career finally went from strength to strength, and he was soon the captain of his own fleet. As the years passed, he became a famed and feared pirate, operating off Madagascar and seizing a fortune in treasure and vessels.

Nine years after he met Kidd about Sainte

Rose, the men were to meet again off the coast of Madagascar. Now Kidd was a feared pirate hunter, and when he heard that Culliford was in the area, he was determined to get his revenge. He had not forgotten the mutiny all those years ago, nor Culliford's part in it, and he was sure that the time had come to make Culliford pay. In fact, once Kidd's crew heard of Culliford's determination and the success of his recent endeavours, he became a rather attractive prospect. With Kidd powerless to stop them, the majority of his crew abandoned their pirate-hunting master and signed on to sail with Culliford instead.

With his newly enlarged crew, Culliford sailed from Saint Mary's Island off the coast of Madagascar in 1698. Alongside him was another pirate, Dirk Chivers, and together the two men made for the Red Sea, where they engaged Great Mohammed. That ship was carrying a fortune in cash, and Culliford and Chivers captured it with ease. Emboldened and fired up by this enormous haul, Culliford continued to sail the waters around Madagascar, terrorising shipping and bringing in plenty of booty.

DEFINING MOMENT

Capturing Great Mohammed

After years of ill fortune that included mutiny, marooning and a four-year spell in a Mughal prison, Culliford teamed up with pirate captain Dirk Chivers and sailed for the Red Sea. They captured Great Mohammed, a ship groaning under the weight of its treasure. The bounty of £130,000 made the captains and crew rich men.

1698

Culliford's reign of piratical terror couldn't last forever, and in 1699, the British arrived on St Mary's Island in search of the infamous captain. Although his first instinct had been to fire on the British ships, when Culliford learned that they were there on a mission to offer him a pardon, he was more than interested. After such an extensive pirate career, Culliford was happy to accept the royal pardon, though some of his crew weren't so sure and fled, happy to remain outlaws.

After years in exotic climes, Culliford returned to England, believing himself to be a free man. Here, however, he found that he had been outwitted. In fact, almost as soon as he set foot on British soil, Culliford was arrested for the attack on the treasure-laden Great Mohammed. The man who had once sailed the open seas was thrown into the festering prison at Marshalsea, his pardon now worthless. It seemed inevitable that Culliford's next stop would be the gallows, but instead he agreed to testify against another pirate, Samuel Burgess, in return for his life.

At this point, Robert Culliford disappears from the historical record, his fate unknown. Although what became of Culliford will likely remain a mystery, it is tempting to speculate about what happened to him once he was released from Marshalsea. Perhaps he went back to sea under another name, or even aboard a naval vessel, or maybe, having cheated death by the narrowest of margins, the hugely wealthy Captain Culliford retired and lived to a ripe old age, happy to live the high life on the spoils of his piratical career.

"The man who had once sailed the open seas was thrown into the festering prison"

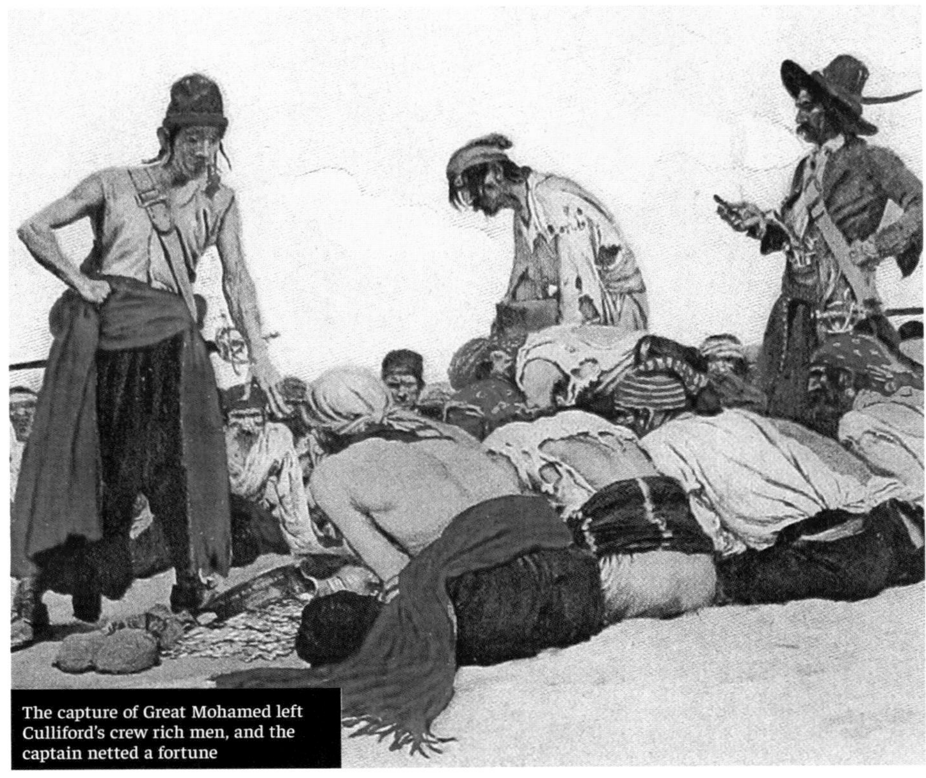

The capture of Great Mohamed left Culliford's crew rich men, and the captain netted a fortune

Culliford returned to London, believing he had been pardoned by King George I

Amaro Pargo was one of the richest, not to mention most charitable, pirates of the age

AMARO PARGO
the charitable captain

Not all pirates spent their days plundering; some consorted with kings and gave a fortune to charity

Born on Tenerife in 1678, Amaro Rodríguez Felipe y Tejera Machado became famed in pirate history by the nickname Amaro Pargo. He was given this name in honour of the largo fish, which was known to move swiftly through the waves, taking its prey by surprise. The ships commanded by this famed privateer were just as swift and just as sure, but not everyone feared this particular pirate.

Amaro was born to wealthy parents on the island of Tenerife, where he was raised in comfortable, privileged surroundings. Like his peers, he was a Catholic from birth and faith, and this was always a defining element of Amaro Pargo's life. As he grew older he sought for a career of his own and, when in his early 20s, took to the ocean as a second lieutenant aboard Ave Maria, known to its crew as La Chata, which translates to The Barge. It was on The Barge that a chance attack by pirates gave the young second lieutenant the chance to prove himself, an event that changed of his life forever. When Amaro's shrewd strategising resulted in the defeat of the pirate attack, the young man was given a ship as a reward, and from that moment, nothing could stop Amaro.

Amaro's career coincided with the War of the Spanish Succession and, for a privateer with ambition and daring, the rewards could be enormous. Amaro, however, wasn't going to rest on his privateering laurels, and had ambitions in business too.

Swiftly he established himself as one of the most accomplished captains at sea, building his fortune on the back of trading between the Canary Islands and the West Indies. He expired brandy and wine made from his own crops, and also became one of the most active slave traders to emerge from the Canary Islands. On the back of these business interests, no matter how unsavoury they seem to us, Amaro Pargo acquired a fortune in goods and property, eventually becoming the richest man in the Canary Islands. So celebrated was Amaro that he was welcomed into the company of King Philip V of Spain, who awarded him a letter of marque.

At the head of a large and richly appointed fleet, Amaro sailed the West Indies, making the very best of the letter the king had awarded him. His fortune meant that he could afford the best of everything, and his ships were some of the best-equipped on the ocean, tirelessly chasing down his Dutch and British quarries. As a loyal subject of King Philip V, Amaro Pargo's targets were any vessel that came from a nation who opposed Spain, and he was merciless in pursuit. If captains refused to capitulate to his demands, he engaged them in battle, seizing their ships, their cargo and a fortune in booty.

But for Amaro, life wasn't all about boarding, looting and battling; he had a philanthropic side too.

From the day of his birth in San Cristóbal de La Laguna, Amaro Pargo was a devoted Catholic. He firmly believed, since God had given him so many blessings and such good fortune, that he was duty bound to give something back in return. Just as in all other areas of his life, Amaro didn't do charity by halves, and he shovelled a fortune into philanthropic works. Amaro's exploits and trade deals were used to bring much-needed relief for the poor and needy, including those held in prison. He ploughed money into religious orders, charitable endeavours and places of worship, even paying for the construction of churches and cathedrals in which he could worship the Lord he believed had raised him to the very pinnacle of wealth and success. After all, he was a favourite of the king himself, not to mention the most wealthy man in the Canary Islands. Thanks to his exploits, Amaro Pargo became a celebrity in his homeland, loved by the people from the richest to the poorest, and hailed as a hero, as well as a man of God.

That man of God found one of his closet friends in the shape of Sister Mary of Jesus, a nun who became his confidante, confessor and spiritual advisor. In return, Pargo funded the building of the Parroquia de Nuestra Señora de Los Remedios, the precursor to La Laguna Cathedral that can be seen on Tenerife today. Amaro remained unmarried and, since his death, historians have sought to find evidence of a romantic connection between the nun and the pirate, though so far, have been unable to do so. There is no denying that Amaro counted Sister Mary of Jesus as a beloved friend, and when she died in 1731, he funded a lavish casket for the woman he considered as good as a saint. Indeed, Amaro always believed that he had been blessed by Sister Mary, and was convinced that she watched over him after death, bringing him luck and good fortune, as well as providing the occasional miracle to see him safely home.

When Pargo died in 1747, he was at home in San Cristóbal de La Laguna, the very place in which he had been born. His funeral was as magnificent as you might expect, and was attended by an enormous crowd of both the rich and poor, all of the town pouring into the streets in order to pay their respects to the man who had given them so much. Amara Pargo, however, left one tantalising mystery behind. In his will, he wrote of a vast treasure that he had accrued and hidden somewhere, a priceless booty of art, money, jewels and every imaginable luxury. To this day, that treasure has not been found; perhaps, one day, Amaro Pargo's fortune will be revealed. Until then, it remains one of the greatest mysteries of the pirate age.

Defining moment

An audience with the king

In 1725, after years spent serving the king of Spain, Amaro Pargo was honoured by Philip V of Spain, who named him Caballero hijodalgo. This title officially recognised Amaro as a nobleman, a hero of the people, and one of the most important people in the land. It was the pinnacle of his achievements.

1725

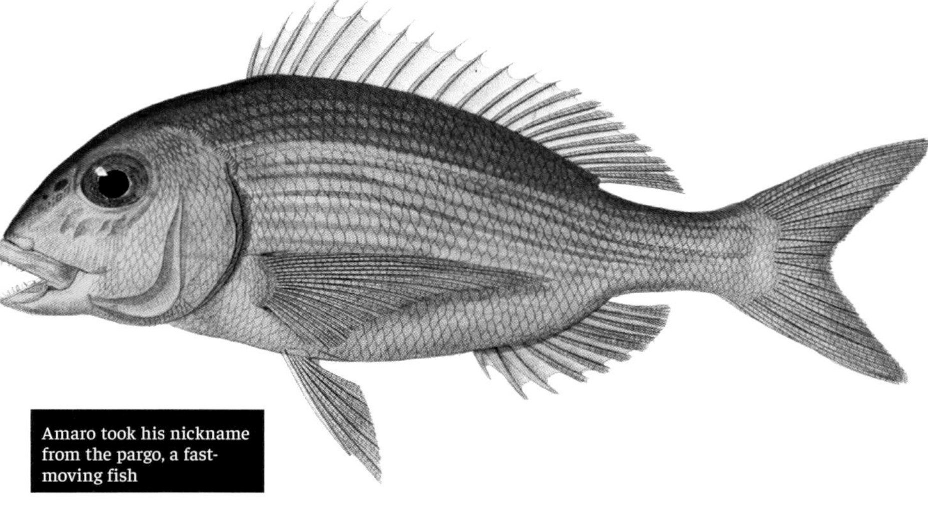

Amaro took his nickname from the pargo, a fast-moving fish

Sister Mary of Jesus was Amaro Pargo's closest friend and spiritual confessor

Amaro's tomb on Tenerife features the unmistakable symbol of the skull and crossbones

The Golden Age

Piracy reached its Golden Age between 1715-1725, when a gang of pirate captains ruled the Caribbean

86

98

138
104
80

THE PIRATE REPUBLIC

The Golden Age of Piracy saw a nest of pirates emerge around the port of Nassau on the Bahaman island of New Providence. Here they formed their own 'pirate republic'...

The Golden Age of Piracy has come to describe the decade between 1715 and 1725 where, with the Treaty of Utrecht bringing an end to Britain's involvement in the War of the Spanish Succession, a number of enterprising and ruthless commodores had taken to the seas for private gain. British sailors had suffered particular hardship with the signing of the Treaty and the Royal Navy's subsequent mothballing of its enormous fleet. This left sailors out of work, and those who did find employment saw their wages slashed in the new economic climate.

Indeed, dissatisfaction was so prevalent among those who sailed with merchant vessels or those still working with the Royal Navy that very often, when captured by pirates (or buccaneers as the Caribbean operatives became known), many men immediately switched sides. On board a pirate vessel, not only would they stand to boost their wages, but they would also enjoy a less stringent brand of discipline. One famous example of maritime defection is the standoff between Bahaman pirates and HMS Phoenix in 1718, where, under the cover of night, a clutch of Royal Navy men sneaked off to join the outlaws.

> "When captured by pirates, many men switched sides"

Many of the early buccaneers had been privateers, operating under license from the crown and granted legal right to harry enemy shipping. During the Golden Age, however, this changed and men took to the sea knowing full well that they were in open revolt against the authorities. As well as out-of-work and disaffected sailors, pirate numbers were boosted by the arrival of runaway slaves, indentured servants and all sorts of other outlaws, including the politically and religiously agitated, many of whom objected to George I's ascension to the throne of England in 1714. He had succeeded Queen Anne at the expense of the house of Stuart, much to the chagrin of Jacobite sympathisers. It is no coincidence that Blackbeard renamed his flagship, the captured slaver La Concorde, as Queen Anne's Revenge.

An 18th century cannon stands in place in Fort Charlotte, New Providence

The authorities regularly painted pictures of these pirates as brutal monsters, bent on rape and pillage, but the truth is often quite different. Many colonists regarded them as folk heroes and though the infamous duo of 'Black Sam' Bellamy and Edward 'Blackbeard' Teach took more than 300 ships between them, there are no reports of their having killed a single captive.

Much to the authorities' annoyance, these pirate gangs enjoyed enormous success,

A flotilla of smaller pirate ships attack a British Royal Navy vessel harrying French, Spanish and English shipping throughout the West Indies and raiding the coast. Chief among them were the pirates who set up in the port of Nassau on the Bahaman island of New Providence. The island was around 60 square miles in size and was situated 200 miles east of Florida, thereby offering a sound base to harass the shipping lanes.

The island offered fresh fruit, meat and water while Nassau's harbour was tailormade for defence and the unloading of booty. It could take around 500 vessels, though it was too shallow to accept large battleships. With Hog Island splitting the harbour into two inlets, it was also difficult to blockade. The surrounding region, meanwhile, offered plenty of protection amid its waterways and no sensible captain would sail these waters without an experienced pilot at the helm.

Buccaneers had long recognised New Providence's strategic importance, though it came into its own when selected as the base of operations by the privateer-turned-pirate Benjamin Hornigold in 1713 (see separate profile on page 92). Hornigold, along with his great rival Henry Jennings (see separate profile on page 96) became the unofficial overlord of a veritable pirate republic, which played host to the self-styled Flying Gang.

In truth, New Providence had suffered greatly during the War of the Spanish Succession and had witnessed Spanish incursions during 1703, 1704 and 1706. By the time Hornigold had set his sights on the island, there was only a skeleton settlement in the town of Nassau, and Thomas Walker was the island's only remaining appointed official. Though the evidence is scant, it appears that he was acting in the role of deputy governor upon Hornigold's arrival and he did not take kindly to the pirates' presence.

Full-on naval battles were typically avoided by pirate crews and captains

He took it upon himself to stand up to the buccaneers and, calling for reinforcements, he penned copious letters to anyone and everyone, sending missives to the proprietors of Bahaman estates, the lords of the admiralty and the press, informing them of the growing pirate menace operating from his island. He whipped up a goodly amount of interest and concern, with the acting governor of Bermuda, Henry Pulleine, writing to officials in London that the Bahamas had become a veritable "nest of pyrates".

Pirates board a vessel under the cover of moonlight

Walker, meanwhile, who lived a few miles from Nassau with his freed black wife and their children, set about planning an attack on the Bahaman pirates and sailing against the men on Harbour Island, due east of New Providence, he captured the pirate Daniel Stillwell, a number of his associates and the pirate ship Happy Return. His luck ran out, however, and while Walker was away on business Hornigold freed Stillwell and hatched his own plan in a bid to rid New Providence of Walker and his troublesome ways. This was a key moment in the history of the island, for with Walker out of the way, there would be no opposition to the Flying Gang, who would rule the Bahamas as they saw fit.

According to a deposition given in Charleston by Walker's son, Thomas Jr, the young man ran into Hornigold in late 1715 in the port of Nassau and the pirate told him that his father was a "troublesome old fart" and that if he did not desist from his meddling ways, Hornigold would murder him, burn his house to the ground and whip his family.

When, in December of that year, Hornigold captured the mighty Spanish warship that he vainly named Benjamin, it looked as though Walker had lost control. By the time Henry Jennings and his men sailed into Nassau in January 1716, their decks laden with Spanish treasure, a new age really had been born. A short while later, Hornigold refortified the harbour, refitting the old fort and arming it with cannons. Walker conceded defeat. He set sail for Charleston with his family, never to return. New Providence, to all intents and purposes, belonged to pirates.

According to Captain Johnson's original source, *A General History Of Pirates* (as it came to be known), by 1716 Nassau played home to not just Hornigold and Jennings, but also to the former's loyal lieutenant Edward 'Blackbeard' Teach, John Martel, Olivier La Buse, Charles Bellamy and Edward England among many others. The island of New Providence also acted as a rendezvous for a clutch of other infamous pirates, including Stede Bonnet, Jack Rackam and the pirate women Mary Read and Anne Bonny.

As 1716 wore on, the outlaw population on New Providence blossomed, boosted by log cutters from Campeche and any number of the disaffected. The citizenry began to drift away, fearful of their treatment at the hands of the swaggering newcomers. One Thomas Barrow, the leader of the men that had worked on the Spanish wreckers, earned

All crewmembers on a pirate ship would fight for their share of the spoils

Tortuga, off the coast of Haiti, is also the site of a pirate base

New Providence

This small island in the Bahamas was to become a pirate paradise

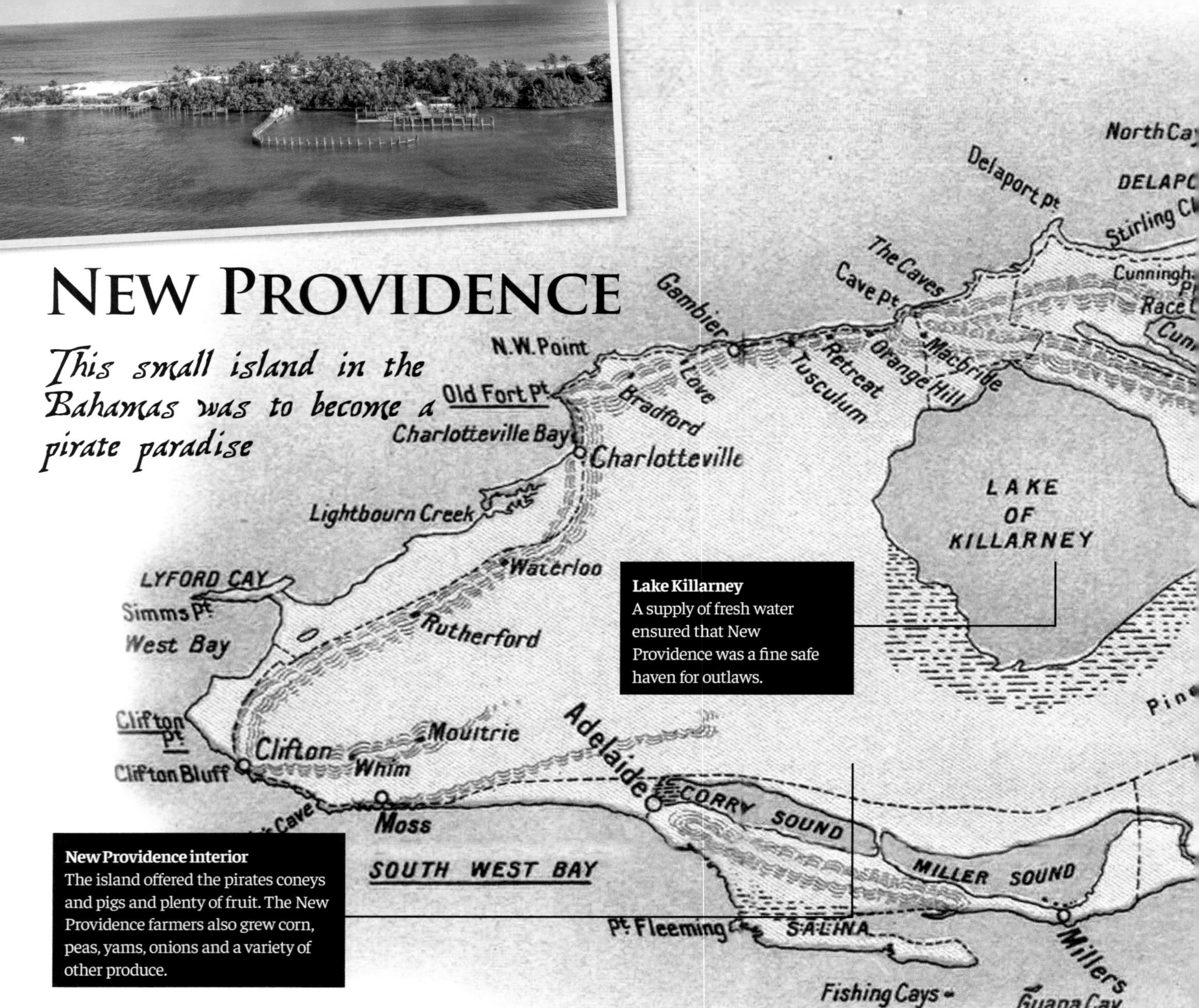

Lake Killarney
A supply of fresh water ensured that New Providence was a fine safe haven for outlaws.

New Providence interior
The island offered the pirates coneys and pigs and plenty of fruit. The New Providence farmers also grew corn, peas, yams, onions and a variety of other produce.

a nasty reputation for extorting the menfolk and upsetting the island's women. Hundreds of tents and huts, houses and hovels sprung up as the pirates made the place their own. Wives and prostitutes moved in and alehouses did a roaring trade.

The better homes in and around Nassau, meanwhile, were populated by the merchants and smugglers to whom the pirates sold their booty and with whom they traded for ammunition and other valuable supplies. However, even the traders were not always ensured safe passage around New Providence. Barrow is said to have robbed a brigantine from New England around this time and to have beaten up the master of a Bermudan trading vessel.

Still, the place was not entirely lawless. Generally, the pirates operated within the rules of an unwritten code of conduct, which ensured that their existence was the very best among sailors, and certainly more profitable and enjoyable than the life of a Royal Navy tar or a merchant. For the Flying Gang came to elect their captains and, if they felt he had failed them, they could depose him. When in combat, the captain was granted full command but the majority of decisions, from deciding where to attack to choosing suitable punishments for transgressors, were made democratically by the ship's crew.

Prizes were split pretty evenly between all crew members, with the captain only taking a little more than his men and the cabin boy taking the smallest share. The crew also appointed a quartermaster to ensure that food and supplies were doled out equitably. Hornigold and Jennings were the pre-eminent pirate leaders, though some have written that Edward 'Blackbeard' Teach was appointed as a magistrate on the island. Whatever the truth of this claim, he certainly became a powerful pirate leader. Such was the power of this pirate republic, and the damage it caused to the ships of all nations, the British authorities finally took a decisive course of action with a three-pronged plan of attack. First, the Navy would dispatch three warships to Caribbean waters. Second, George I would offer the King's Pardon to any surrendering pirate, forgiving them for all piracies committed prior to January 1718. Third, the authorities would appoint Woodes Rogers as governor and garrison commander of the Bahamas with a precise remit: deliver the King's Pardon to any who would accept. Those that did not should be hunted down

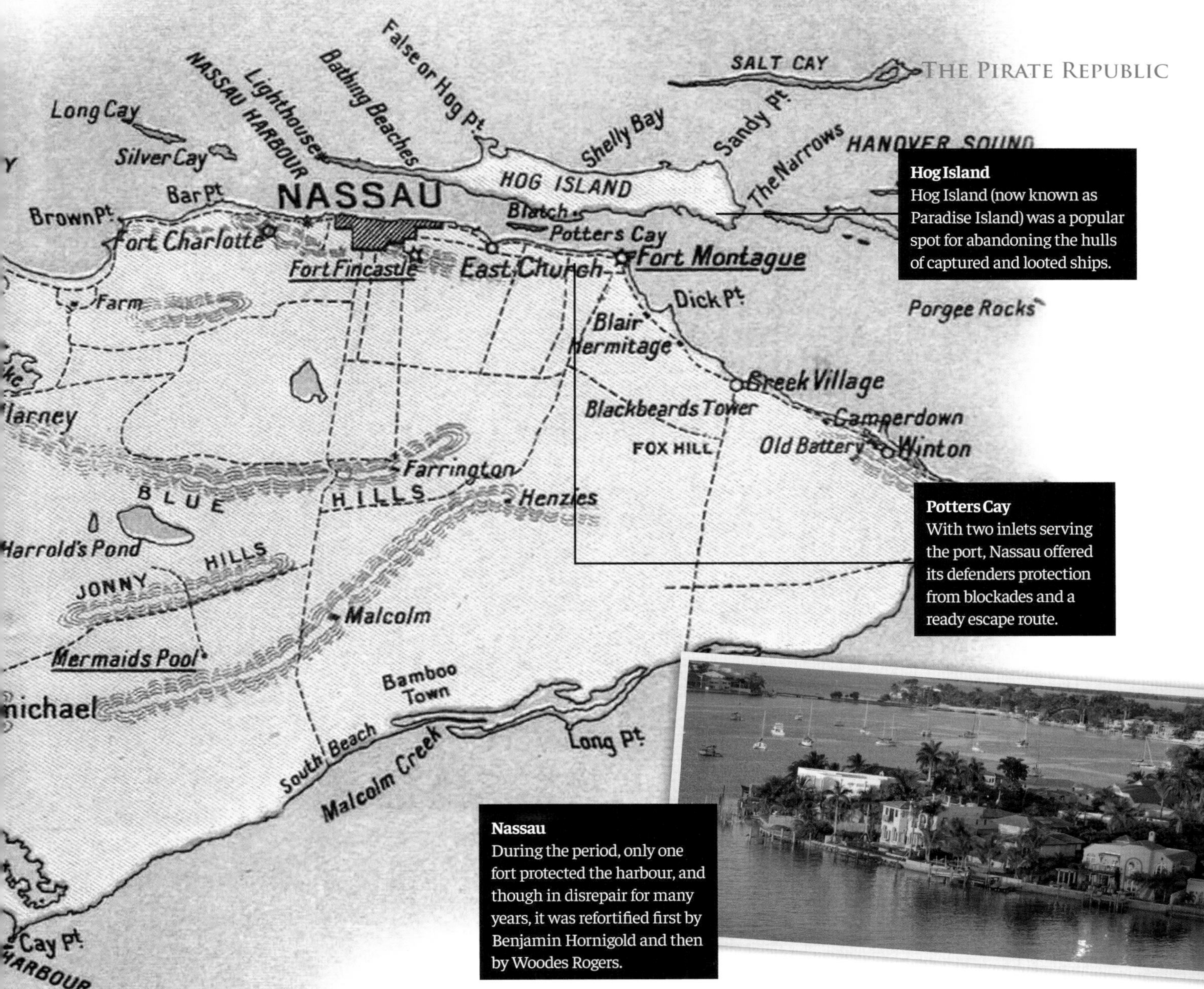

Hog Island
Hog Island (now known as Paradise Island) was a popular spot for abandoning the hulls of captured and looted ships.

Potters Cay
With two inlets serving the port, Nassau offered its defenders protection from blockades and a ready escape route.

Nassau
During the period, only one fort protected the harbour, and though in disrepair for many years, it was refortified first by Benjamin Hornigold and then by Woodes Rogers.

> "George I would offer the King's Pardon to any surrendering pirate, forgiving them for all acts"

via a committed offensive.

Rogers had already proved himself an able commander and had been a successful privateer himself, operating under the sponsorship of the Mayor and corporation of Bristol in years past. He arrived at New Providence in July 1718 on board the Delicia, a former East Indiaman, and was accompanied by the warships HMS Milford and HMS Rose along with the sloop-of-war Shark. In total, he had brought seven armed ships and more than 500 men – more than enough, the authorities reckoned, to take down the republic of pirates.

Several prominent figures, such as Hornigold himself, having already received news of the King's Pardon, decided to turn themselves in. Others, such as Charles Vane and Blackbeard, decided to fight.

Vane was holed up in Nassau upon Rogers' arrival but quickly fired his guns and fled, leaving the island to the new governor who immediately set about reassuring the civilians, and also rebuilding the crumbling fort that overlooked the growing town. He recruited Benjamin Hornigold and Captain Cockram as pirate hunters and sent them after Vane. Though Vane eluded him, in October Hornigold caught up with a clutch of pirates on the island of Exuma. These men had accepted the King's Pardon before swiftly going back to their old ways. They included two notable men, John Augur, a former commander of the sloop Mary, and William Cunningham, who had been one of Blackbeard's gunners. Rogers hanged them, a total of eight recidivists swinging on the gallows on the morning of December 12.

Rogers' arrival and his execution of these Nassau pirates did not bring an end to the age of buccaneering, but it terminated New Providence's position as a haven for outlaws and scoundrels. Though the likes of Blackbeard and Vane remained at large for a while, the Pirate Republic had breathed its final breath, before finally succumbing to the sea's pounding waves.

The Flying Gang

After the Wars of Spanish Succession drew to a close, many British privateers who preyed on the Spanish New World shipping were left feeling rather listless. With no more state-sponsored raiding to fill their wallets, many of these men decided to turn their ships and crew to a less salubrious form of money making – piracy. As there was a collection of these men and women around the Caribbean, they decided to form an organisation, taking the moniker 'The Flying Gang'. Masterminded by Benjamin Hornigold and Henry Jennings during the salvage of the 1715 Spanish Treasure Fleet, the gang consisted of the most cunning and fierce buccaneers of the day and would terrorise the Caribbean until the Royal Navy and infighting brought them to justice. Not all famous pirates would be in the gang however, with men like Black Bart forging their own destinies.

Benjamin Hornigold

Nationality: British
Born: c.1680 **Died:** 1719

One of the founders of the Flying Gang, Benjamin Hornigold served as a mentor for other members, including the terrifying Edward Teach. Aboard his 30-gun sloop Ranger, he menaced merchants but always avoided attacking British vessels in what is usually seen as patriotism. Ignoring tempting targets wasn't popular among his booty hungry crew, however, and they mutinied and cast him out as captain. Taking up the 1718 Pardon, Hornigold became a pirate hunter, spending the rest of his life hunting down his old prodigy and other famous buccaneers.

Henry Jennings

Nationality: British
Born: Unknown **Died:** Unknown

The other founder of the Flying Gang, Henry Jennings' first act of piracy was to seize some of the 1715 Treasure Fleet plunder. He became the unofficial mayor of Nassau and Hornigold's rival, mentoring men like Charles Vane and Jack Rackham. Jennings became infamous after a botched attack on a French merchant vessel. Betrayed by Sam Bellamy, who made off with Jennings' loot, the captain reportedly slaughtered 20 French and English sailors and put an English merchantman to the torch. Jennings took the 1718 Pardon and retired from pirating.

Edward Teach

Nationality: British
Born: c.1680 **Died:** 1718

Better known as Blackbeard, Teach could hold the title as the most famous and feared pirate of all time. Under the tutelage of Benjamin Hornigold, Teach took over some of his mentor's small fleet when Hornigold retired in 1717.
By attacking and capturing a French ship, he gained his notorious flagship, Queen Anne's Revenge. Decked out with 40 guns, this ship was a force to be reckoned with. Preferring to use his fearsome reputation rather than violence to claim his booty, Blackbeard nevertheless fought the British Navy that was sent after him, finally submitting after a frenzied fight.

Charles Vane

Nationality: British
Born: c.1680 **Died:** 1721

The epitome of the romantic pirate image, Vane found his fortune in the sunken 1715 Treasure Fleet with other members of the Flying Gang. After being captured by the British in 1718, he hoodwinked them, spinning a story that he wanted to surrender. Back on the seas, Vane carved out a reputation for cruelty and violence on friend and foe alike. Always refusing to bow to authority, he dodged the 1718 Pardon by breaking the blockade of Nassau. Stuffing a ship with gunpowder and explosives, he directed it at the British, blowing a hole and making his escape.

Stede Bonnet

Nationality: Barbadian
Born: c.1688 **Died:** 1718

A landowner before turning to a life of crime, Bonnet was known as the 'gentleman pirate'. After raiding ships on the Eastern seaboard of the USA, he began raiding with Edward Teach, after meeting the man in Nassau. While plundering, Bonnet had sustained wounds that made him unable to command, but still followed Blackbeard and his crew in many successful raids. Bonnet almost lost everything to Blackbeard, with his disgruntled crew joining the Queen Anne's Revenge and then Blackbeard himself betraying Bonnet and making off with their ill-gotten loot.

'Calico' Jack Rackham

Nationality: British
Born: 1682 **Died:** 1720

So named for his flashy, colourful calico clothes, Jack Rackham is most remembered for his flag, the Jolly Roger, and his unisex crew. He came into his own as a pirate when he mutinied against Charles Vane, who lost his crew's faith when he refused to attack a French ship ripe for the taking. Raiding around Nassau, Rackham would start an affair with Anne Bonny and the two would escape to the high seas, recruiting volunteers from the ships they attacked. After a heavy bout of drinking in port, Rackham's ship was seized and its captain sent to Port Royal to dance the hempen jig.

Mary Read

Nationality: British
Born: c.1690 **Died:** 1721

Starting her life at sea as a sailor in the Royal Navy (disguised as a man), Mary Read turned to piracy after being captured by buccaneers and had eventually signed up with Jack Rackham by 1720. She would only reveal her sex to Anne Bonny, and the two may have had an affair, which they kept secret from Rackham to avoid his jealous feelings. After the whole crew was captured after a heavy night of drinking, Read claimed she was pregnant, known as 'pleading the belly' to avoid execution but fell ill and died in captivity.

Sam Bellamy

Nationality: British
Born: 1689 **Died:** 1717

As is the case with many pirate nicknames, 'Black Sam' Bellamy got his name from his rather distinctive appearance. Favouring black coats, Bellamy also shunned the fashionable powdered wigs of the day, and instead he embraced his natural black hair, which he would regularly tie up to keep out of his face. After a 1716 mutiny against Benjamin Hornigold, Bellamy set about becoming the richest pirate who ever lived. Recent excavations of his flagship, Whydah, show that at the time of his death in 1717, he had amassed five tons of booty.

Paulsgrave Williams

Nationality: American
Born: 1676 **Died:** 1724

An accomplice of Sam Bellamy, Williams sought his fortune in the sunken Spanish treasure fleet of 1715. Disappointment racked the man as both he and Bellamy found that most of the treasure had been secured before their arrival. Not one to be deterred, Williams decided to 'salvage' loot from ships that were still afloat and so fell into piracy. Unlike his partner, Williams was known to always sport a white, powdered wig in the sweltering Caribbean sun. Contemporaries commented on the sharp contrast between his white hair and sun-baked skin.

Olivier 'La Buse' Levasseur

Nationality: French
Born: c.1688 **Died:** 1730

Like many British privateers, Levasseur did not want to desist his actions for the French crown when the War of Spanish Succession drew to a close. He was nicknamed 'the buzzard' for his quick and fearless attacks. Levasseur is rightly famous for his substantial buried treasure, to which he created a string of clues. Leaving behind cryptic hints, ciphers, rock carvings and a lost necklace, many have followed the trail in the hopes of discovering his wealthy legacy, although nobody has succeeded – yet.

Captain Sam Bellamy

the pirate in black

Sam Bellamy might have landed the biggest treasure haul ever known, but he lost it all – and his life – during a violent storm

Born on Long Island, a Cape Cod resident raised on the area's rich heritage related to pirates and shipwrecks, Barry Clifford hit the news in July 1984. An avid explorer of the deep blue sea, he'd discovered the remains of Captain Sam Bellamy's famous ship, Whydah, wrecked by sand shoals and a tempest more than 200 years before, on 26 April 1717.

Clifford recovered 200,000 artefacts and plenty of treasure. While many pirate tales of plunder and buried treasure exist in the collective pop-culture ether, mainly thanks to books and films, the rediscovery of Whydah and its bounty is quite extraordinary. Here was an authentic pirate ship as evidence that pirates could get their grubby mitts on some serious booty, and there was a kernel of fact – a shred of truth – to the stories. This was the first authenticated find from the golden age of piracy. Captain Sam Bellamy (1689-1717) earned the distinction – and long-lasting fame – as the pirate who captured the largest haul ever known.

Many yarns begin on a dark and stormy night, and Whydah's demise is no different. As pirate tales go, there's something almost tragic about Bellamy's death and the loss of all that beautiful treasure. Captain Sam Bellamy – known forever as the pirate 'Black Sam Bellamy' (because of his penchant for black clothing) – and his crew sailed up the east coast to Block Island, to the north of Cape Cod, where Bellamy intended on careening and refitting two large ships in his four-ship fleet. The rain lashed down harshly like a cat o' nine tails on a sailor's bloodied back, visibility was extremely poor, and the wind rose dangerously. The areas in which the ships were sailing virtually blindly were known as treacherous waters, for sand shoals could ground a ship. Caught in a lee shore (where the wind rips in from the open ocean and pushes vessels towards land), one of the ships

Defining moment

Treasure hunter turns pirate

Having sailed from England to Cape Cod, at the northern tip of Long Island, to track down relatives who lived there, Bellamy joined an expedition to recover treasure from a Spanish wreck down in Florida. With the project a failure, the crew turned pirate, joining forces with Benjamin Hornigold and Edward Teach, aka Blackbeard.

1716

"Captain Sam Bellamy earned the distinction – and long-lasting fame – as the pirate who captured the largest haul ever known"

Captain Sam Bellamy went down with his ship on 26 April 1717

– a sloop traditionally known as Mary Anne – threatened to be smashed among breaking waves. The crew attempted to save the ship, by cutting down the masts, and hunkered down for the night. They survived.

Miles further up the coast, Whydah – pitching and rolling – was dragging towards the shore. Not even anchors, deployed against the storm in an attempt to steady the ship, could help them. The laws of physics came into play. A ship its size could not survive a lee shore. Striking a shoal, the boat was a few hundred yards from land, and quickly ripped asunder. Two men made it to safety. Over the course of several days, bloated bodies washed up on the beaches, the crabs and other sea life having feasted upon an unexpected human banquet.

As a Devonshire lad, born in Hittisleigh, circa 1689, Bellamy was destined for a life at sea. After years in the Royal Navy, where he fought against the Spanish in the West Indies, aboard the sloop Barsheba, Bellamy turned pirate and spent his 20s earning a reputation as a dashing and good-natured pirate, which is unusual. He took no prisoners when raiding ships, and liked to think of himself as a Robin Hood figure, making his crew the Merry Men.

Bellamy's career into pirate history began when he took over Benjamin Hornigold's sloop, an eight-gun vessel, Mary Anne. Because Hornigold, a former privateer gone rogue, was an avowed patriot – even when he himself turned pirate in Jamaican waters – he refused to attack English merchant vessels. Among Hornigold's crew was a black-bearded chap by the name of Edward Teach, who distinguished himself in service, and was awaiting a promotion from Hornigold. He would go on to be known by his nom-de-pirate, Blackbeard, the most famous buccaneer of them all.

Hornigold's no-English-ships rule caused disagreement and rupture between Bellamy and his compatriot. But for a time, Hornigold, Bellamy and a Frenchman named Olivier "La Buse" Levasseur joined forces as a troika of three pirate ships: The Benjamin, Mary Anne (also spelled Marianne) and La Buse's Postillon. In the Yucatán Channel (the strait between Mexico and Cuba), the three pirates captured an English vessel (against protestations from Hornigold) and several Spanish ships. Bellamy also made daring

Defining Moment

Capturing Whydah

Whydah, sailing with an abundance of riches, was spotted between Cuba and Hispaniola. Captain Bellamy ordered a pursuit and chased for three days. Rather than kill the captain or Whydah's crew, though, Bellamy swaps his old ship for Whydah. Making for the US coast, to meet an old friend, the ship sets its course to disaster.

1717

Whydah's galley bell

Treasure from Whydah, on display at Field Museum in Chicago, 2009

"They spread a large, black flag with a death's head and bones across, and gave chase," as recounted by Bellamy's crewman Thomas Baker

Defining Moment

Whydah lost at sea

A storm destroyed Whydah, but a few hundred yards from the beach. The ship took on too much water and capsized, sending the crew into a panic and attempting to swim for it. Of a 145-man crew, only two survived. Captain Sam Bellamy was among the dead. Whydah's companion ship, Mary Anne, was also lost in the storm.

1717

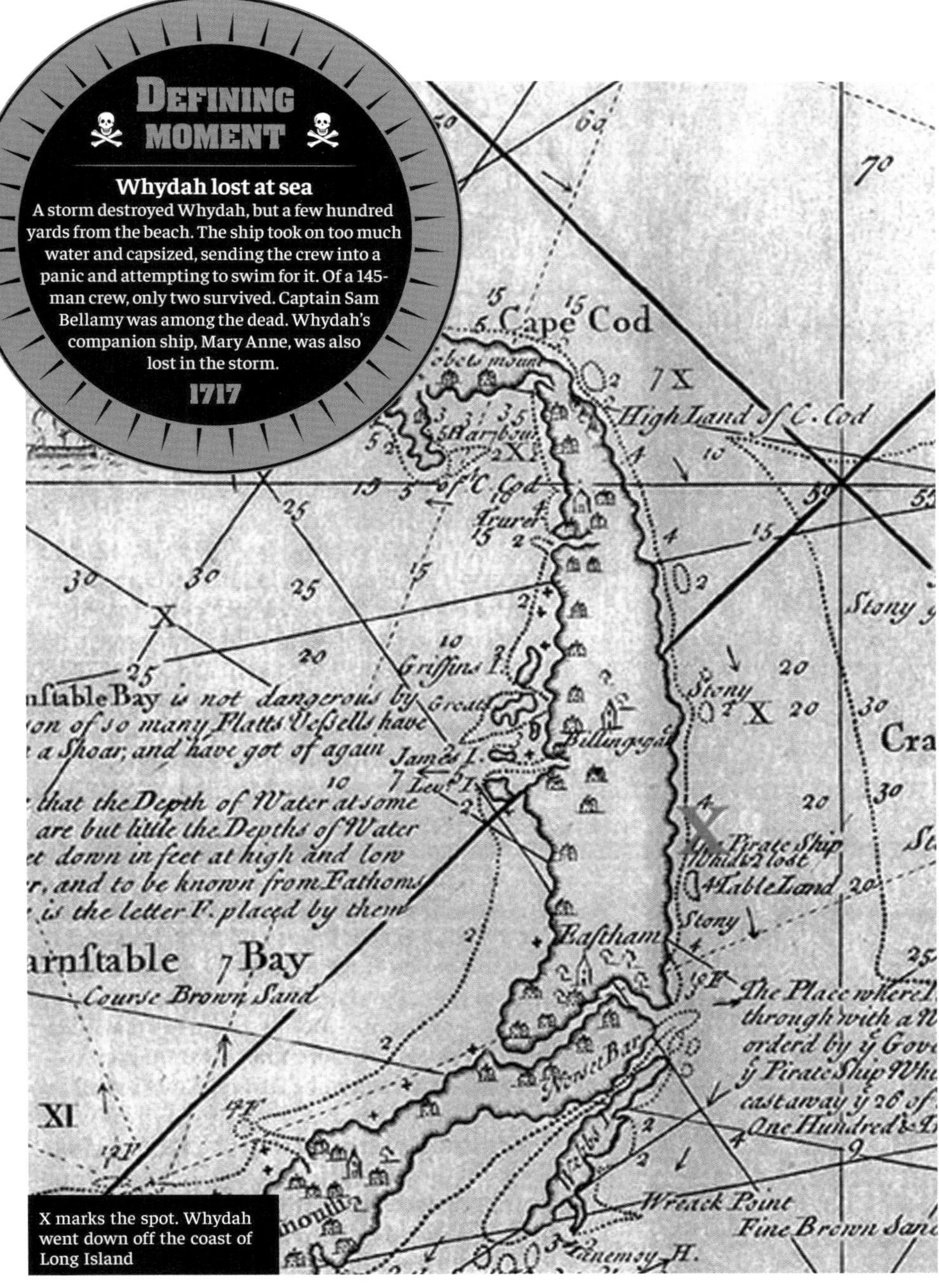

X marks the spot. Whydah went down off the coast of Long Island

raids in smaller vessels known as piraguas. They also, on one occasion, joined forces with privateers – led by Henry Jennings – to tackle a French merchant ship, La St Marie, commanded by Captain D'Escoubet. Firing musket shots and cutting La St Marie's anchor, the pirates and privateers boarded a 16-gun ship loaded with 30,000 pieces of eight. There was no violence meted to the crew, something detailed time and time again during Bellamy's days as a pirate, where he captured more than 50 ships.

Thanks to Barry Clifford's excavation of Whydah, its bounty is known to the world. And what a haul! Some 8,397 coins from several countries, 8,357 coins of Spanish silver, nine gold coins, 4,131 pieces of eight, 17 gold bars, 14 gold nuggets, 6,174 'bits' of gold, and gold dust. The treasure also included African jewellery. Bellamy and his men mustn't have believed their luck. While they never got to spend any of it, as fortuitous events conspired against them, Captain Bellamy must surely have considered this amount of treasure as a retirement fund.

Whydah was on its maiden voyage. Built in England, and put to sea in 1716 as a slaving ship, it was named after a west African trading post. A three-masted, 300-ton, ten-gun vessel of about 100 feet in length, Whydah was on its maiden voyage. Having crossed the Atlantic from the west coast of Africa, picking up slaves for the West Indies plantations, it was sailing in the Windward Passage (between Cuba and Haiti) when Bellamy's crew saw it. As a large vessel, it would provide an upgrade to their current ship – Sultana – and Bellamy ordered to give chase. Three days later, Whydah was in sight and offered little resistance. Taking the 10 guns from Sultana, Whydah was now Bellamy's. He was now in charge of a powerful 28-gunner. Along with the treasure, he must have felt like fortune was smiling down upon him.

In Cape Cod, local folklore and tradition has it that Bellamy was returning to the area because he was deeply in love with an American woman, Maria Hallett. Either way, he met his end close to the shore of Long Island, Whydah going down in the storm and just two crewmen surviving the wreck. Mary Anne's seven-man crew, who had seen out the storm, were rescued the next day by two fishermen and given over to the authorities. The two Whydah survivors, Thomas Davis and John Julian, were also handed over to local law enforcements and subsequently tried. Davis wasn't a pirate. Employed as a carpenter aboard St Michael, a ship Bellamy captured and forced the carpenter to work on for him, Davis protested so much, Black Sam assured him that he'd be replaced as soon as possible. At trial, he produced witness testimonies, asserting to his good character and was found not guilty of piracy. John Julian was a slave and never tried, instead he was sold back into slavery as was typical at the time. He died in 1733. The Mary Anne crew were tried in Boston and six of them hanged. Reverend Cotton Mather of the Second North Church in Boston visited Mary Anne's men as they awaited the scaffold. Publishing a pamphlet of his conversations with Bellamy's surviving – and condemned crew members – he cautioned "All the riches which are not honestly gotten must be lost in a shipwreck of honest restitution, if ever men come into repentance and salvation."

Captain Sam Bellamy, like so many buccaneers, lived a short and eventful life. It was a hard life and far from romantic. His temperament might have been good-natured compared to others, but a thief is still a thief. His career as a pirate was equally short. He was roaming the Caribbean as a pirate captain aged 27 and was dead at 29.

If Blackbeard is the quintessential pirate baddie, Bellamy is the archetype for the dashing pirate anti-hero of Hollywood movies. The Robin Hood comparison is bunkum, but the good pirate – the pirate who takes it to the enemy and does so with panache and humour – captured the imagination, more so than the grim realities of buccaneer tradition and life.

Benjamin Hornigold

poacher turned gamekeeper

The Caribbean privateer turned to piracy, mentoring the infamous Blackbeard before accepting the King's Pardon and becoming a ruthless pirate hunter...

Benjamin Hornigold turned to piracy in the aftermath of the War of the Spanish Succession, which came to an end for the British with the Treaty of Utrecht in the spring of 1713. This worldwide conflict had left the Royal Navy financially drained and the Admiralty mothballed its fleet and released over half of its labour force. Thousands of sailors, all across the globe, were suddenly out of work, while those who retained employment saw a sharp fall in wages. Privateers were no longer set to work.

In the West Indies, sailors found themselves in a perilous state. Spanish vessels continued to seize British shipping and, adding insult to injury, the owners of the vessels often withheld sailors' wages during their incarceration. For many, piracy was the only way out. Certainly, Hornigold, a successful privateer during the war, saw this as his best option and, taking with him one Edward Teach (later known as Blackbeard), in late 1713 he embarked on his new career.

He chose as his base of operations the Bahamas, which were strategically well placed to intercept Spanish and French shipping, and which offered plenty of protection amid their myriad waterways. Only a fool would enter these waters without an experienced Bahaman pilot. The Bahaman island of New Providence had suffered greatly during the war and there was only a skeleton settlement in the town of Nassau. This was to be Hornigold's haunt.

Hornigold's career in piracy began in a humble fashion with the acquisition of three long canoes, equipped with oars and simple rigging, which allowed the marauders to move quickly against small sloops and the Spanish plantations that dotted the Caribbean coast. Splitting into three different parties, Hornigold's men launched a year-long reign of terror, capturing booty estimated at more than £60,000. News of an impending retaliatory attack by the Spanish authorities saw the group fragment, though Hornigold stayed put, settling on the readily defendable Harbour Island. Teach, it is thought, stayed with him.

By the summer of 1714, Hornigold had been given control of a small sloop, the Happy Return, and set sail to harry the Spanish colonies in Florida and Cuba. In the autumn, he acquired a ship of his own and in December snatched a tiny Cuban fleet laden with treasures. His haul of over £10,000 is said to have established his glowing reputation as the pre-eminent pirate operating in Bahaman waters.

His career took a darker turn in late 1715. Up until this point, Hornigold regarded himself as a privateer, still at war with Spain, even if his remit was unofficial. But in November he seized the English ship Mary, a sloop with capacity for 140 men and six guns, and this he sailed into Nassau harbour along with a captured Spanish vessel. There, he declared that every pirate in the area would fall under his protection.

This group of ruffians called themselves the Flying Gang and they made Nassau their own. Other rogues and seadogs came pouring in and Nassau witnessed a true gathering of pirates. Hornigold soon captured another Spanish sloop, even bigger than the Mary, which he named the Benjamin.

DEFINING MOMENT

Treaty of Utrecht

This series of treaties brought to an end the War of the Spanish Succession and, with it, a close to the act of privateering in the West Indies. This in turn forced many seamen to turn to piracy, including Hornigold and his loyal lieutenant Edward Teach, who sallied forth from the Bahaman island of New Providence.

1713

"Hornigold's men launched a year-long reign of terror, capturing booty estimated at more than £60,000"

With the ever-expanding band of pirates transforming Nassau into a den of iniquity, Hornigold prospered, and in April 1716 he snatched the French sloop the Marianne, bagging a cargo amounting to more than £12,000. This ship he turned over to the pirate Sam Bellamy, whom he had met off the coast of Cuba and who had impressed him with his tales of derring-do. Hornigold promoting him ahead of his own followers, including Teach.

It is thought that Bellamy may have been key to Hornigold's subsequent alliance with the French pirate Olivier La Buse. Despite his nabbing of the Mary, Hornigold liked to think himself a privateer, maintaining hostilities against his nation's traditional enemies, Spain and France. He was reluctant to attack English shipping and yet urged on by his two new allies, his men agreed to target another English ship in the Yucatán Channel.

DEFINING MOMENT

Unleashing Blackbeard

Edward Teach proved a loyal servant to Hornigold and remained faithful even when others mutinied. Hornigold rewarded that loyalty in 1716 when he granted Teach his own ship, thereby igniting the career of the man who would become most synonymous with Caribbean piracy, the infamous Captain Blackbeard.

1716

Hornigold captured the French-owned La Concorde, which he turned over to Edward Teach

This motley group also captured a pair of Spanish brigantines, brimming with cocoa, which they took without firing a shot. As the year stretched on, he traded the Benjamin, which was showing signs of damage, for the slightly smaller Adventure. Soon, however, the tenuous friendship between Hornigold, Bellamy and La Buse began to fray.

Hornigold's reluctance to attack English shipping was an irritant to his two allies and the men on his own ship began to question his authority. He reticence was costing them loot, and some may have blamed his negligence for the loss of the Benjamin. After a meeting aboard the Adventure, a ballot was held and Hornigold was deposed. The majority of his men voted to join Bellamy and La Buse. Hornigold was allowed to keep the Adventure, but was told to leave the alliance. With lieutenant Edward Teach on board, he limped back to Nassau.

He was soon on his feet again, however, and it was at this time that he elected to fortify the harbour at Nassau, making it a true bastion of piracy. The people of Nassau fled to safer land. As he set out to sea again in late 1716, he captured a sloop capable of carrying six guns, which he turned over to Teach. Once in charge of his own vessel, Teach adopted the now-legendary moniker of Blackbeard.

The duo operated in consort through 1717, pillaging six prizes off the American coast and then raiding back in the Caribbean. By the April of that year, Hornigold had upgraded the Adventure to the Bonnet and had captured the treasure-stuffed sloop, Revenge. By the year's end the pair ended up with a haul totalling in excess of £100,000. They were the masters of the Caribbean, Hornigold every inch the equal of his great rival, Henry Jennings.

Hornigold and Teach sailed together throughout 1717 and towards the end of the year near Martinique they captured the English-built frigate, now in French hands, La Concorde de Nantes. This was a fine prize, and the two men divided their haul and parted ways, Teach retaining the ship, renaming her Queen Anne's Revenge and installing 40 cannons.

Such was the prevalence of piracy in the region that King George I decided to take action and in September 1717 issued a proclamation granting a royal pardon for all piracies committed prior to January 5, 1718. Known as the King's Pardon, it was announced in Nassau by the son of the governor of Bermuda and divided opinion among the seamen living therein. For the more moderately minded men, including the rivals Jennings and Hornigold, this was welcome news.

Despite the occasional lapse, Hornigold liked to regard himself more privateer than pirate, and, like many in the Nassau gang, saw an opportunity to invest his plunder in legal trade. Hornigold accepted the King's Pardon and sailed to Jamaica, where he struck up a positive relationship with the newly appointed governor Woodes Rogers. Indeed, as Rogers cracked down on those who had refused the King's Pardon, he turned to those that knew the pirates' ways. Who better to catch a pirate than a former pirate? Hornigold answered his call. The poacher turned gamekeeper, and in the autumn of

> "By 1719 Hornigold had returned full-time to the life of the privateers"

William Hogarth painted this picture of the governor of the Bahamas, Woodes Rogers (right), whose son is showing him plans for the port of Nassau

Defining Moment

The King's Pardon

Put together by King George I in a bid to curb the blight on West Indian shipping, the King's Pardon was carried to the Nassau pirates by Captain Vincent Pearse in February 1718. A potentially tense engagement was eased with the help of Hornigold who advised fellow pirates to accept the olive branch, even if they later recanted.

1717

1718 he set sail in a bid to bring the notorious Charles Vane to justice. It was while conducting this mission that he captured the 30-ton sloop Wolf and the recidivist pirate Nicholas Woodall, who was smuggling supplies and ammunition to Vane's base at Green Turtle Cay. In the winter of that same year, he captured yet more recidivists, including Blackbeard's one-time gunner named William Cunningham.

By 1719 Hornigold had returned full-time to the life of the privateers, operating under Rogers' commission, sailing against the Spanish from his old haunt of Nassau. According to the famous fact-cum-fiction that is Captain Charles Johnson's *A General History Of The Robberies And Murders Of The Most Notorious Pyrates*, Hornigold may well have perished in a shipwreck, although modern historians disagree with this idea, and it is thought that he more likely met his end after an engagement with a Spanish brigantine near Havana, either dying in combat or soon after in a Cuban prison. Certainly, this once-famous pirate and a key member of the infamous Flying Gang was never heard of again.

Men were often press-ganged into joining the Royal Navy during the Age of Sail

Under the rule of Jennings, New Providence became a pirate paradise

HENRY JENNINGS

mastermind of the pirate haven

Henry Jennings was an unusual pirate because he lived long enough to enjoy old age

Like so many famed names from the golden age of piracy, the life of Henry Jennings is shrouded in mystery, his origins lost in the mists of time. Where he came from and what his life was before he came to prominence as a privateer during the War of Spanish Succession is largely unknown, but all sources agree that he was a wealthy plantation owner of Jamaica, so why he decided to leave it all behind for a life of adventure at sea remains a mystery. Whatever lay behind Jennings' decision, the life of a privateer proved financially fruitful for this famed captain. For all his escapades though, perhaps Jennings' fearsome reputation rests on one particularly audacious raid that took place in 1715.

On 31 July 1715, the Spanish Treasure Fleet was attempting to navigate the coast of America, carrying a fortune in booty. Having survived bad weather around the Bahamas, things only got worse when a hurricane blew up as the fleet reached Florida. Battered by the terrible conditions, the fleet was reduced to matchwood and its enormous cargo of gold and treasure was lost in the wreck. When King Philip V of Spain heard of the loss of his fleet, he immediately declared that the treasure was the rightful property of Spain and that no other country should try and take so much as a peso. Meanwhile, Spanish crews were immediately dispatched to salvage the treasure they could find. They successfully located the flagship, Urca de Lima, and began salvaging its priceless cargo. In order to keep the booty safe, a fort was built at St Augustine, where the treasure was stored as salvage efforts went on.

Of course, commands issued by the Spanish king cut little ice with his opponents when it came to enormous sums of money, and soon privateers and ships from across the globe were heading for Florida, where the fleet had been lost. Jennings emerged into the historical record in Jamaica at the head of a fleet of his own, his sights set on the lost fortune. As captain of the sloop named Bathsheba, he headed out towards the stricken fleet, determined to make himself a fortune at sea.

When Jennings reached the coast, he took one look at the Spanish fort and knew that he could easily crush it and claim the treasure held there. With his crew outnumbering the Spanish soldiers by more than four-to-one, Jennings demanded the surrender of the salvage crew. At first the crew refused, but after a short conflict that made Jennings' point, the soldiers backed down, leaving the crew to pile their ships high with treasure before heading back to Jamaica. With Britain and Spain at peace at the time of the wreck, Jennings' actions were illegal, but went unpunished. In fact, it wasn't until he later seized a French ship and caused a diplomatic stink that things took a turn for the worst for this fearsome, fortunate pirate.

As half of a partnership with Black Sam Bellamy, Jennings was no gentleman privateer and was happy to wreak violent revenge on those who attempted to oppose him, slaughtering his enemies and ruthlessly deserting their ships. Eventually Bellamy's greed got the better of him and he double-crossed his old partner in crime, leading Jennings to brutally kill a group of captured French and British prisoners in retaliation.

Although his actions against the Spanish Treasure Fleet had been sanctioned by the governor of Jamaica, Lord Archibald Hamilton, when Jennings reached the island after his latest raid, he discovered that he had been declared a pirate by order of King George I. Should he drop anchor and set so much as a foot on land, he risked the gallows. Forced to leave behind his comfortable life, he fled for the Bahamas and set up home on New Providence, focusing his efforts on the sleepy backwater town of Nassau.

DEFINING MOMENT

Accepting the amnesty

After years living as the unofficial pirate mayor of New Providence, Jennings was wealthy beyond imagining, and feared and celebrated in equal measure. When the governor of the Bahamas, Woodes Rogers, offered an amnesty, Jennings accepted it and retired to Bermuda, where he could freely enjoy his wealth.

1718

Here, he established himself in what was to become a legendary pirate haven, eventually becoming its unofficial mayor and the man to whom all paid court.

Jennings lived the high life as ruler of New Providence, famed for his cruelty as much as his fortune.

All of those who took shelter there paid him a hefty share of their booty in return for protection, and he became enormously wealthy on the profits of his diplomatic endeavours. Why this wealthy plantation owner became first a privateer and then a pirate, history doesn't tell, but Jennings embraced the life with everything he had until offered the opportunity to return to something vaguely resembling respectability.

When Woodes Rogers was appointed governor of the Bahamas and offered an amnesty, Jennings accepted it. He took his formal pardon and changed allegiances, becoming a pirate hunter who pursued those he had once called friends. Rich beyond his wildest dreams, he lived the life of a privateer at sea while maintaining an opulent island home to which he could retire between expeditions.

Eventually, Jennings gave up his seafaring life and retired to enjoy a life of luxury on his plantation in Bermuda. Some tales, perhaps seeking a suitably moral ending to a career that had been so steeped in violence and crime, claimed that Jennings couldn't resist the pirate's life. Supposedly, he was eventually captured by the Spanish and left to rot in a prison cell. In fact, it's far more likely that Henry Jennings received no such punishment and lived out his old age in relative yet happy obscurity, growing older and richer in his Bermuda home.

Jennings became the unofficial mayor of the pirate haven in New Providence

After a short fight, the Spanish soldiers surrendered, handing their salvaged fortune to Jennings

The Flying Gang

"Despite his fearsome appearance, there are no verified accounts of Blackbeard ever having murdered or harmed those he held captive"

Blackbeard's appearance, no less than his reputation, instilled fear in any enemies he came across on the seas

DEFINING MOMENT

Teach becomes a pirate
Teach moves to the uninhabited island of New Providence, within easy reach of major shipping lanes and home to pirates, traders and transients. Here, he meets renowned pirate Benjamin Hornigold and joins his crew. They go on a pillaging rampage through the waters of Havana, Bermuda, Madeira and Virginia.

1716-1717

BLACKBEARD
the legendary pirate

Was Blackbeard a formidable pirate or a masterful image cultivator?

Fearsome pirate and terroriser of the oceans, Blackbeard has become a legendary figure in seafaring stories, making his mark on history books despite a career spanning just two years.

Little is known about the early life of Edward Teach – the moniker 'Blackbeard' not coming to life until many years after his birth, which historians estimate to be around 1680. Little is known of his true identity, either. Records exist for Edward Teach, Thatch and Thack, and it was common at the time for pirates to use fake names, so as not to tarnish their family's reputation. His real identity will probably always be unknown.

Teach was raised in the sea port of Bristol and likely began his career as a privateer, or 'corsair' – a person authorised by a government to attack foreign vessels during wartime – during the Spanish War of Succession, also known as Queen Anne's War.

> "Teach was raised in Bristol and likely began his career as a privateer"

After the war, he set off to New Providence, a largely uninhabited area home only to pirates, traders and transients, where law and order dared not tread. Here he met renowned pirate Benjamin Hornigold, and like others looking for a life of adventure and riches, joined his ship as a crewman. But Hornigold saw something special in Teach. As historian Charles Johnson wrote in his 1724 book, *A General History Of The Robberies And Murders Of The Most Notorious Pyrates*, Teach "had often distinguished himself for his uncommon boldness and personal courage." Hornigold put Teach in command of a sloop, and together they began a reign of terror along colonial shipping lanes.

The duo were successful, but inconsistent. Ships at the time very rarely carried precious cargo – and certainly it would be rare to happen upon chests of gold and silver – so pirates relied on looting general goods such as cocoa, cotton and rum, either for their own use, or to sell for reasonable amounts at ports. Hornigold and Teach's strategy, however, seemed mixed. In September 1717, for example, they captured the ship Betty, from Virginia, but only took its stores of Madeira wine before sinking the ship and its remaining cargo.

Come the end of 1717 – by which time Teach, now known as Blackbeard thanks to his impressive facial hair, had his own ship – the valuable cargo from British ships had become too tempting for the fleet's crew. Fearing mutiny, Hornigold retired from piracy, leaving Teach in charge and accepting a royal pardon. It was around this time that Stede Bonnet, also known as 'The Gentleman Pirate', joined Teach. A land owner and military officer from a wealthy family, Bonnet was unable to control his rowdy crew and so ceded control to Teach. The expanded party sailed together as one.

Up until now, Teach, or Blackbeard, as official reports had begun referring to him, had proven himself to be a strong, respected leader

Blackbeard's famous ship was the illegally obtained Queen Anne's Revenge

Life in the time of Blackbeard

Queen Anne's War
Blackbeard's career as a pirate coincided with the end of the War of the Spanish Succession, which meant thousands of seamen were relieved of military duty, creating a huge number of highly trained, but bored sailors at a time when the cross-Atlantic colonial shipping trade began to boom. As such, pirate captains had a constant pool of recruits.

Pirates as patrons
While pirates of the time were often viewed as despicable rogues of the sea, official views were sometimes quite different, with the English government considering privateers who became pirates a kind of informal 'reserve naval force'. Royal pardons were regularly issued to pirates and public opinion was often favourable toward them.

Female pirates
Piracy was certainly seen as a man's game, which is why the two famous female pirates – Anne Bonny and Mary Read – disguised themselves as men. When their ship was assaulted in 1720, the two women – along with just one other man – were the only ones to defend it, as the other crew members were too drunk to fight.

A pirate's life
Life aboard a sailing ship was anything but comfortable. The crew lived in cramped and filthy quarters, food spoiled quickly and fresh water was hard to come by (which is why so many pirates drank rum instead). One dietary staple was 'hard tack', a type of biscuit that sailors often ate in the dark to avoid seeing the weevils infested within.

Superstition at sea
Pirates and sailors were notoriously superstitious, believing that having women on board their ship was bad luck – which was surely a problem for the crew of the womanising Blackbeard – and that whistling on a ship would create a storm, hence the phrase 'whistle up a storm'. Many pirates also believed having pierced ears would improve their eyesight.

and a capable pirate, but it was in November 1717 that the legend really came to life. After attacking French merchant vessel La Concorde off the coast of Saint Vincent, Teach took the ship as his own, renaming it Queen Anne's Revenge and equipping it with 40 guns. It was a large, imposing vessel, flying a sinister flag showing a skeleton spearing a heart – an image that quickly became synonymous with terror on the high seas the world over, and one that perfectly fit the image Blackbeard had cultivated.

A tall, broad man with a thick beard covering most of his face, Blackbeard was a frightening figure – something he played to during battle, when he wore three pistols across his chest and put lit matches under his hat to create a terrifying mist from which he would emerge like the devil himself. As Johnson wrote, he was "such a figure that imagination cannot form an idea of a fury from hell to look more frightful." Blackbeard was a man who understood the importance of appearance, and thought it better to strike fear into the hearts of his enemies than rely on skill alone.

But despite his fearsome appearance, there are no verified accounts of Blackbeard ever having murdered or harmed his captives – although the cannon fire involved in forcing other ships to give up no doubt killed many. Those who surrendered were allowed to sail free, albeit without their possessions. Those that resisted were marooned and their ships torched, but still they escaped with their lives.

However there are numerous legends and newspaper clippings that suggest – despite his relative mercy toward captured ships – he was a man of cruelty. One story claims he shot his own first mate, saying "if he didn't shoot one or two [crewmen] now and then, they'd forget who he was." Another says that after a long drinking session he challenged his crew to sit in the ship's hold while they set alight several pots of sulphur. All except Blackbeard scrambled out for fresh air, with the captain later emerging, snarling, "Damn ye, I'm a better man than all ye milksops put together!"

In May 1718, Blackbeard once again demonstrated his dual personality, during the Blockade of Charleston where he showed both mercy and menace. His flotilla blocked the port of Charleston, and with no guard ship at the port the pirates had their pick of ships. They took over the Crowley, bound for London carrying a group of prominent Charleston citizens, including Samuel Wragg, a member of the Council of the Province of Carolina. Blackbeard demanded medical supplies from the South Carolina government, and threatened to execute his captives if his demands were not met.

Wragg – acting as spokesperson for the hostages and no doubt using his social standing to his advantage – agreed, and one hostage, Mr Marks, was sent with two pirates to retrieve the supplies. Blackbeard imposed a deadline of two days. After three days, the party hadn't returned, and the hostages became frantic, fearing Blackbeard's wrath. Eventually a message arrived: Mark's boat had capsized. Blackbeard granted a reprieve of two further days, but still the party did not return.

Yet the captain did not brutally execute his hostages, as threatened. Instead, he moved a number of his ships into the Charleston harbour, causing panic in the town. Eventually Marks returned with the medical supplies. It emerged that on his arrival to South Carolina's government offices the drugs had been provided swiftly, but the pirates he had travelled with

Defining moment

Blackbeard gets his treasure

On 28 November, Blackbeard's two ships attack French merchant vessel La Concorde transporting slaves off the coast of Saint Vincent, firing cannons across its bulwarks and forcing its captain to surrender. Blackbeard gives the crew of La Concorde the smaller of his two ships and renames La Concorde 'Queen Anne's Revenge'.

1717

Legend has it that his skull was used to make a silver chalice, with one 1930s judge in Carolina claiming to have drunk from it

"Teach took the ship as his own, renaming it Queen Anne's Revenge and equipping it with 40 guns"

Timeline

1680

- **Edward Teach is born**
There's no firm record of Edward Teach's birth, but historians suspect it was likely around 1680, and that he was probably born in Bristol, an important international sea port at the time.
1680

- **Learning the ropes**
Teach serves as a privateer during Queen Anne's War, a struggle between France and Britain for control of North America. This period of his life gives rise to the name of his ship, Queen Anne's Revenge.
1701-1714

- **A legend is born**
The name 'Blackbeard' enters official records for the first time in a report to a British colonial council about Hornigold's operations.
Spring 1717

- **Going it alone**
As his crew becomes disgruntled with the lack of pillaging, Benjamin Hornigold steps down as pirate captain and retires from piracy, leaving Blackbeard in charge. The pair never meet again.
Late 1717

- **The blockade of Charleston**
Blackbeard strikes terror into the town of Charleston after blockading its wealthy port, plundering merchant ships and seizing passengers and crew of the Crowley. After his demands for medicinal supplies are met, he releases the hostages, without their valuables – or clothes.
May 1718

had disappeared to go drinking. They were finally discovered, drunk and entirely incapable of manning a boat back to Blackbeard. The pirate captain kept his word, though, and the ships and prisoners were released.

However, while Blackbeard was to some extent an honourable man, he was still a pirate, and his willingness to double-cross others – his own men, in fact – was never clearer than in June 1718. His former captain and mentor Benjamin Hornigold had previously accepted a royal pardon, and it seems likely that around the time of the blockade of Charleston, Blackbeard had been considering seeking one, too. Pardons were regularly issued, with officials in England taking a rather relaxed view of piracy. For example, pirate Francis Drake was knighted by Queen Elizabeth in 1581 when he returned from a round-the-world expedition with a booty of more than £1 million.

The pardon was open to all pirates who surrendered before 5 September 1718, but also stipulated that immunity was only assured on crimes committed before 5 January of that year. In theory, this would mean death for Blackbeard for his actions at Charleston. It was likely that this misdemeanour would be waived, but he wanted his safety assured. After discussing the matter with Bonnet, he sent his companion to Bath Town to surrender. Bonnet received a full pardon and then travelled back to Blackbeard to collect his ship, the Revenge, and the remainder of his crew.

Upon his return, however, he found that Blackbeard had disappeared, having stripped the Revenge of its provisions and marooned its crew.

Blackbeard wasn't the most successful pirate ever – Henry Every once took more wealth in just a single ship

Blackbeard, without knowing the outcome of Bonnet's pardon, then sought his own from Governor Eden in June 1718, and settled in the town of Bath, where he took a wife and found work as a privateer – an industry that was helpful in keeping restless former pirates occupied.

While out on an expedition, he encountered Charles Vane, and he, Vane and a group of other notorious individuals, including Israel Hands, Robert Deal and Calico Jack, spent several drunken evenings together. This party of dangerous figures caused panic for local officials, in particular Governor Alexander Spotswood of Virginia. The governor commissioned Lieutenant Robert Maynard to capture Blackbeard and his crew, offering a hefty incentive from the Assembly of Virginia.

But Blackbeard was outsmarted. Believing that Maynard had only a small crew with him, the pirates boarded Maynard's ship. No sooner had they set foot on the vessel than a veritable army came bursting forth from the ship's hold, shouting and firing, overpowering the pirates with superior training and weaponry. Blackbeard and Maynard fought head-to-head, and as Maynard drew back to fire at the pirate, Blackbeard advanced and was cut down by one of Maynard's men before being brutally attacked – and eventually killed – by Maynard's crew.

It was a grisly death for the legendary pirate, but he fought to the end: his body revealed at least five bullet wounds and 20 stab wounds suffered before he was brought down. His head was hung from the bow of Maynard's ship – the final humiliation for a man who had for so long dominated the seas.

DEFINING MOMENT

The beginning of the end

Blackbeard parties at Ocracoke Island with a cohort that includes dubious characters Charles Vane, Israel Hands and 'Calico Jack' Rackham. The governor of Virginia had issued a proclamation that all former pirates not travel in groups larger than three. The governor orders a number of captains to capture Blackbeard.

1718

1719

Double cross
Queen Anne's Revenge runs aground, and while his partner Bonnet is away seeking a pardon from Governor Charles Eden, Blackbeard strips his ship of valuables and maroons Bonnet's men.
June 1718

A quiet life
Blackbeard seeks his pardon from the governor of Virginia, and finding kind hospitality from a town in need of an economic boost, decides to settle down in Bath and take a wife.
June 1718

Off the wagon
After months of relative peace and quiet, Blackbeard sails to St Thomas on a sloop he renames Adventure, seeking a commission as a privateer. He returns to piracy, and the governor of Pennsylvania issues a warrant for his arrest.
Summer 1718

The end of a golden age
Maynard tracks Blackbeard down, and the pirates open fire. Mistakenly believing they've won the battle, the pirates board Maynard's ship, but are quickly overpowered. Blackbeard is killed after a brutal fight.
November 1718

Setting an example
Blackbeard's associates are tried in Williamsburg, Virginia. Records show that one is acquitted and one is pardoned, but the rest are hanged.
March 1719

THE QUEEN ANNE'S REVENGE

The infamous pirate ship of the most notorious buccaneer around, 1710-18

The scourge of the Atlantic and the Caribbean, Queen Anne's Revenge was a mighty vessel. Constructed in 1710 by the Royal Navy, the frigate was first stolen by the French, renamed La Concorde de Nantes and used as a slave ship before making its way into the hands of Blackbeard in 1717.

Much has been made of the fearsome pirate (real name Edward Teach) and like his famous flagship, he was originally part of the Royal Navy. However, the lure of plunder and booty was too much for this young privateer who decided that a pirate's life was for him. He added 26 guns to the vessel giving it a total of 40, and its size meant it could take up to 300 tons of precious loot. Its main hunting ground was the North Carolinian coast and the ship's clever tactic was to hide in inconspicuous inlets before launching a devastating broadside on unsuspecting passing ships. Reeling from the attack, the ship would then be boarded and stripped of its wealth and booty. Queen Anne's Revenge was only Blackbeard's ship for a short time but its speed and strength helped him in his most audacious mission: the blockade of Charleston Harbor.

In 1718, Blackbeard steered the ship into the South Carolinian port in league with three other pirate ships. Five merchant ships were plundered by the corsairs as traffic came to a standstill in the dock for a week. Blackbeard made his escape, taking many Charleston citizens as hostages for ransom. He then marooned his ships and many of his crew about 300 miles north and took the treasure for himself. The infamous pirate had escaped once again but Queen Anne's Revenge had made its final voyage. It was rediscovered in 1996.

Shipwreck

The shipwreck was studied for many years before it was confirmed that it was indeed Queen Anne's Revenge. The recovered artefacts are now on show at the North Carolina Maritime Museum.

Sailing speed

With three masts and eight sails, Queen Anne's Revenge could achieve high speeds when in pursuit of an enemy or fleeing the long arm of the law.

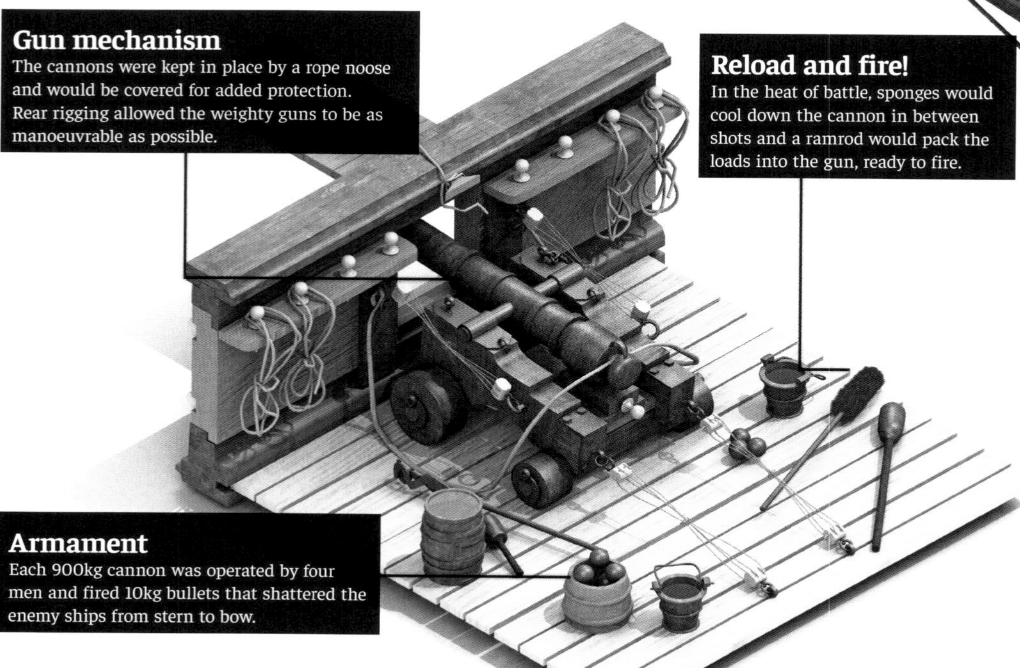

Gun mechanism

The cannons were kept in place by a rope noose and would be covered for added protection. Rear rigging allowed the weighty guns to be as manoeuvrable as possible.

Reload and fire!

In the heat of battle, sponges would cool down the cannon in between shots and a ramrod would pack the loads into the gun, ready to fire.

Armament

Each 900kg cannon was operated by four men and fired 10kg bullets that shattered the enemy ships from stern to bow.

Blackbeard's quarters
Located at the rear, the captain's cabin was the most secure place in the event of a mutiny, but only the bravest would dare rebel against Blackbeard.
Supplies
Extra rigging, food and drinking water were kept in the hull while heavier materials like ammunition were kept midship for ballast. Food supplies consisted of salt pork, salt beef and hard tack (unleavened biscuits).
Anchor
The ship's anchor alone weighed 1,500kg. Its sheer bulk meant raising it took about an hour of hard work.
Seizure
Blackbeard first came into contact with the ship off the coast of Martinique. The pirates, aboard two sloops, took over the ship easily as the crew had been severely weakened by scurvy and dysentery.
Galley
Fire was constantly a threat on board these wooden ships, so the stove was made of brick and a bucket of sand was kept nearby to extinguish flames.

"In reality, the pirates of the Caribbean and the Atlantic were, like the Barbary pirates of North Africa, slavers as well as thieves and murderers"

It wasn't uncommon for slaves to become part of the crew on pirate ships, though depending on their captors they might still remain slaves for trade

THE LEGEND OF BLACK CAESAR

Was Black Caesar a vicious pirate, or was he an accidental victim of Blackbeard? And what role did slaves play in piracy?

The truth about the golden age of piracy is often stranger and crueller than the fiction. Piracy became a profitable business in the Caribbean in the mid-1600s because of two other profitable businesses; shipping and slavery. The first business supplied the pirates' targets, the constant supply of valuable cargo in the 'triangular trade' between Africa, the New World and Europe. Ships in this trade were exposed at sea on the long passages between Africa and the New World, and the New World and Europe. The European empires had the technology to create the shipping networks, and an economy sophisticated enough to render all three legs of the triangular trade profitable. But they did not yet have the military means to secure the vast oceans.

The second business was integral to the triangular trade: a supply of African slaves. The legends of piracy depict the pirate's ill-gotten gains as gold or jewellery. In reality, the pirates of the Caribbean and the Atlantic were, like the Barbary pirates of north Africa, slavers as well as thieves and murderers. The growth of the Atlantic trade triangle depressed sailors' wages, while periodic wars between European empires raised and then dashed hopes of employment. Many pirates were out-of-work sailors, reduced by necessity to take the lowest and most dangerous of sailing jobs.

There may be, as the saying goes, no honour among thieves, but there is a curious equality among them. Anyone could choose to become a pirate. Some, slaves included, could be made into pirates without their choosing. Once aboard, all received equal shares of the loot, and all faced the gallows if they were caught. But not all were hanged. After being captured in 1720 because their crew were too drunk to fight, the notorious female pirates Anne Bonney and Mary Read dodged the noose by claiming pregnancy. While women pirates benefitted from a humane impulse, black pirates were saved by inhumanity. Too valuable to execute, they were often sold into slavery, or returned to their owners.

> "Slaves could be made into pirates without their choosing"

Black sailors constituted between a quarter and a half of Caribbean and Atlantic pirate crews. Some were volunteers, others slaves who had been forcibly conscripted. In 1717, black sailors numbered 60 of Edward 'Blackbeard' Teach's 100 crewmen. Many black pirates were 'cimarrons' or 'maroons', escaped slaves

THE MAROONS OF JAMAICA

Black pirates were not the only escapees from the slave trade to create their own societies. All over the New World, escaped slaves and freemen formed communities that the Spanish called 'cimmarons', and the English 'Maroons.'

In Jamaica, escaped slaves intermarried with Taino natives. The settlements of Maroons in the island's interior were large enough to block the expansion of the colonial economy from the coasts. In 1731, the British sent troops into the hills in the First Maroon War, but failed to defeat the Maroons. Instead, the British granted the Maroons a form of recognition. The colonial authorities granted the Maroons local autonomy in return for military service if needed. This balance held until the Second Maroon War of 1795.

The immediate cause of the war was a dispute over two stolen pigs. A black slave whipped two Maroons suspected of stealing the pigs. Six Maroon elders came to the British to complain, and the British arrested them. A revolt broke out. For eight months, 5,000 redcoats and militiamen struggled to defeat the Maroons, tracking the fugitives with bloodhounds imported from Cuba.

One improbable outcome of the war was the return of some of the Jamaican Maroons to Africa. When the Maroons surrendered in December 1795, the British deported the 600 Maroons of Trelawney, where the rebellion had begun, to Nova Scotia in Canada, where they joined communities of Black Loyalists who had sided with the British against the American Revolution. In 1800, the British deported the Jamaican Maroons again to the new colony of Sierra Leone. Landing at Freetown, they were added to the Register of Liberated Africans.

The Maroon settlement of Accompong abided by the terms of the 1739 treaty, and survived, along with several other smaller Maroon communities. When Jamaica became independent in 1962, the new government confirmed Accompong's autonomy. In 2005, UNESCO, the United Nations' cultural body, declared the music of the Moore Town Maroons to be a "Masterpiece of the Oral and Intangible Heritage of Humanity." In 2016, a delegation of Maroons from Accompong travelled to the Kingdom of Ashanti in Ghana. Once there, they set about renewing ties with the Akan and Asante peoples, who number among their ancestors.

from Spanish, French and English plantations. Others were captured as part of a slave ship's cargo. In 1717, the pirate captain Samuel 'Black Sam' Bellamy took 25 African slaves from a 'Guinea ship'. Some slaves were sold on, but others remained on board, signing the 'articles of agreement' as equal members of the crew. In 1721, Bartholomew 'Black Bart' Roberts, the most successful of all Golden Age pirates, had 88 black crewmen in a crew of 368. In 1722, Roberts was killed in an encounter with three Royal Navy ships off the coast of Ghana. Fifty-two white crewmen were hanged. His 65 black crewmen were given to the Royal Africa Company, and sold into slavery.

The pirate known as Black Caesar emerged from this brutal context. He too became a legend, though all that is known for certain is his death – or, at least, the death of a black pirate named Caesar. Nevertheless, the legend of Black Caesar reflects the realities of slavery and piracy.

On 22 November 1718, Blackbeard's ship, Adventure, was taken in Ocracoke Inlet in North Carolina by HMS Jane, a Royal Navy ship under Lieutenant Robert Maynard, and HMS Ranger. Blackbeard was killed – shot five times and cut with more than 20 sword and knife wounds – and his severed head hung from HMS Pearl's bowsprit. A few days later, 15 of Blackbeard's crew were tried at Williamsburg, Virginia. Thirteen were convicted. Four months' later, they were hanged. Between five and seven of the hanged pirates were black, and one of the condemned was named Caesar.

Six years later, the legend of Black Caesar was born in Captain Charles Johnson's *A General History Of The Pyrates*. In Johnson's telling, Black Caesar was an African chieftain. In the late 1600s, a slave trader tempted him and 20 warriors onto his ship by showing him a watch and promising further gifts. Once aboard, Black Caesar and his men were plied with food, drink and offers of jewels and silks. The slavers cast anchor, and allowed their ship to drift from the shore. By the time the Africans realised they had been abducted, it was too late. Weeks later, a hurricane came as the ship approached Florida. A sailor who had befriended Caesar freed him, and the two commandeered the ship, probably at gunpoint. They escaped in a longboat, and were driven to shore by the oncoming storm. The slave ship seems to have been destroyed on the reefs.

Caesar and his friend used the longboat as a miniature pirate ship. When a sail approached, they rowed out and posed as shipwrecked sailors. Once their would-be rescuers were at hand, they pulled out their weapons and demanded food, ammunition, and valuables. They then escaped into the mangrove swamps of Elliott Key, the northernmost point of the Florida Keys, to bury their loot. On one of these raids, Caesar's accomplice abducted a young woman. The two pirates fell out over her. Caesar killed his friend, and took ownership of the woman.

Caesar now expanded his operation. He recruited a crew, and intercepted ships on the open sea. If he was chased, he would either lose his pursuers by cutting into the creeks and swamps – Caesar Creek, to the north of Elliott Key, is named for him – or disappear into the mangroves. To hide his boat, he either lowered the mast and sank the boat in the shallows, or alternatively affixed a metal ring to a rock and, using a heavy rope, turned his boat upside down; an 18th century map of southern Florida marks 'Black Caesar's Rock', apparently in reference to this trick.

According to the legend, Black Caesar established a tyrannical private kingdom on Elliott Key. His settlement included a harem of over 100 women, abducted from passing ships. Many, it can be assumed, were slaves who had

Slaves are forcibly led to an auction to be sold

exchanged one kind of servitude for another. He also took hostages, and erected stone huts in which to imprison them while awaiting ransom payments. When he left on a raid, he made no provision for these hostages. Many of them starved to death.

In a further gruesome twist, some of the children escaped from the camp. Subsisting on berries and shellfish, they formed their own feral society, speaking its own language. While Elliott Key is reputed to be haunted by the inmates of Black Caesar's camp, the image of a camp of fugitive children was to reappear in the Lost Boys of JM Barrie's *Peter Pan*.

The rest of Black Caesar's story might all be fiction too, or at least a composite of different stories. The elements of the story are representative of the intertwined histories of slavery and piracy. Slaves frequently were abducted from west Africa after being tricked onto ships. Members of the crew and the cargo of a slave ship could be cast ashore as survivors of a shipwreck. The slave name 'Caesar' was not uncommon, either. Slavers often gave mock-classical nicknames to their slaves, and Black Caesar was an imperious figure, a man of 'huge size, immense strength, and keen intelligence.'

Many slaves would not survive the crossing

No trace of Caesar's stone prison has been found on Elliott Key, but Johnson's descriptions of Caesar's hideout and settlement echo accounts of Maroon settlements. Escaped slaves did flee to the swamps of Florida, or the hills of Jamaica. Once there, they established societies and subsisted by raiding plantations and piracy on the seas. In Florida, escaped slaves intermarried with Seminole Indians, forming the Black Seminoles, a hybrid of African and Native American culture. Their descendants live among the Seminole Nation of Oklahoma; one of their two communities is named Caesar Bruner Band.

"No trace of Caesar's stone prison has been found"

In 1716 or 1717, Black Caesar left his swampy kingdom and signed up with Blackbeard. The legend places Caesar on Blackbeard's ship, Queen Anne's Revenge, a 40-gun vessel, but he may equally have been commanding one of the smaller ships which Blackbeard formed into a fleet in March 1717. Working their way northwards from Belize, they attacked ships off Jamaica, Cuba, and the Florida coast, before blockading the port of Charles Town (modern Charleston) in South Carolina. 'Commodore' Blackbeard and his confederates looted ships that attempted to enter the port, took local dignitaries hostage and demanded medical supplies for his fleet, and successfully extorted a ransom from the residents.

With Blackbeard and his allies continuing to wreak havoc, Alexander Spotswood, the governor of Virginia, set two Royal Navy sloops, HMS Jane and HMS Ranger, on his trail. On the evening of 21 November 1718, Lieutenant Maynard of HMS Pearl found Blackbeard's Adventure in its anchorage at Ocracoke Island. Blackbeard was taken by surprise – he was drinking with guests – and short of men. One of his officers, Israel Hands, was ashore with some 24 of the crew; in *Treasure Island*, Robert Louis Stevenson names one of Long John Silver's men after Hands.

The battle began the next morning. A broadside from Adventure devastated Maynard's crews, rendering HMS Ranger unable to continue the fight. But small arms fire from HMS Jane may have damaged Adventure's sails and rudder, because Blackbeard's ship ran aground. Maynard steered HMS Jane alongside, launched grappling hooks and grenades, and boarded Adventure.

In Johnson's *A General History Of The Pyrates,*

Did free slaves willingly choose a life of piracy?

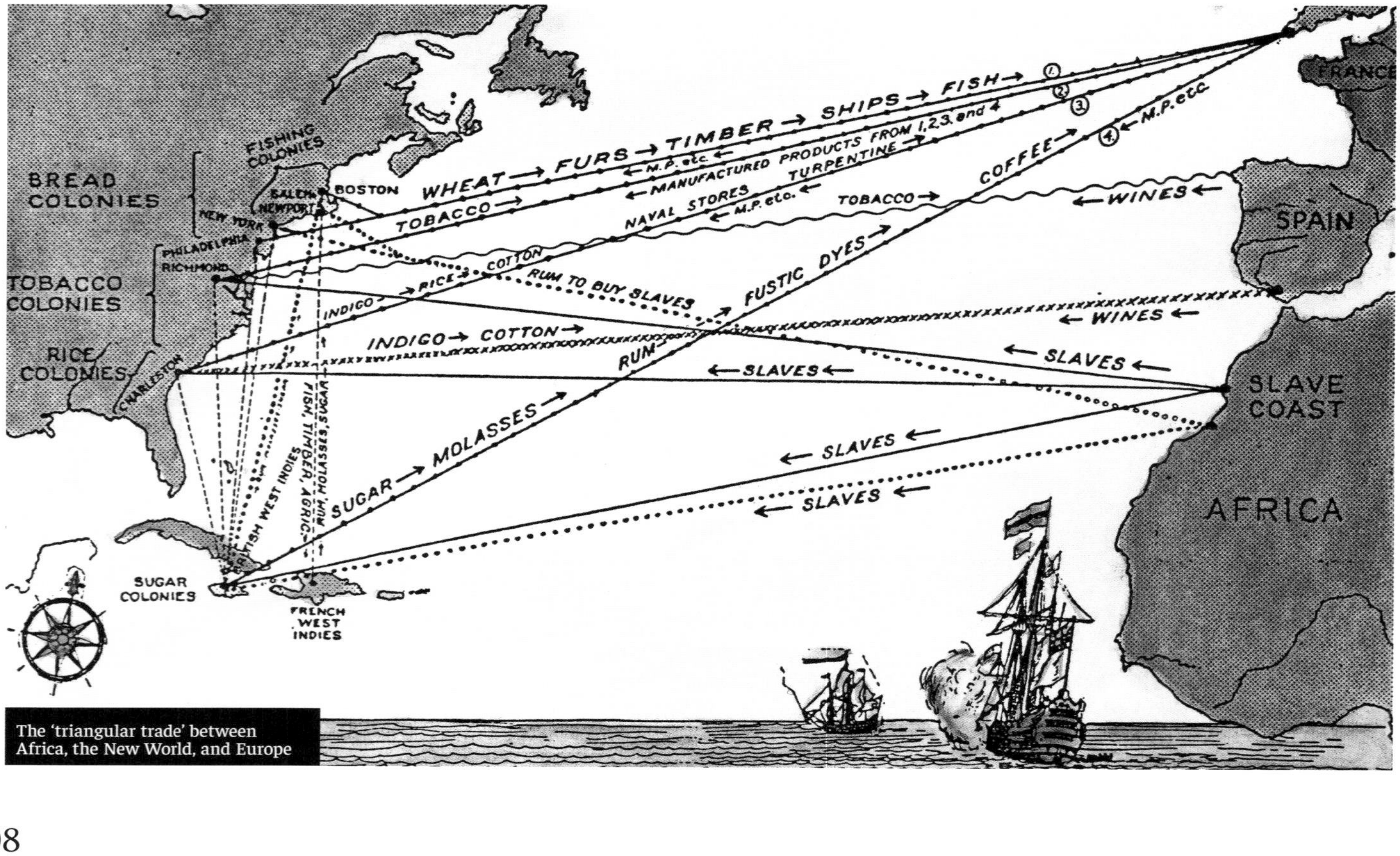

a 'negro' stays in the powder room below decks on Blackbeard's ship. Blackbeard has ordered him to blow up the ship, but he doesn't. Is this the same Caesar tried and hanged at Willliamsburg? And why was that Caesar not among the convicted pirates who made statements to the colonial authorities during their four-month

The 'triangular trade' between Africa, the New World, and Europe

The slave trade in numbers

≈ 1 million

European traders enslaved an estimated 12.5 million Africans between the early 1500s and the late 1800s

10.7 million of those slaves survived the Middle Passage between Africa and the New World colonies.

Of the 54,000 slaving voyages across the Atlantic, Portuguese slavers carried the most slaves, 4.65 million in 30,000 crossings.

Just over half of all slaves worked in sugar plantations.

British slavers carried 2.6 million slaves in 12,000 crossings.

Only 500,000 (4.5%) worked in cotton plantations.

One in three of all slaves (4 million people) taken to the New World went to Brazil.

Half a million slaves went to British possessions in the Caribbean and North America.

In 1772, a judge in London ruled in the Somerset v. Stewart case that slavery was illegal in the British Isles.

The British parliament freed all British slaves in 1833.

imprisonment?

When Adventure was attacked, Blackbeard was on board with 18 other men. Six, according to the Admiralty report, were "Negroes". Blackbeard's crew contained many black pirates, but he also plundered slave ships and dealt in slaves. In 1717, he took 60 slaves from the French slaver Concorde off the island of Saint Vincent. As he left Charleston that year, he took another 14 from Princess. So at least some of Adventure's six 'negros' may have been slaves. Furthermore, none of the black men on board Adventure were killed or wounded in the battle. It is likely that the 'negro' in the powder room was a slave, imprisoned below decks.

Nine of the 15 men tried at Williamsburg were captured in the fighting. The remaining six were arrested on shore at Bath Town, under suspicion of piracy. Two were acquitted; one was Israel Hands, who noted that Blackbeard had recently shot him in the knee. It is possible, then, that Caesar was not even on Adventure during the battle?

In the four months between conviction and execution, three black pirates, James Black, James White and Thomas Gates, made depositions. Presumably, they hoped that by cooperating they might save their lives. The pirate named Caesar did not do this. Was this because he was a notorious pirate, who knew that no amount of collaboration would spare him the noose? Or was it that he was a slave who spoke little or no English and, having been captured by Blackbeard and then held below decks, knew nothing about his captors?

The answer, like Black Caesar's treasure, may still lie buried in the swamps of Elliott Key.

DEFINING MOMENT

Collaboration with Blackbeard
When an injured Stede Bonnet agreed to temporarily cede control of his ship to Blackbeard and stay on as his guest, it was a fateful decision. Blackbeard cheated him not once but twice, stealing his booty and even his crew. Despite stating he would avenge himself, Blackbeard escaped Bonnet's justice and sailed into the sunset.

1717-1718

An engraving of Stede Bonnet, surely one of the most ill-equipped pirates to ever set sail

STEDE BONNET

the gentleman pirate

Stede Bonnet wasn't a very good pirate, but he was certainly a stylish one

Stede Bonnet, the gentleman pirate, wasn't your run-of-the-mill seafaring rogue. A wealthy and educated plantation owner with time on his hands, Bonnet's domestic life was far from an idyll and, after one-too-many arguments with his wife, his mind was made up. He left his spouse and three children at home in Barbados, he purchased the sloop Revenge, replenished his fashionable and fine wardrobe, and set out to be a pirate.

Although the crew of Revenge didn't think much to their dandyish captain's seafaring skills, they were among some of the most well-paid men on the Caribbean waves. Bonnet's generosity secured the support of his men and for this reason, they stayed loyal to their captain through thick and thin.

In 1717, Bonnet reached Nassau after a brutal battle with a Spanish vessel. With Revenge battered from the engagement and Bonnet suffering from injuries, the captain met Edward 'Blackbeard' Teach and the infamous pirate made him an offer he couldn't refuse. Blackbeard offered to take control of Revenge so Bonnet could have time to recover. Indeed, he suggested that Bonnet might remain aboard the vessel as his guest, sailing as some sort of pirate tourist whilst Blackbeard called the shots.

Bonnet accepted the offer and together the two men set out to sea. With one of Blackbeard's most trusted lieutenants serving as caretaker captain of Revenge, Bonnet joined Blackbeard's own ship as a guest. Although Bonnet had enjoyed some small successes as a captain, under Blackbeard's command Revenge truly found her purpose. With the convalescing Bonnet pottering about ineffectually in his nightclothes and Blackbeard striding the deck barking orders, the two men made a strange sight as they looted ship after ship, the hold soon filling will all manner of precious booty.

This collaboration went on for months and it was whilst he was in control of Revenge that Blackbeard engaged and seized the magnificent Concorde, later to become his legendary flagship, Queen Anne's Revenge. What Bonnet made of all this we can only guess but his time as a cruising passenger was coming to an end and, eventually, Bonnet and Blackbeard went their separate ways. Flushed with success, Bonnet went down to the hold of Revenge to count his loot and he found it empty, Blackbeard having cheated him.

After months of successful piracy under Blackbeard, Bonnet's crew were about to face a stark reality. Used to victories with the legendary captain, now the Gentleman Pirate had resumed control, there was precious little triumph and plenty of frustration as their quarry continually outwitted Bonnet, leaving the pirates empty-handed. When Bonnet met Blackbeard again, his crew swiftly deserted him and joined the famous captain.

Although Bonnet had already been betrayed by Blackbeard once, when Blackbeard offered him passage aboard Queen Anne's Revenge if he would cede command of Revenge, he accepted. Left with little crew, of course, he had no choice but to agree. Once again, Stede Bonnet became a tourist aboard Blackbeard's ship and this time, he began to get a little tired of the pirate life. Perhaps he longed for the wealthy plantation he had left behind, even if he didn't long for the wife he had abandoned there, but life as a pirate hadn't proved to be the successful adventure he had dreamed of.

In the company of Blackbeard, Bonnet sailed for North Carolina. It was here that the two men were granted a pardon. Bonnet then received permission from the governor to travel on and secure his letter of marquee, which would leave him free to legally operate as a privateer. He returned to Revenge to share the news with his crew and found that Blackbeard had outwitted him once again. He had stripped the ship of the supplies and treasure and left the crew marooned, leaving Bonnet to re-equip his vessel at his own expense. Although Bonnet swore to take revenge on the man who had twice robbed and humiliated him, he never saw Blackbeard again.

Deprived of most of his crew and all of his booty, Bonnet and Revenge set to sea once more, but their captain was as inept now as he had ever been. As soon as he realised that privateers were a little more governed than pirates, Bonnet cooked up a scheme to go back to his pirate life. He assumed a pseudonym and even referred to his ship as Royal James in an effort to fool the British into thinking that he was nothing but an innocent merchant. Desperate to preserve his pardon whilst continuing his pirate lifestyle, it was a subterfuge that the occasionally inept Bonnet couldn't hope to pull off.

Bonnet was captured in 1718 and sought to save his skin by claiming that he was an innocent man, forced into piracy by his wilful crew. Although members of that same crew admitted that he certainly wasn't the strongest captain around, they passionately refuted claims that he was naught but a bystander. During his trial in Charleston, people called for his release and a desperate Bonnet wrote letters in which he begged for his freedom, promising he would be a model citizen if his life would only be spared.

Sentenced to death, Stede Bonnet's wits deserted him. He was finally hanged on 10 December 1718, the gentleman pirate now a broken man.

The moment Stede Bonnet was hanged in Charleston

Bonnet is pictured here, captured by Colonel Rhett

Captained by Rogers, the Duke lost no time in attacking Spanish shipping in the name of the English crown

Woodes Rogers

the governor privateer

From the Bahamas to the real Robinson Crusoe, Governor Woodes Rogers lived a life at sea

Businessman, privateer, island governor and rescuer of the real-life Robinson Crusoe, Woodes Rogers longed for adventure. Born in the late 1670s and growing up just in time to see the War of Spanish Succession, he came into the world at just the right time to find adventure. Raised in a wealthy household with a rich nautical heritage, by the time Rogers was a young man, he was already in charge of the family seafaring business and his future looked bright. In fact, over the years that followed, bright was the last thing his life seemed to be!

Rogers became famous for a voyage he began in 1708 at the invitation of family friend Captain William Dampier, who asked him to captain a privateering expedition that would circumnavigate the globe. Rogers seized the challenge with both hands and took two ships, Duke and Duchess, out to sea. As captain of the former, he was given a Letter of Marque and threw himself whole heartily into life as a privateer.

The voyage took three years and made Rogers into a celebrity in his homeland. His was not an easy expedition and he found himself enduring challenges including scurvy, freezing temperature, empty cargo holds and even mutinies. Perhaps the most famous story associated with the expedition, however, is the tale of Alexander Selkirk.

In 1704 a Scottish sailor named Alexander Selkirk had been sailing master aboard the Cinque Ports under the command of Captain Thomas Stradling. By sheer coincidence, Stradling had also sailed with William Dampier, the same man who commissioned Rogers to undertake his voyage round the world. Selkirk had been on that voyage too and had turned his

Sailing as a privateer, Woodes Rogers arrived in California in 1709

Rogers was twice appointed as Governor of Nassau

back on Dampier, believing him incapable of leading an expedition. Now that was a distant memory and when the ship made a stop for provisions at the Juan Fernández Islands, Selkirk told Stradling that he would go no further. He believed that the vessel wasn't fit to go back out to sea and Stradling thanked him by marooning him on a nearby deserted island named Isla Más a Tierra. Selkirk's was a lonely life and as the years passed, and no doubt he began to wonder if he would ever be rescued at all. Rogers, meanwhile, was battling with scurvy aboard his ship and determined that he had to replenish his stock of limes as a matter of urgency. He took the fateful decision to land at the Juan Fernández Islands and, as they sailed along the empty coastline of Isla Más a Tierra, spied a campfire on the supposedly uninhabited island. Rogers was sure that this meant there were Spanish vessels in the area, yet when he sent a landing party onto the island, they discovered not Spanish sailors waiting to be plundered, but the sorry figure of Alexander Selkirk.

The marooned and desperate Selkirk welcomed the newcomers with open arms, even when he realised that the crew included his old shipmate, Dampier, whom Selkirk had thought so little of. Offered passage home on board, Selkirk thanked the crew with a gift of fresh wild goat meat, which did wonders for their scurvy-ridden teeth. His story later became immortalised in the tale of Robinson Crusoe, of course, but Woodes Rogers had other things on his mind.

DEFINING MOMENT

A trip around the world

When he inherited his father's businesses, Rogers found himself facing financial losses caused by the loss of his ships to the French. He accepted an offer from William Dampier to captain an expedition, determined to make a success as a privateer and replenish his coffers. His dreams of making a fortune remained unfulfilled.

1707-1711

After rescuing Selkirk, the expedition continued, but it seemed to be beset with bad luck, culminating in a legal battle upon Rogers' return to England. His career didn't end here and, faced with financial ruin due to mounting legal costs and the failure of his business and privateering exploits, he returned to the ocean.

Rogers left behind his life as a businessman and privateer and went into politics, becoming the royal governor of the Bahamas, a largely lawless place where pirates ran riot with little censure. At the head of a fleet of ships he sailed for the Caribbean and successfully took the pirate haven of New Providence, quelling any resistance thanks to his ability to grant royal pardons to those he found there. Not everyone wanted to be pardoned though, and Rogers faced threats from pirates who were determined to take back their old haunt and establish the pirate haven once more. In fact, their efforts failed and Rogers showed no mercy to those who challenged his rule. They were put to death, this demonstration of Rogers' power leaving the other residents of the island in no doubt that their new governor wasn't a man to be trifled with. He fortified the islands of New Providence and Nassau, holding back the threat from Spanish forces until the Spanish and British crowns finally made peace.

In fact, Rogers never fully shed the bad luck that seemed to follow him around and was always in financial trouble of one sort or another. When he visited England in March 1721, he was placed in debtors' prison for old debts and lost his office as governor. With nothing better to do upon his release from prison, he wrote the legendary book, *A General History Of The Robberies And Murders Of The Most Notorious Pyrates*, but fate had one more twist in store for Woodes Rogers.

In 1728, after seven years out of office, he was suddenly made governor of the Bahamas again, but the preceding years had exhausted him. He battled with island politics, finding them far more troublesome than any attack from pirates had ever been, and died in 1732, having lived a life full of drama, heartbreak and precious little triumph.

The Flying Gang

Charles Vane was one of the most ruthless pirates of his time

CHARLES VANE

despised by his fellows

The pirate so prolific in his plundering that lawful trade in the Caribbean was brought to a standstill

Charles Vane was one of the most ruthless and uncompromising of all pirates. During his three-year career, he captured or looted more than thirty ships, with no regard to nation or allegiance. Vane frequently ignored the Pirate Code and treated his own crew with almost as much contempt as those of the ships he plundered.

Reports of his early life are sparse, but Vane probably came to the West Indies during the War of the Spanish Succession. In 1716 he was a sailor under Captain Henry Jennings, a British privateer, but with the war now over, privateers were out of a job. After the 1715 Spanish Treasure Fleet sank off the coast of Florida, Jennings and his crew turned pirate and raided the Spanish camps that were attempting to salvage the shipwrecked treasure. They made off with 350,000 silver pieces of eight and sailed for Jamaica. On the way they attacked a Spanish ship and plundered another 60,000 pieces of eight. With his share of the money from these raids, Vane outfitted his own ship, which he named the Ranger. For two years he used Nassau as his base and plundered merchant shipping, along with several other famous pirates collectively known as the Flying Gang. Each time he captured a better ship, he took it as his own, but he always renamed them Ranger.

Then, on 22 July 1718, a new governor of Nassau was sent from Britain to stamp out piracy. He was a formidable former sea captain called Woodes Rogers, and he brought with him ten ships, including two Royal Navy warships and 100 soldiers. Charles Vane was caught by surprise with his fleet in Nassau harbour. Most other pirate captains surrendered immediately and accepted the King's Pardon, but Vane sent a letter to Rogers demanding to keep all of his pirate booty. This was probably just a stalling tactic because Vane then set fire to the largest of his own ships, a 20-gun ship called Lark, and set it drifting towards Rogers. As the British frantically cut their anchors to move out of the path of the fireship, Vane took a six-gun sloop and slipped out to sea, firing his cannons in a parting shot of defiance.

Instead of lying low, Vane immediately began seizing new ships and recruiting enough men to retake the port. He captured a sloop to use as a consort ship for his raids and promoted his quartermaster Yeats to captain it. He also wrote to governor Woodes Rogers to brag that he would soon be joined by the pirate Stede Bonnet, and would then attack Nassau. The truth, however, is that he was not well liked by other pirates. For the ordinary crew, part of the attraction of turning pirate was the more democratic rule aboard the ship. But Vane was autocratic and treated even his officers with contempt. His crews complained that he didn't share out the plunder fairly and he was often unpredictable and capricious in his choice of targets. On one occasion he captured a ship full of logwood (a valuable plant dye), but instead

DEFINING MOMENT

Vane pretends to take the King's Pardon

The 20-gun Royal Navy warship HMS Phoenix captures Vane and his crew as they return to Nassau. Charles Vane claims that he is on his way to accept the King's Pardon. He is released on the spot, but Vane has no intention of turning straight and immediately resumes piracy.

February 1718

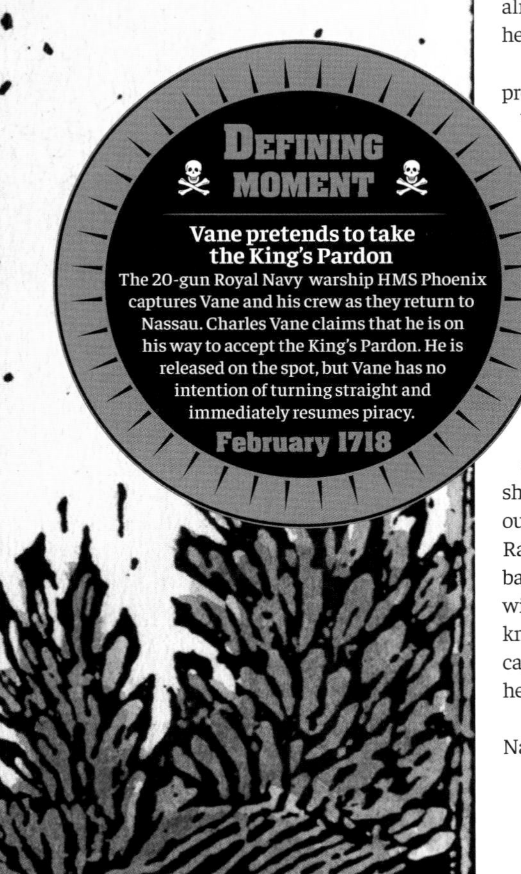

Vane's piracy actually almost halted the slave trade at one point, because so few ships ever made it to port

of taking the cargo, he ordered his prisoners to throw it overboard so he could use the ship for his own purposes. Halfway through the process, he changed his mind and allowed the captain to keep both his ship and the remaining cargo. At other times he promised the crews of captured ships that they would be well treated if they surrendered quietly, and then had them all murdered anyway.

In August 1718, Vane began attacking the ships entering and leaving Charleston, South Carolina. One of these was a large brigantine with 90 slaves from west Africa. Vane ordered them all transferred to Yeats' sloop, ignoring the captain's complaints about the overcrowding. Yeats had finally had enough and he sailed off one evening, abandoning the Ranger. Vane gave chase but Yeats escaped up the North Edisto river towards Charleston, where he and his crew all accepted the King's Pardon from the governor of South Carolina. Charles Vane lurked for several days at the mouth of the river, hoping to catch Yeats and have his revenge, but he was forced to break off when the governor of South Carolina sent out two well-armed ships under the command of Colonel Rhet, on a mission to track down and capture vagrant pirates.

Then in November 1718, confidence in Vane's command crumbled altogether. Having sailed for several weeks without seeing a ship, they sighted a target and hoisted their pirate flag, expecting a speedy surrender. Instead, they promptly received a broadside and the ship hoisted its own flag, revealing it to be a French warship that significantly outgunned them.

Vane wanted to flee but his quartermaster Calico Jack Rackham argued that they rush in and board the warship, since their fighting skills would carry the day. Vane insisted that they would be sunk by its cannons before they could get there. Since pirate law at the time was that the captain's decision was final when it came to fighting, chasing or being chased, Vane got his way and the Ranger escaped. But the following day, the crew accused him of cowardice and voted Jack Rackham the new captain of the Ranger. Vane was put aboard a small sloop with the few crew who took his side.

Defining Moment

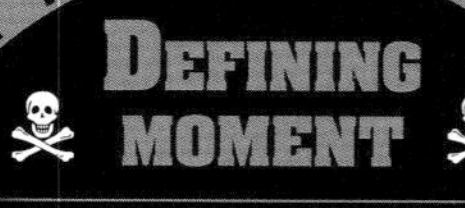

Vane slips his pursuers

Colonel William Rhett was a famous pirate hunter, with a particular grudge against Vane. While hunting him, Rhett comes across two ships that have been recently plundered. The crew tells Rhett that Vane is planning to hide upriver, to the south. But Vane has deliberately planted this false rumour, and Vane heads north instead.

15 September 1718

Gold and silver coins from the wrecked Spanish Treasure fleet provided the starting capital for Charles Vane's pirate career

The party at Ocracoke Island went on so long that merchants set up shop to sell food and liquor to them

DEFINING MOMENT

The Ocracoke Party

Vane joins Blackbeard and hundreds of other pirates for a non-stop rolling party at Ocracoke Island, North Carolina that lasts for weeks. As well as food and drink, more than 50 prostitutes have been brought from nearby Bath Town. Vane tries to persuade Blackbeard to join forces with him and take back Nassau, but Blackbeard declines.

October 1718

In 1718, Charles Vane took over Nassau harbour and flew his pirate flag from the fort

"Vane's fierce reputation allowed him to take ships simply by firing a few warning shots, or even just hoisting his pirate flag"

Undaunted, Charles Vane had the sloop upgraded in Honduras and immediately began looking for fresh targets. Within three days he had captured three small ships off the northwest coast of Jamaica. He kept the largest one and persuaded the crews from all three to join him and by mid-December had captured two more. Vane's fierce reputation allowed him to take ships simply by firing a few warning shots from his cannons, or even just hoisting his pirate flag. With his unquenchable ambition he would soon have been in a position to take revenge on the disloyal Yeats and Rackham. But in February 1719, his ship hit a violent storm and he was wrecked upon an uninhabited island near Honduras. Almost all of his crew were drowned and Vane only survived thanks to the fishermen who occasionally visited the island to catch fish and turtles. Contemporary accounts don't make it clear whether Vane depended on intimidation or charity to feed himself, but he was stranded for several weeks. Eventually a ship arrived, captained by an old pirate acquaintance of Vane's, named Holford. Unfortunately, Holford had since turned honest and flatly refused to take Vane aboard, except in chains, saying "I shan't trust you aboard my ship... for I shall have you caballing with my men, knock me on the head and run away with my ship a pyrating". Instead, he gave Vane a month to make his own escape and warned that he would take Vane prisoner for the bounty on his head, if he was still on the island when Holford returned. Vane protested that there was no way to escape except by stealing one of the fisherman's small boats. Holford apparently replied "Do you make it a matter of conscience... when you have been a common robber and pyrate, stealing ships and cargoes and plundering all mankind that fell in your way? Stay there and be damned, if you are so squeamish!"

Vane does indeed appear to have been too squeamish – or proud – to make off with one of the tiny fishing boats, because he was picked up instead by a different ship that arrived at the island not long afterwards. Vane used a false name and was taken aboard as crew, but the captain of this ship also happened to know captain Holford and when the two ships met at sea, Holford was invited to dine aboard the ship carrying Vane. He was recognised almost immediately and Holford summoned his ship's mate with a pistol to take Vane away in irons. Vane spent some time in jail at Port Royal, Jamaica before being tried and hung.

At his trial, many of his former accomplices, who had since taken the King's Pardon, spoke out against him. Charles Vane said nothing in his own defence, nor called any witnesses. In terms of the sheer number of ships captured, Vane's career had been one of the most successful of any pirate. But his ego and his capriciousness cost him his allies and his life. He died almost as poor as he began.

Calico Jack

the charismatic pirate

He was quick witted and smooth talking, but this dashing corsair let his heart rule over his ambition

John Rackham went by the nickname of Calico Jack because of the colourful striped trousers that he wore, which were made of Indian calico cloth. His career was short and not especially successful but he stands out as a flamboyant and charismatic character. Rackham was the first to use the famous skull and crossed swords design on his pirate flag and he was also the only pirate captain known to have women in his crew.

We know from his trial records that Rackham was born in 1682 but nothing is known of his early life until he turns up as the quartermaster of Charles Vane's ship, Ranger, at the age of 35. Rackham had probably been a pirate for several years at this point, slowly working his way up the ranks to one of the most senior positions in Vane's crew. Then in November 1718 he accused his captain of cowardice and persuaded the crew to vote him as their leader instead. Calico Jack's first month in command was not terribly impressive. He attacked mostly very small ships and didn't make much money from them. On one occasion Rackham captured a ship, only to discover that it was full of prisoners being deported from Newgate gaol in England to work on the plantations. Not only was this a decidedly worthless cargo, but he didn't even manage to hang on to the ship itself as it was recaptured a few days later by an English naval warship.

In December he had better luck and captured the Kingston just outside Port Royal in Jamaica. This had both a valuable cargo and was also a much better ship. Rackham took the Kingston as his new flagship and sailed off to sell his booty, but the attack had been seen from shore and local merchants clubbed together to fund two pirate-hunting ships to go after him. These eventually caught up with him in February 1719, while he was anchored at the Isla de los Pinos, near Cuba. Rackham and his crew were ashore at the time so they escaped capture, but the Kingston was taken back to Jamaica.

Some sources state that Rackham and his crew returned to Nassau in New Providence after this to accept the King's Pardon. This would have been after the 5 September 1718 deadline for the pardon, so they would have been technically ineligible, but Rackham may have claimed that they had been forced into a life of piracy by Charles Vane. The governor of New Providence, Woodes Rogers, detested Vane and so it's possible that he accepted this excuse and pardoned them anyway. It's around this time that Calico Jack encountered

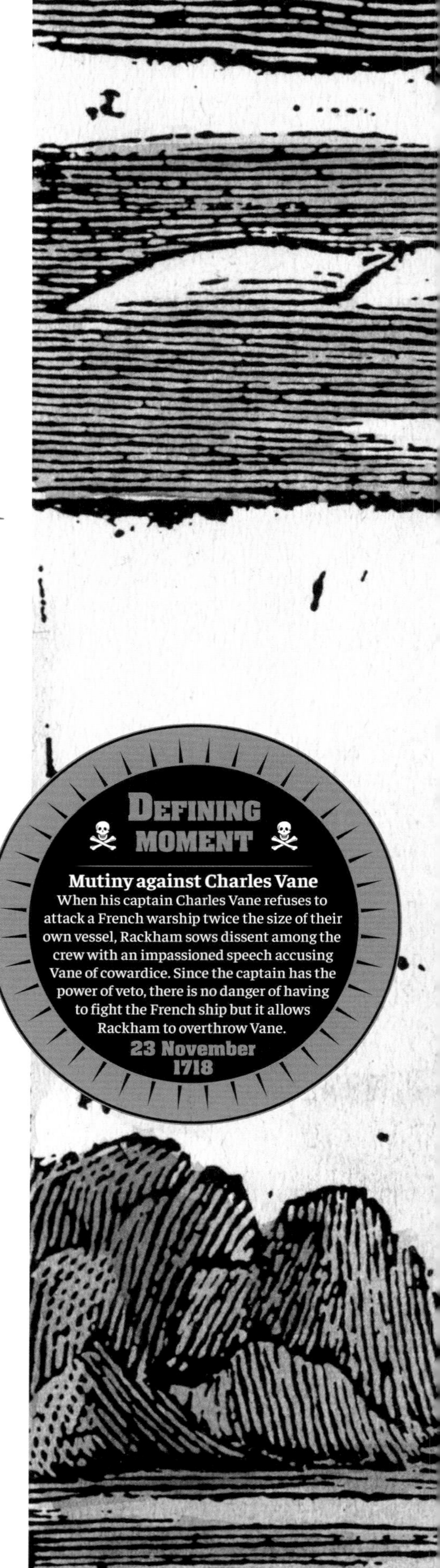

Defining Moment

Mutiny against Charles Vane

When his captain Charles Vane refuses to attack a French warship twice the size of their own vessel, Rackham sows dissent among the crew with an impassioned speech accusing Vane of cowardice. Since the captain has the power of veto, there is no danger of having to fight the French ship but it allows Rackham to overthrow Vane.

23 November 1718

“ “Rackham took the Kingston as his new flagship and sailed off to sell his booty”

the first of the women that would later sail with him. Anne Bonny was the wife of James Bonny, a pirate who had turned honest and made a small living informing on his former shipmates to Governor Rogers. Rackham and Bonny began an affair, and when her husband found out, Rackham tried to buy her divorce. James Bonny refused this offer and instead complained to the governor, demanding that Rackham be publicly flogged. To escape this fate, Rackham dressed Anne Bonny as a man, rounded up eight other pirates, and stole a small ship called The William. Of course this immediately voided his pardon and Rackham went straight back to minor piracy. It isn't clear whether Mary Read was one of Rackham's original crew aboard The William, or whether she transferred later from a captured ship, but contemporary accounts state that Calico Jack was completely fooled by her disguise as a man.

It's worth taking a moment to consider how credible this is. Female crew were unheard of aboard sailing ships at the beginning of the 18th century and Mary Read both dressed and swore like a man. But Rackham already knew he was smuggling Anne Bonny aboard in men's clothing, so he might be expected to be more suspicious. A witness at their trial testified that both women looked exactly like men, apart from "the largeness of their breasts", which is a fairly big hint.

Life aboard a small sailing vessel wasn't anywhere near private enough for a woman to go unnoticed for long, no matter how gruff her appearance. Another witness said that in any

DEFINING MOMENT

Fooling the Spanish coastguard

Calico Jack is trapped in a small bay by a heavily armed Spanish coastguard ship, together with a small sloop that it had captured. In the night, Rackham and his crew row over to the sloop, board it and silently slip away. When dawn breaks, the Spanish ship opens fire with all cannons on Rackham's old ship, now luckily abandoned.

c.1719

> "By keeping so close to the shore, Rackham had attracted attention from the authorities"

Rackham's body was displayed at the entrance to Port Royal harbour as a warning to other pirates

Rackham left the defence of his ship, The William, to Anne Bonny and Mary Read

Jack Rackham captures a Spanish ship

Calico Jack's flag is one of the most iconic pirate emblems today

DEFINING MOMENT

Birth of Rackham's son

Calico Jack has an informal marriage to Anne Bonny while at sea and she gives birth to a son in Cuba, but she rejoins him shortly afterwards. It isn't clear what becomes of this son, but Rackham's attachment to Bonny sets him apart from the murder that defines many of the other famous pirates.

Early 1720

case they only dressed as men when attacking or chasing other ships.

Whatever the living arrangements aboard The William, Rackham and his crew spent some time ashore in Cuba, while Anne Bonny gave birth to a child. In August 1720 they were back at sea and looking for prey around the coast of Jamaica. The William had just four guns and 14 crew so they were forced to hunt small game close to the shore. In September they stole the catch and tackle from seven small fishing boats, worth just £10, but after that they were able to capture two small merchant sloops, worth £1,000. But by keeping so close to the shore, Rackham had attracted attention from the authorities. The governor of Jamaica sent a pair of pirate-hunting ships, commanded by Captain Jonathan Barnet aboard the Snow-Tyger, to sail around the island after him.

On 20 October 1720, Rackham was rounding Negril Point at the western end of Jamaica when he saw a small flat-bottomed boat with nine men aboard. The charismatic Calico Jack hailed them with a mixture of menace and persuasion, and insisted that the men come aboard and drink with him. He probably intended to persuade them to join his crew, but they were sufficiently suspicious to come fully armed with muskets and cutlasses. Nevertheless, they seem to have got on well, and as night fell the pirates and sailors got royally drunk together. Then at around 10pm, Captain Barnet caught up with the pirates and found The William at anchor in the bay. He ordered all lights to be extinguished on the Snow-Tyger and slipped quietly alongside. The first the pirates knew of his presence was when he loudly demanded their surrender. Rackham's crew leapt to battle stations and managed to fire a couple of times from their small swivel-mounted guns, but the Snow-Tyger out-gunned them and after unleashing a broadside, Barnet moved in to board them.

Most of the crew of The William were still below decks and almost the only ones to put up a fight were Anne Bonny and Mary Read. Calico Jack seems to have kept well out of the way during the battle and Barnet managed to capture all of them with no casualties among his own men. Rackham and his crew were taken to Port Royal in Jamaica and tried at St Jago de la Vega (now Spanish Town) on 16 and 17 November 1720. Bonny and Read were tried two weeks later. The entire crew were found guilty of piracy and sentenced to hang. Even more unfortunate was the fate of the nine other men who had come aboard to drink with Rackham that night. They were swept up with the others and charged with piracy, just like the rest of the crew. At the trial, they loudly protested that they were just turtle fishermen who had been compelled to come aboard The William. They pointed out that they had immediately surrendered to Captain Barnet when The William was boarded and had refused Rackham's orders to help him weigh anchor and outrun the Snow-Tyger.

It's impossible to know for sure whether these men had intended to join Rackham's pirate crew or not, but the fact that they were armed at the time of their capture counted heavily against them and all nine were sentenced to hang along with the rest of the crew. Ironically, the two pirates that fought the hardest to evade capture – Anne Bonny and Mary Read – both escaped the hangman's noose by "pleading the belly", in other words they claimed to be pregnant. But Calico Jack was hung, disembowelled and his body displayed in a gibbet on a tiny islet at the entrance to Port Royal, which became known as Rackham's Cay.

John Rackham's career began when he accused Charles Vane of cowardice but in the end he was branded a coward himself for refusing to put up a fight aboard the William. Mary Read is reported to have said "If he had fought like a man, he need not have hanged like a dog".

Anne was one of the fiercest crew members on board the Revenge

ANNE BONNY

disappearing pirate queen

Irish Anne Bonny became famed across the Caribbean for her exploits, but what became of her?

When Anne McCormac was born in Cork, Ireland in 1689, her life was one of adventure from the start. Anne was born to a respectable married lawyer named William McCormac and his maid, so when news of the pregnancy broke, McCormac's orderly world was plunged into scandal.

Separated from his wife and facing public ruin – not to mention the fury of his spouse's family – McCormac and his lover decided to elope. They set their sights on Charles Town, South Carolina, where they were sure that they could make a new start. In fact, Anne's mother died in Charles Town when her daughter was just 13 years old, leaving her entirely in the care of her father. By this time, McCormac – now known as Cormac – had enjoyed enormous success in the new world and he was determined to ensure that his daughter married well. He arranged a marriage to a respectable, wealthy acquaintance, but the girl had absolutely no intention of submitting to her father's wishes.

For all his careful planning, William Cormac had reckoned without Anne's lust for adventure and while he made his fortune as a plantation owner in this respectable new world, Anne had longed to escape it. She turned her back on the suitors her father selected and chose instead James Bonny, a dissolute soldier and would-be pirate. Furious at her disobedience, Cormac disowned Anne and turned her out of his house, swearing that she would not get a penny from him.

As their male crew mates fled, Anne and Mary Read fought valiantly against their captors

With James scheming to get his hands on his new wife's money frustrated, the couple left Charles Town and headed off in search of adventure. Seeking a fortune of their own, they soon arrived in the Bahamas, where Anne threw herself headlong into the wildest parties she could find. She soon discovered that there was more to life than James Bonny and became a regular fixture in pirate drinking dens. Surrounded by tales of adventure and fortune, Anne Bonny set her sights on a far higher prize than any her husband could offer.

With James busy acting as an informant for Governor Woodes Rogers, Anne instead fell head over heels for the infamous pirate, Calico Jack Rackham. Threatened with public flogging for her dalliance with Jack, Anne stole away with her lover and took to the waves. Once again disguised as a man, Anne proved herself to be one of the most fearless and fierce members of Rackham's crew. She loved the thrill of a fight and never shied away from combat, standing firm beside her mates.

Rackham and Anne were separated briefly when she fell pregnant. Believing that a pirate ship was no place for a pregnant woman, Calico Jack left her in Cuba, promising to return once she had given birth. He kept his promise, but history does't record what became of the child she had been carrying when she left the ship.

Anne wasn't the only woman sailing with Calico Jack Rackham, and she was joined on board his ship, Revenge, by Mary Read. Read was easily her equal in terms of temperament, courage and ambition, and soon the crew of Rackham's Revenge became moderately successful in the West Indies. Rather than pursue huge and well-defended bounties, they focused on smaller raids and soon the ship's hold contained a respectable amount of treasure.

The career of Read, Bonny and Rackham came to an abrupt end in October 1720 when the Revenge lay at anchor. A ship captained by the British Navy's famed pirate hunter, Jonathan Barnet, sighted the vessel and stole upon it by night. In fact, the vast majority of the crew was passed out drunk after celebrating a successful attack on a Spanish ship that had netted a small fortune in treasure. Only Mary and Anne were still sober and though they fought valiantly, they were easily overpowered by the larger and, crucially, more sober crew of the British ship.

The captured crew was taken to Spanish Town to face trial, where the revelation that the captured pirates of the Revenge included two women caused a sensation. This was utterly unheard of, and people watched the proceedings with interest, wondering what would become of these most unusual ladies.

The trial was short and the entire crew were sentenced to hang, Mary and Anne included. In one last desperate attempt to save their lives, the two ladies both pled their bellies, meaning that they claimed to be pregnant. No pregnant woman would be hanged and the execution of both was postponed until they had given birth.

Stricken with fever while in prison, Mary died before her baby was born, but Anne's story takes a strange twist. The infamous Anne Bonny disappeared from the historical record immediately following her appearance in court and the decision to commute her death sentence, yet rumours of her fate abounded. The most likely explanation for her sudden disappearance is that Anne's wealthy father took pity on his daughter in her time of most need. Unwilling to see his child go to her death or see her child born in the festering confines of a Port Royal prison, some claim that he pulled some strings among his rich and powerful friends, essentially buying her freedom. Released from jail, Anne returned to America and the shelter of her father's planation. Here, she took a new name and began a new life as a respectable wife and mother, far from the pirate ship where she had once known such peril and adventure.

DEFINING ☠ MOMENT ☠

Anne and Calico Jack fall in love

In 1720, the pirate captain, Calico Jack Rackham, and Anne Bonny fell in love. Jack offered Anne's husband a payment if he would divorce her, but instead he threatened her with a flogging. Calico Jack didn't waste a moment and he and Anne stole a sloop, William, from the harbour at Nassau, and took to the sea.

1717-1718

When British forces boarded the Revenge, Anne fought furiously to save her crew mates

"Only Mary and Anne were still sober, though they were easily overpowered"

Anne was a disobedient daughter, and turned out of the house by her father

MARY READ

the female buccaneer

Cutting a swath in the macho world of pirates were rare women like Mary Read

Mary Read hadn't exactly envisaged a career as a pirate. She was a victim of circumstance and, some might say, opportunity. Sailing aboard a ship to the West Indies, a gang of pirates attacked the vessel and took her captive. From here, Read's life headed on a drastically different course from the one she'd imagined. Her fame, however, was less for her piratical deeds and misadventures and more because of the unusual relationship with fellow sea-rovers: Anne Bonny and Jack Rackham.

Read is a something of a mystery before she turned up in the Caribbean and struck up an ill-fated but deeply romanticised partnership with her pirate cohorts. A life as set down in the classic *A General History Of The Robberies And Murders Of The Most Notorious Pyrates* by Captain Charles Johnson, written three years after Read's death, proved the major contributor to her myth. The problem is that virtually none of it is verifiable, with only court documents and records available from time spent in the West Indies and the trial which saw her, Bonny and Rackham sentenced to death for their crimes.

Johnson sets out Read's life before turning pirate as a melodrama full of tragedy, bravery and crossdressing. Born circa 1691, it is said she was the illegitimate daughter of a sea captain. Mary's mother was unwed at the time and decided to dress her daughter as a boy in a bid to fool a relative into contributing to her upbringing. Moving to London, young Mary was raised as a lad. This ruse became a life-long undertaking. Although dead by 31 or roughly thereabouts, Mary continued crossdressing as and when it suited. Employed as the footman to a female French aristocrat, when she got bored of all that, she enlisted as a cadet in the British army, then at war with the French. The story goes that she fell in love with a Flemish soldier, presumably she revealed to him her big secret, and they went off to run a tavern in the Netherlands together. When this man died, she dragged up again and joined a foot regiment before heading out to the Caribbean. It's a rich tale, one fit for a grand picaresque 19th century novel, but how true is it? Maybe buried somewhere is the truth, or maybe none of it is true.

It is quite incredible that a woman could pass for a man for so long while sailing the seven seas. To be aboard a cramped ship with all sense of personal space obliterated by necessity and hierarchy of the crew, the ingenuities involved in masking the truth from others must have been truly extraordinary and stoked by a constant fear of being found out. Yet ships are full of dark corners and crannies and it is feasible Mary Read and others developed their own tricks and seadog personas

DEFINING MOMENT

Towards piracy

Read's ship was sailing to the West Indies when it was attacked by pirates and she, as an assumed Englishman, was captured and forced into piracy. In 1719, she took the King's Pardon and wished to assume a career as a privateer. The crew mutinied against the captain and Read joined in. She earned a reputation as a good fighter.

c.1719

Mary Read, the female pirate who wore men's clothes

Nassau Harbour, the Bahamas. From here, Rackham, Read and Bonney stole an armed sloop and set sail for pirating adventures

to ward off inquisitive prying. But when toilet facilities were boxes overhanging the bow and small platforms for urinating into the ocean, such daily challenges were fraught with risk. But there was a greater danger than going to the bathroom. Women were forbidden from pirate ships. Being found out could possibly lead to sexual assaults. Also, taking women to sea knowingly was frowned up by pirates, despite their democratic ways when dealing with decisions. Anybody caught smuggling a woman was to be put to death, as the pirate's code rule drawn up by Bartholomew Roberts stated: 'If any man were found seducing any of the latter sex, and carry'd her to sea, disguised, he was to suffer death.'

A way of stopping any of this malarkey was to hire unmarried pirates. But women at sea and working aboard vessels was not uncommon or completely unknown. It worked out well enough for Read. One 19th-century female seaman, named Mary Ann Arnold, was uncovered by Captain Scott of the ship the Robert Small, when they crossed the equator and celebrated with what could be an at times vicious ceremony, involving beatings with wet rope, dunking and in some cases, being chucked overboard. Scott and his crew were shocked, but he later declared Miss Arnold to be among the finest mariners he ever knew: 'I have seen Miss Arnold among the first aloft to reef the mizen-top-gallant sail during a heavy storm in the Bay of Biscay.' If they proved their worth and did a good a job as a man, some captains were suitably impressed. Captain Scott was not a pirate, of course, and Mary Ann Arnold no buccaneer, but both Arnold and Mary Read's exploits show that they competed and worked and fought for respect.

Defining Moment

Meeting Calico Jack

Read meets Jack Rackham in Nassau and turns pirate. Rackham threatened to kill Read because he noticed Anne Bonny, his lover and fellow pirate, who sometimes dressed as a man, was attracted to her. When Jack discovered Read was a woman, they kept it secret from the rest of the crew. Read's pirating career lasted barely a few years.

1720

Read met Jack Rackham and Anne Bonny in Nassau and soon joined forces. Their first course of action was to steal a sloop from Nassau harbour and slink off into infamy. When captured and put on trial at Spanish Town, Jamaica, Read and Bonny were described as fearsome creatures, a world away from ladylike grace and femininity. One witness in court, who was attacked by the pirates, named Dorothy Thomas, provided the judge with a description of Read and Bonny, which might have shocked folk. 'The two women, prisoners at the bar, were then on board the said sloop, and wore men's jackets and long trousers, and handkerchiefs tied about their heads; and that each of them had a machet and pistols in their hands, and cursed and swore at the men, to murder the deponent; and that they should kill her, to prevent her coming against them, and the deponent further said, that the reason of her knowing and believing them to be women then was by the largeness of their breasts.' Thomas's account provides an interesting detail: the pair did not hide their sex.

> "When put on trial, Read and Bonny were described as fearsome creatures, a world away from grace"

19th Century illustration of Mary Read baring her breast before a defeated, startled male pirate

A pirate's end

Having escaped the hangman, Mary Read was sent to prison to carry out the commuted sentence. In April 1721, not long after the trial, it is said she died from a violent fever while languishing in her cell. There is no information as to whether she gave birth or not. Read was buried on 28 April in St. Catherine's church.

April 1721

It is said when Mary Read first joined Calico Jack's crew, and Anne Bonny took a shine to their new recruit, Jack was jealous and threatened to cut Read's throat. Only when it was revealed Read was really a woman in disguise did he stop his threats and allow her to remain aboard. The situation is certainly unique and leads to all sorts of questions. Were Read and Bonny lovers?

On 16 November 1720, the crew were faced with four charges of piracy, after being captured off the coast of Jamaica. Presiding over the court was Sir Nicholas Lawes, the island's governor, and 12 commissioners. Rackham was found guilty and swiftly executed. His body was placed in a cage and hung from a gibbet at Deadman's Cay.

Read faced charges relating to attacks against seven fishing boats, two sloops off the island of Hispaniola, a schooner and a merchant sloop (named the Mary) close to Dry Harbour Bay, Jamaica and kidnapping. She pleaded not guilty, but was found guilty on two counts (relating to the schooner's capture and the Mary episode). She was sentenced to death with the others. Read and her pal Bonny were not mere passengers, as Dorothy Thomas and others attested, but very much in the fray and made themselves known during skirmishes and missions to attain the property of vessels. A French witness, speaking through an interpreter, told the courtroom how the women 'wore men's clothes, and at other times, wore women's clothes'.

Then, like many highly charged courtroom dramas, Mary Read and Anne Bonny played their ace card: they were pregnant and therefore could not be killed by the state. After an examination confirmed the matter, they were carted off to prison.

How much of Mary Read's story is true may never be known, but she entered pirate lore for she was among the very few female pirates who operated during the golden age of piracy, and proved herself as good a fighter and pirate as the man next to her. While her career was small-time and the plunder hardly worth risking death for, Read's place in history is affirmed. The relationship with Calico Jack and Anne Bonny is the most unusual facet of her short but fascinating life.

Read sailed with the famous Captain 'Calico Jack' Rackam

Bartholomew Roberts was the most successful pirate of the era in terms of vessels captured, the final count numbering more than 400

Defining moment

Death of Howell Davis

Although initially an unwilling pirate, Roberts was both esteemed and trusted by the captain who captured him. When Davis was killed during a bungled attempt to kidnap the governor of Principe, Roberts was catapulted to the position of captain: his first act was to avenge the death of Davis before going on to make his own reputation.

1719

Black Bartholomew Roberts

the prize king

Reluctant at first, 'Black Bart' overcame his qualms to become the pirate with the largest capture count of the Golden Age

Knowledge of Roberts' early life is somewhat unclear. Born in Wales as John Roberts in 1682, he is believed to have begun his career at sea at the age of 13. After that, however, the trail runs decidedly cold for the next 23 years, and it is not until 1718 that he next enters the scene, serving as a mate on a sloop out of Barbados.

The following year saw Roberts as third mate aboard Princess, a slave ship, and it was then that fate, rather than natural inclination, intervened to throw him into a life of piracy. The Princess was captured by pirates while at anchor off the Gold Coast, by an attacking force led by captain Howell Davis. Perhaps because Roberts was a fellow Welshman or just because Howell recognised in Roberts a man of great capabilities, he was spared the sword and taken along with the departing pirates as part of their crew.

Roberts quickly became a trusted favourite with Davis, and it is said that the captain took advantage of the opportunity to speak Welsh to Roberts, confiding in him whenever he did not want the rest of the crew to hear. Whatever his initial qualms regarding piracy may have been, it seems that Roberts was quick to overcome them, warming to his new, albeit unexpected, role. So much so, in fact, that six weeks later, when Davis was killed during a botched attempt to capture the governor of the island of Principe, Roberts was quick to accept the position of new captain of Royal Rover. Further highlighting the esteem Roberts' held for his mentor, vengeance was the first thing on his mind: Roberts and his men stole ashore, killing many of the men of Principe and looting the place before fleeing into the darkness.

Operating off the coasts of West Africa and the Americas, Roberts established a name for himself as lucky and profitable, and his men were more than willing to follow him after a string of captures helped cement his position. Like most pirates, his career was relatively short, spanning just three years from 1719 to

Celebrating a recent victory, many of Roberts' crew were said to have been drunk on the day of their fateful encounter with the Swallow

Despite his death, Black Bart's reputation lived on, inspiring many to embark upon a life of piracy on the high seas

his death in 1722. However, if the amount of ships captured is the measure of success for a pirate, then Roberts is the most prosperous ever. During his career he was known for the capture of at least 400 vessels, albeit losing out on the title of most loot stolen, which goes to Samuel Bellamy. There were definite perks to a life of piracy over that of a common seaman, and a quote attributed to Roberts has him comparing the relative poverty of a normal seaman to the wealth obtainable under a pirate flag.

Several flags have been attributed to Roberts during his three-year career. This one shows an hourglass held between death and a pirate

A skilled navigator and leader of men, Roberts was not above a touch of subterfuge to achieve his aims, and it was this streak of daring that led to the success of his most audacious raid.

Roberts and his crew had spent a disheartening two months watching the coast of Brazil for potential sport, but had so far been unlucky. Patience was rewarded, however, when a Portuguese fleet of more than 40 ships was discovered in the Bay of All Saints, the largest bay in Brazil. The ships were awaiting an escort to accompany them safely to Lisbon, and Roberts was quick to seize the advantage. Boarding one of the small vessels of the fleet, he quickly ascertained from a stunned mate which of the other ships was the biggest prize: the Sagrada Familia. Attacking and taking the ship before anyone could raise the alarm, Roberts had hit the jackpot. The captured ship turned out to hold not only 40,000 gold moidores but also jewellery of great worth intended for the king of Portugal himself.

There was, however, a fly in the ointment; following the encounter and no doubt hoping for yet greater treasures, after spending some of their ill-gotten gains, Roberts and some of his crew set off to pursue another ship that they hoped would also be profitable. Not only were they unsuccessful, but Roberts returned to find that the man he had left in charge, Kennedy, had taken off with one of his ships and what was left of the captured treasure from the Sagrada Familia.

With his lesson well learned, Roberts and

DEFINING MOMENT

Taking the Sagrada Familia

Generally held to be Roberts' most audacious victory, the wily captain quickly infiltrated the Portuguese fleet and identified the biggest prize among it. Attacking before anyone could realise what was happening, he seized a sizable treasure haul, only to lose part and the ship when another of his crew absconded with it some time later.

1720

DEFINING MOMENT

Capture of Neptune

The capture of this merchant vessel proved to be Roberts' final victory and the beginning of his downfall. Celebrating their prize, most of the crew of Royal Fortune were drunk when the British ship of the line, Swallow, came into view, and despite a bold attempt to escape to freedom, Roberts was killed in a vicious broadside.

February 1722

"A skilled navigator and leader of men, Roberts was not above a touch of subterfuge"

the renamed Fortune set sail once more. It was believed to be in the wake of this unfortunate incident that Roberts embarked upon the creation of a pirate code, a set of rules by which the pirates under him would agree to abide. Different captains had different codes over the years, but in the one attributed to Roberts, no boys or women were allowed on board the ship, and gambling for money with either dice or cards was strictly forbidden. Burned no doubt by Kennedy's betrayal, defrauding the company would be punished by the offending party being marooned, and deserting the ship during battle carried with it the penalty of marooning or death. Robbing another man was also not to be tolerated, and would result in the guilty party having their nose and ears slit before being sent ashore to fare as best they could.

Roberts was not to be kept down for long, and Newfoundland was his next destination. There, he took many ships and managed to force the surrender of Trepassey harbour, it was said, without the need for bloodshed. Moving onwards into the Caribbean, over the next year Roberts and his crew were perhaps too successful: their activities so impacted trade in the West Indies that they were left without worthy quarry, forcing them to move on to West Africa to find more lucrative pickings. Off the coast of Guinea, the Royal Fortune was pursued by two French ships. Roberts' luck held, however, and the two ships were captured, being taken by Roberts, with one being made use of as a store ship.

During his career, Roberts had several ships named Fortune or variations of this, and it seemed a well-chosen name for this luckiest of pirates. Even Roberts' luck had to run out at some point, though. On 9 February 1722, Roberts and his crew had captured the Neptune. Due to much celebration, the following day the men were still worse for wear, many said to have still been drunk. They were therefore badly prepared for the appearance of Swallow, a ship that had taken Ranger, one of the ships under Roberts' command, a few days beforehand. Roberts' boldness came to the fore once more and a daring plan of escape was fixed upon, one that involved sailing right past Swallow in an attempt to reach freedom. Things did not go according to plan, and when Swallow was able to fire a second broadside at the ship, Roberts was killed – the famed pirate who everyone had thought invincible cut down like so many before him. As he had requested if it should ever come to it, Roberts' body was thrown overboard rather than allowed to be taken, and so the career of one of the most renowned pirates of his age came to an end.

Bold and daring, Roberts was well known for speaking his mind, and his renown is illustrated by the fact that not only did many attempt to emulate him, but also the one occasion on which several pirates sought him out for help and advice, which Roberts duly gave. The nickname Black Bart, although much in use and known today, was not actually used by or about Roberts during his lifetime.

Of the four flags that have come to be associated with Roberts, the one most often linked to him is black with a white skeleton and white pirate who are holding an hourglass between them. Another features a pirate standing on two skulls, with initials underneath that made no secret of his dislike for Martinique and Barbados due to their moves against him. The flag that was flown on the day of the fateful meeting with the Swallow was somewhat fitting, depicting a skeleton and a man holding a burning sword. Roberts' name is still known today, with homage paid to this pirate of great renown in pop culture throughout the centuries since his death – proof that his deeds live on.

Fly began his pirate career with mutiny

WILLIAM FLY

the last pirate of the Golden Age

When William Fly went to the gallows, the Golden Age of Pirates died with him

William Fly isn't famous for his piratical exploits or his seafaring adventures, but for his death that marked the end of the golden age of piracy.

Hailing from Jamaica, Fly wasn't particularly remarkable but he was ambitious and he took to the ocean in May 1726 determined to make his fortune. As a lowly boatswain aboard the slave ship Elizabeth, Fly was at the mercy of its captain, James Green. A brutal man who ruled through fear and tyranny, Green worked his ill-treated crew to the bone and Fly soon realised that he would never achieve his dreams while serving under the captain. Perhaps for the first time, the ambitious young man realised that the road from boatswain to captain was a long one and he determined instead to become a pirate, seeing it as a shortcut to fame and fortune.

Unable to hold his tongue in the face of Green's tyranny, Fly led a mutiny against him and seized the ship en route to Africa. The mutineers dragged the hated Captain Green up onto the deck. Drunk and insensible, Green recovered his wits and begged for his life, but his men were deaf to his entreaties and hurled him into the ocean to die. He was soon joined by the first mate and as the two men sank beneath the waves, the mutineers imprisoned any remaining loyal crewmen and celebrated uproariously. Then they raised the Jolly Roger, renamed the ship, Fame's Revenge, and set a course for America under the captaincy of the newly-elected William Fly.

In fact, the piratical career of Fame's Revenge was short. The reign of the pirates was coming to an end and in the dying days of the golden age, there was no chance that any newly-minted pirate ship could hope to remain at large for long. After successfully seizing four ships during their journey to North Carolina, the crew engaged a fifth and forced some of its men to join their crew. One of these men,

William Atkinson, was to prove the undoing of them.

Atkinson soon saw that Fly's men weren't happy under his command. Their hauls were small and the new captain was every bit as brutal as the man they had overthrown and drowned. Atkinson waited for his moment and remained patient as Fly divided his crew between the Fame's Revenge and a newly-captured vessel. Atkinson secretly released some of the prisoners that had been taken on board and, when he gave the signal, the escapees subdued Fly and what remained of his crew.

Atkinson's audacious plot succeeded and he successfully navigated the ship, along with its four captive pirates, to Boston. Placed on trial for his life, Fly wasn't about to start begging and pleading like Stede Bonnet, but was determined to remain as piratical as ever. He behaved as though this was a walk in the park, showing little interest in the trial nor his ultimate fate. The pirates were sentenced to death after a short trial and flung into a jail cell to await their date with the gallows.

During his spell in prison, William Fly was visited by the preacher, Cotton Mather. Mather, of course, was famous for his prosecution of the Salem witches and he was determined to make Fly repent and save his immortal soul. He lectured the four pirates on their ungodly behaviour, telling them to repent and secure salvation. While his three crewmen eagerly devoured Mather's sermon, keen to end up on the right side of the Almighty, William Fly was having none of it.

He listened as Mather rained down fire and brimstone on his deed until, tired of being berated for the death of Green and the first mate, he informed Mather he hadn't personally killed either. Instead, he claimed, one of the other pirates had thrown the two men into the sea, he had merely stood by and watched. This made no difference, Mather told him, and he continued to sermonise as Fly railed and ranted against William Atkinson, the man he believed had betrayed his trust. He was obsessed with the hopeless idea of realising his revenge on Atkinson, even though he surely knew that he would not live to exact it.

In the face of Mather's preaching, Fly alone refused to be moved. With his men keen to escape the threat of eternal damnation, the former captain continued to argue with Mather, who eventually gave up his mission to save William Fly's soul.

When the day of execution came, Fly strolled through the gathered crowds like a true celebrity, waving to those who had come to witness his death. Smiling and prancing, when he reached the scaffold he hopped nimbly up to take his place, every inch the showman. He examined the noose from which he would soon dangle and declared it a poor job. Carefully, he re-tied the noose until it was to his liking and then placed it around his own neck

As his crewman meekly repented and told the spectators to follow the path or righteousness and the law, Fly looked on in amusement. He sought no pity, nor offered repentance and instead warned any seafarers among crowd to treat their men with dignity and respect, for it was they who were to blame for mutiny and piracy. After all, he pointed out, if he had not faced the tyranny of Green, he would have remained a loyal and law-abiding crewman all those months ago.

Fly was hanged on 12 July 1726, unrepentant to the last. His body was gibbeted as a warning to others and with him, the golden age of piracy finally breathed its last.

DEFINING MOMENT

The refusal to repent

Fly's refusal to repent and his last words suggest that he wasn't driven purely by ambition, but by his own moral code. He believed to the last that he was not to blame for his fate, and warned that those in positions of authority should treat those below them properly, or leave them with no choice but to revolt.

12 July 1726

Fly led a mutiny on his first ship, casting the hated captain into the sea

"When he reached the scaffold he hopped nimbly up to take his place"

The remains of Fly and his executed crew men were taken out to Nixes Mate in Boston Harbor following their execution

OLIVIER LEVASSEUR

the buzzard

How one pirate has been leaving clues to the whereabouts of his two million dollar booty long after his death

When you think of piracy, what specifically comes to mind? Peg legs, eye patches and hooks for hands are staples for movie pirates, but real life was rarely so imaginative. However, feared and renowned pirate Olivier Levasseur procured himself an eye injury, and therefore an eye patch, before he had barely started dabbling in buccaneering. Continuing the swashbuckling stereotypes, he also managed to secure himself one of the biggest treasure hauls in pirate history before being captured and sentenced to death in 1730. If this were a movie, Levasseur would have made a brave escape, swaggered aboard his ship and sailed off into the sunset for one last adventure. In actuality, Levasseur wasn't so lucky. But that doesn't mean his story wasn't stranger than fiction.

Nicknamed La Buse and La Bouche – French for 'the Buzzard' and 'the Mouth' because of his speed and ruthlessness when it came to attacking his enemies – Levasseur spent much of his life as an outlaw. However, his rather fortunate upbringing helped him carve out a respectable sailing career. Born in Calais to a wealthy bourgeois family during the Nine Years' War (1688-1697), he received an excellent education and became a naval officer some years later.

During the War of the Spanish Succession, Levasseur procured both a scar across one of his eyes and a Letter of Marque from King Louis XIV. The Letter of Marque meant that he was licensed to attack and capture enemy vessels before bringing them before admiralty courts for condemnation and sale, and so he became a privateer for the French crown. But when it was time to return home with his ship when

Defining moment

A change in career

Having fought as a French naval officer during the War of the Spanish Succession, Levasseur made a rather surprising career change when he joined Benjamin Hornigold's Flying Gang instead of returning home. He quickly became known as La Buse because of the speed and ruthlessness with which he attacked his enemies.

1716

Levasseur's grave can be found at Saint-Paul, Reunion, in France

Basil Rathbone played Levasseur in the film *Captain Blood* starring Errol Flynn

John Cruise-Wilkins has attempted to find La Buse's hidden treasure after his father started a search in 1947

La Buse left a cryptogram for people to solve

DEFINING MOMENT

An enormous booty

A career highlight for Levasseur and his partner John Taylor was their attack on the Portugese great galleon Nossa Senhora do Cabo, which contained treasures belonging to the Bishop of Goa and the Viceroy of Portugal. Levasseur, Taylor and their crew managed to get away with a huge fortune thought to be now worth over $2 billion.

April 1721

the war eventually ended, Levasseur decided that life wasn't for him. Instead, he signed up with the infamous Flying Gang in 1716, and befriended fellow crew members Sam Bellamy and Edward Teach, who would later come to be known as the notorious pirate Blackbeard.

After a year of looting the party split (Hornigold becoming a pirate hunter had something to do with it), but that wasn't the end for Levasseur. In 1719, he decided to try his luck out on the West African Coast, and formed a partnership with Englishmen and fellow pirates Howell Davis and Thomas Cocklyn.

The three pirates had a short but successful run, with their biggest victory being their attack of the slaver port of Ouidah, a city on the coast of the republic of Benin. They managed to capture the slave ship Bird Gallery at the mouth of the Sierra Leone River, and were so thrilled by the attack that they celebrated for a month before finally releasing its captain, William Snelgrave, who had been beaten and shot but ultimately spared. According to writings from Snelgrave after the ordeal, Howell has said, "their reasons for going a pirating were to revenge themselves on base merchants and cruel commanders of ships."

> "They managed to capture the slave ship Bird Gallery, and were so thrilled by the attack that they celebrated for a month"

Like his compatriots in the Flying Gang, Levasseur, Howell and Cocklyn's partnership eventually came to an end, this time due to a falling out after a drunken argument. Not long after setting out on his own, Levasseur found himself shipwrecked in the Mozambique Channel, stranded on the island of Anjouan. It was during this time that his bad eye became completely blind and Levasseur started wearing his signature eye patch.

Very little is known about how he got himself off Anjouan, but things started to look up again for Levasseur after that point. According to legend, the Frenchman became instrumental in the building of a pirate fortification on the island of Sainte-Marie, just off the coast of Madagascar. From 1720 onwards, Levasseur began plundering from the safety of the Sainte-Marie base with a new set of pirate partners, John Taylor and Edward England.

Together, the trio and their crew captained three ships and 750 men, and successfully plundered the Laccadives, selling the loot to Dutch traders for an impressive £75,000. Once again, the partnership came to an end, but this time it was England who was cast out; Levasseur and Taylor grew tired of his kindness towards their captives and so decided to maroon him on the island of Mauritius to teach him a lesson.

It was with Taylor that Levasseur perpetrated one of the greatest exploits in piracy history, securing them enough booty to fulfil any buccaneer's wildest dreams. In April 1721, the

Reginald Cruise-Wilkins first found a pirate marking on some rocks near his home at Bel Ombre

pair made plans to capture the Portuguese great galleon Nossa Senhora do Cabo – known in English as Our Lady of the Cape – which was loaded with gold and precious stones belonging to the Bishop of Goa and the Viceroy of Portugal, who were both on board on a return trip from Lisbon. The ship seemed like no easy conquest, with its 74 gun ports in contrast to Levasseur's 26 cannons.

Luckily for the pirates, the Nossa Senhora do Cabo had been damaged in a storm, causing the crew to dump all 74 cannon overboard and then sit it on a sandbar while it underwent repairs. In one of the most opportune captures of all time, Levasseur and his crew managed to seize an absolutely preposterous haul, with each crew member receiving a whopping £50,000 and 42 diamonds each. The stolen fortune is believed to have been worth well over $2 billion in today's money.

Having pulled off the biggest and most impressive exploit of his career Levasseur decided he deserved a break, and settled down in secret on the Seychelles archipelago where he started attempting to spend his money. But, like most pirates, he didn't quite manage a happy ending; his dangerous and very illegal lifestyle finally caught up to him in 1730, when he was captured near Fort Dauphin, Madagascar, and hanged for piracy on 7 July.

But Levasseur's story doesn't end there. Mere moments before he was hanged and with a rope around his neck, the pirate threw a cryptogram, contained within a locket, from the scaffold into the crowd that had gathered to watch his execution, and yelled: "Find my treasure, he who may understand it!" Those served as Levasseur's final words.

Since the bizarre event, many people, both pirates and otherwise, have attempted to crack the code and seek out the treasure. Some even claim to have been partly successful, but there is no evidence that the booty of gold and precious stones has ever been discovered. However, several may have come close.

According to legend, a woman named Rose Savy came across some mysterious carvings in the rocks at Bel Ombre beach near Beau Vallon on the island of Mahé during the 1920s while the tide had been unusually low. After hearing of the carvings – which represented a dog, snake, turtle, horse, fly, hearts, a keyhole, a staring eye, a ballot box, a woman's body and the head of a man – a public notary in Victoria, Seychelles, made a connection through searching his archives and concluded that the symbols had been made by pirates.

Savy also happened across the last will of a pirate named Bernardin Nageon de L'Estang, who had died 70 years after Levasseur, and claimed to have obtained some of the hidden treasure. Within the will was the following message to his nephew: "I've lost a lot of documents during shipwreck. I've already collected several treasures; but there are still four left. You will find them with the key to the combinations and the other papers." The will also contained Levasseur's original cryptogram, which accompanied Savy on a steamboat to Kenya and a flight to the national library of Paris so its origin could be verified.

In 1947, Savy's neighbour, Reginald Cruise-Wilkins attempted to decipher the cryptogram, and discovered a connection with the Zodiac, the Clavicles of Solomon and the Twelve Labours of Hercules. In order to find the treasure, he believed a series of tasks had to be carried out in a strict order, with the treasure chamber being buried somewhere underground. Cruise-Wilkins eventually died in 1977, but his son John, a history teacher, has dedicated part of his life to continuing his father's quest. His search has so far been futile.

Throughout his life, Levasseur had no need for the treasures he acquired by way of buccaneering. Everything he did, he did for fun. The cryptogram was no different: with people still trying to crack its code and find the fortune it conceals, the cryptogram ensured he could continue having fun long after his death, even if he wasn't there to witness it.

DEFINING MOMENT

The story continues

Levasseur's life may have ended in execution for piracy in 1730, but his legacy continues. After throwing a cryptogram into the crowd just moments before being hanged, La Buse continues to perplex. Several pirates claimed to have already discovered the booty, but there has been no evidence supporting those boasts.

7 July 1730

Pirates in the Caribbean

Nautical treasure hunters, or anarchic outlaws? Meet the pirates who dominated the Caribbean in the 18th century and discover their hideouts

Today when we think of the Caribbean, we might imagine endless golden beaches and turquoise seas. However, if you had set sail at the start of the 18th century and survived the long arduous journey across the Atlantic, you would not find solace and tranquillity, but instead an anarchic wilderness, overrun with pirates.

Far from the eccentric, adventure- and treasure-seeking rogues that pepper our cultural imagination, pirates were violent outlaws who sailed the shallower waters in sloops, ready to pillage anything they could get their hands on and wreaking havoc across the Atlantic and further abroad.

The origins of piracy lie with state governments. While the act itself was illegal, in England state-sponsored attacks on the ships of national enemies were made lawful by Letters of Marque and Reprisal. These gave former naval officers and merchants the right to pillage enemy vessels, carrying valuable cargo like indigo, tobacco and sugar. These privateers, or buccaneers, often targeted Spanish ships, as they controlled much of South America and the Caribbean. But the English wanted in on the action and in the 1620s Thomas Warner settled St Kitts whilst the neighbouring island of Nevis followed shortly after.

Edward Teach's severed head hangs from a bowsprit

> "He pillaged 18 kilograms of gold dust, a great quantity of brandy, elephant teeth and 14 men to beef up his crew"

Capture of the Pirate, Blackbeard, 1718, Jean Leon Gerome Ferris, which was painted in 1920

The Museum of the London Docklands' exhibition 'London, Sugar and Slavery' highlights the extremely lucrative nature of colonisation and how it kick-started the industrial revolution back home. Rich in resources, the Caribbean islands were ripe for exploitation and those who weren't up for a bloody fight with the local Carib or Arawak tribes on unsettled islands could simply pillage goods from Spanish and French ships. The exhibition includes original letters of marque and a gibbet that was used for displaying dead bodies of condemned pirates around Wapping. The National Maritime Museum in Greenwich is also plays host to displays about how 17th-century British naval culture encouraged privateering.

The island of Tortuga off the coast of modern day Haiti became an informal buccaneer's capital or 'pirates' den' during this period. A Brethren of the Coast was set up by

Lettre de Marque.

The Letter of Marque, which gave privateers a license to attack and pillage enemy vessels

Today, the Caribbean is largely a tranquil holiday destination, but its past is rather more bloody

Captain Henry Morgan – a Maritime Robin Hood – and even supposedly respectable men such as Captain Anthony Hilton, the first governor of Nevis, decided his time was better spent in Tortuga. By working together, targeting trade routes and overpowering ships, these buccaneers became extremely successful. However, it would soon start to get out of hand. A law unto themselves, buccaneers soon started pillaging anything they could get their hands on, regardless of the diplomatic consequences.

Two buccaneers who effectively brought this early era to a close were Captains Henry Every and William Kidd. Every was a mariner on the King Charles II. When the crew mutinied, Every was elected as the new captain and set off on a pirating expedition, first to the Portuguese island of Príncipe, off the coast of Africa, where he captured his first ships and pillaged gold dust, brandy and elephant teeth before heading to the Red Sea to attack ships leaving Mecca on their way back to the Mughal Empire. Every attacked the Ganj-i-Sawai and this time he was rewarded with between 23,000 and 27,000 kilograms of gold and silver. The Mughals complained and the English realised they had to act or risk losing vital trade with Asia.

Every and his team sailed to Saint Thomas in the Danish-controlled Virgin Islands, and perhaps to the Bahamas, before heading home. Today on Saint Thomas you can take a guided tour of Skytsborg Tower, also known as Blackbeard's castle. This was a lookout built in 1679 to warn the Danes about pirates but, legend has it that it was later used by Blackbeard. From the top you can see out as far as St Cruix and Puerto-Rico. A similar tower – Bluebeards Castle – is now a luxury holiday resort open to guests.

These lookouts, however, did little to stop Every. When his men arrived back in England, they were arrested, put on trial and hanged at Wapping – a commonly known sight for the execution of pirates, called Execution Dock was used for over 400 years – but Every escaped. Stories abound of him having moved to Ireland, headed home to Plymouth or even back to Saint Thomas. His fate remains unknown.

The incident brought home the risks involved with privateering for the government and it was hoped the trial of Every's men would act as a show trial. Instead, the story of ordinary men making their fortune on the high seas, visiting exotic lands and eluding justice, was lapped up by the press.

A few years later the exploits of another privateer turned pirate, William Kidd, would again capture the public's imagination, and launch the so-called golden age.

Kidd set off from London in 1696 with his own Letters of Marque, ready to turn pirate on the pirates and re-claim stolen loot. King William III was to receive ten per cent of the profits. It did not quite work out that way...

Pirates at the end of the 17th century sailed on a well-known route called the Pirate Round. Pirates would cross the Atlantic, sail around the Cape of Good Hope and then

Henry Morgan was a prominent Welsh privateer of the 17th century

"The sensational story of ordinary men making their fortune on the high seas was lapped up by the press"

The pirate Captain Henry Every, taking the Great Mogul's ship

La Crique beach, in Île Sainte-Marie (known in English as Saint Mary's) near Madagascar

This painting depicts pirates attacking an English naval vessel

Captain Kidd depicted in a scene, welcoming women on board to see his ship in New York

make a stop either in Madagascar itself or on the small island of Île Sainte-Marie. Here they would boost supplies and congregate, before they headed off up the coast of Africa towards the Red Sea and onto India where Mogul ships were a-plenty. The Pirates Museum in Antananarivo highlights why Madagascar was the perfect hideout. When the British began re-asserting their authority over Nassau, legend has it that pirates formed another republic here called Libertaria, though this has never been verified. English speaking visitors to the museum can have all the exhibits explained to them by one of the museum staff at no extra cost.

Kidd soon caused suspicion because he was spotted by naval ships carrying on further north, past Madagascar to the Comoro Islands. The pirate hunter had turned pirate himself.

Some argue that Kidd's conversion to piracy was not necessarily voluntary: a third of his crew perished with cholera and all of his replacements turned out to be pirates themselves. Frustrated after months at sea, Kidd followed Every's footsteps and headed straight for the Red Sea where he plundered the wealthy Quedagh Merchant before heading back to Madagascar and then the relative sanctity of the Caribbean.

It was while on Anguilla that Kidd heard that the English government had declared him a pirate and had issued an

William III saw the Piracy Act of 1698 come into action during his reign

Kidd's treasure

Some of the treasure captured by William Kidd, one of the most notorious of all pirates, has recently been uncovered by divers

The privateer is said to have acquired a vast treasure when he turned to piracy but by the time he was arrested, the infamous loot had vanished.

During his incarceration, Kidd wrote to Sir Robert Harley, the Commons Speaker of the time, offering the location of his £100,000 loot (which is about £10.5 million in today's money) if his sentence was commuted; unfortunately for him the offer was declined.

The so called Kidd-Palmer charts, discovered by Hubert Palmer in a bureau purportedly from Kidd's ship The Adventure Galley – which was purchased in 1935 – allegedly pointed to the treasure being in the China Sea.

The charts vanished in 1957, as has any evidence of a historical evaluation by the British Museum, who were long purported to have verified the charts as genuine.

Other islands that have been searched include Oak Island, Nova Scotia, Hon Tre Lon, Vietnam and Bonaire, the Lesser Antilles. Kidd was known to have stopped off in the Caribbean to unload The Quedagh Merchant and his letter to Harley implies the treasure is in the West Indies.

In 2015, divers believed they had found treasure from the Adventure Galley, off the coast of Madagascar. The UN, however, dismissed the discovery, stating that the silver bar the divers had discovered was 95 per cent lead and the wreck is a broken port construction.

William Kidd and his buried treasure

arrest warrant; the Moguls had threatened to cut off trade which could have bankrupted the East India Company. Kidd was arrested in America and transported back home where he was tried, found guilty and hanged.

The trial and capture of Kidd, however, did little to dissuade privateers and mariners from going rogue. In fact, once again it had the opposite effect. Newspapers turned Kidd into a celebrity and transcripts of his trial sold out, while rumours spread that Every had escaped to the Caribbean where Kidd's treasure allegedly lay hidden.

Privateers soon began to congregate in Nassau in the Bahamas, living by their own pirates code. By 1716, pirates in Nassau outnumbered citizens by ten to one. Some describe it as a pirate's republic; others condemned Nassau as a failed state.

Nassau, however, was certainly not a meritocratic utopia if you were a local. The pirates looted whatever they could, burned down houses of settlers and reportedly even raped local women. The closest thing the pirates had to a leader was Captain Benjamin Horingold, another privateer. Horingold, however, was the subject of an effective coup when he refused to attack English – now British – ships. The pirates reasoned that most of the ships coming in and out of the Caribbean with the biggest loots were British since Britain was now the dominant force in the Caribbean.

Indeed once they started raiding British ships, the Nassau pirates captured 70 per cent of all the treasure that would be looted in the whole era. All the big names congregated in Nassau during the 1710s so the Pirates of Nassau Museum in Nassau is well worth a visit. A life size model of Nassau's

Blackbeard's black flag encapsulates his vicious, brutal reputation. A white skeleton holds an hourglass in one hand, signalling that your time in this world is running out while the other hand holds an arrow pointing at a bloody red heart

Quayside has been reconstructed. There is also a replica pirates flag room, priceless treasure from the golden era and exhibits on Woodes Rogers, Horringold and female pirates Anne Bonny and Mary Read. If you're in Nassau it is also worth hopping across the sea to Florida where pirates would hide out amongst the shallow keys. The Tampa Bay History Centre features many rare artefacts washed up on Florida's shores and will soon open a new gallery, featuring a 60 foot replica sloop and a cartographic centre showcasing some of the earliest maps of the New World and the Caribbean.

It was during the golden age that the most notorious pirate of them all arrived on the scene: Blackbeard. We cannot be certain of his real name, though multiple sources give variations on Edward Teach. What we do know is that Blackbeard was a contemporary of Hornigold and gained a reputation for his courage, brutality and striking appearance: he sported a dirty, long beard, tangled into knots, and would place lit matches under his hat. Indeed, the contemporary pirate biographer Charles Johnson

> "By 1716, pirates in Nassau outnumbered citizens by ten to one. Some described it as pirate's republic"

Nassau Harbour in the late 19th century

Pirates boarding a Spanish vessel in the dead of night. Taken from Lives of the Most Notorious Pirates by Charles Johnson

Edward Teach, known as the formidable Blackbeard

Wreck of the Queen Anne's Revenge

The discovery of Blackbeard's ship boosted our understanding of this infamous yet mysterious figure

Blackbeard's ship was discovered after cannons and other artefacts were salvaged from the coast of North Carolina in 1996.

Originally a French slave vessel known as La Concorde, the ship is most famed for only having made three journeys since its 1710 launch.

In 1717, having set sail from Nantes, near Brittany in France, and stopping off in Africa to pick up slaves, it was attacked by Blackbeard about 160 kilometres from Martinique. With some of the crew having already perished, and Blackbeard boasting two ships with a total of 150 men and 20 cannons, Captain Pierre Dossett did not stand a chance. He surrendered the ship to the pirate.

After stopping on the island of Bequia, Blackbeard renamed the ship, unloaded the slaves and some, but not all, of the crew.

With the newly-named Queen Anne's Revenge, Blackbeard took ships in Saint Vincent, Saint Lucia, Nevis, Antigua and Hispaniola. In South Carolina, he blockaded Charleston's port for a week with his crew.

When Blackbeard headed to Beaufort Inlet, North Carolina, the Queen Anne's Revenge finally met its end when it ran aground in the notoriously shallow waters.

Today you can visit the North Carolina Maritime Museum in Beaufort, which houses more than 300 artefacts from the wreckage.

Illustration of Captain Kidd burying his Bible, because – according to legend – of its opposition to his way of life

The life of a pirate was not easy, with violence and theft a part of the job

wrote that Blackbeard was "...altogether such a figure, that imagination cannot form an idea of a fury from hell to look more frightful."

By now the situation in the Caribbean was out of hand. The British had to act. They made a former privateer, Woodes Rogers, governor of the Bahamas and ordered him to bring back law and order. However, fighting every single pirate who had made Nassau their base would have been an insurmountable task. Instead a compromise was reached. If a pirate would switch sides and work for the government to go after other pirates, they would be offered a pardon. Horingold accepted such a pardon and agreed to start hunting down his former partners in crime.

For a while, Blackbeard also accepted a pardon from the governor of North Carolina, and he settled down in Bath Town. However, this wasn't to last. Soon Blackbeard was back to his old ways.

He met his end at Ocracoke Inlet when the Governor of Virginia sent Royal Navy Lieutenant Robert Maynard to bring him down. On 22 November 1718, in an infamous bloody showdown aboard Blackbeard's ship, one of Maynard's crew put an end to the notorious pirate by hacking off his head. North Carolina is the best place to learn more about Blackbeard. Visit North Carolina have suggested an epic four day itinerary including visits to the Maritime Museum – which houses artefacts from the Queen Anne's Revenge – his final home in Bath and a ferry trip out to the site of Blackbeard's final battle.

After Blackbeard's death, piracy fell into decline. Without a base or the camaraderie of the major players, it no longer seemed so attractive a venture. The pirates that weren't caught absconded on their ships and disappeared into the ether, never to be heard of again, leaving generations of us to fantasise about their lives on the run in exotic lands.

VTRAQUE VNUM
1739
GENV DVX ET GVB REIP
N
N.W
N.E
W
E
S
S.W
S.E